Integrating CORBA®
and COM Applications

Integrating CORBA® and COM Applications

Michael Rosen

David Curtis

WILEY COMPUTER PUBLISHING

JOHN WILEY & SONS, INC.

New York • Chichester • Weinheim • Brisbane • Singapore • Toronto

Publisher: Robert Ipsen

Editor: Robert Elliott

Assistant Editor: Pam Sobotka

Managing Editor: Angela Murphy

Electronic Products, Associate Editor: Mike Sosa

Text Design & Composition: SunCliff Graphic Productions

This text is printed on acid-free paper.

Published by John Wiley & Sons, Inc.

Published simultaneously in Canada.

This publication is designed to provide accurate and authoritative information in regard to the subject matter covered. It is sold with the understanding that the publisher is not engaged in professional services. If professional advice or other expert assistance is required, the services of a competent professional person should be sought.

Library of Congress Cataloging-in-Publication Data
Rosen, Michael
    Integrating CORBA and COM applications / Michael Rosen, David
Curtis.
        p.   cm.
    Includes index.
    ISBN 0-471-19827-7 (pbk./online : alk. paper
    1. CORBA (Computer architecture)   2. COM (Computer architecture)
3. Object-oriented programming (Computer science)   I. Curtis,
David, 1957–   .   II. Title.
QA76.64.R677   1998
005.2'76--dc21   98-24818

Printed in the United States of America
10 9 8 7 6 5 4 3 2 1

Contents

CHAPTER 3

Interworking Architecture   27

CHAPTER 4

Basic Mappings   67

CHAPTER 5

Complex Data Types 89

CHAPTER 6

COM Data Type Mappings 121

CHAPTER 7

Integrating COM and CORBA 145

CHAPTER 8

Exceptions 183

CHAPTER 9

Bidirectional Integration 217

Foreword

This is an important book because it helps developers understand how they can (and can't) knit the two most widely used object systems, COM and CORBA, into distributed applications. To understand why the book is so important, consider a true story about the nature of distributed object systems.

A development manager at Pacific Gas & Electric once told me a story about distributed objects. Several members of his development team were avid wind surfers, and wanted to easily monitor weather conditions at the beaches near their office in San Luis Obispo, Calif. One of the wind surfers built a "weather server," a piece of software running on the network that reported wind, tide, temperature, and so on in the waters off San Luis Obispo.

The weather server ran on a PC sitting under the guy's desk, and one day he kicked the power cord and unplugged the PC. Within moments, the manager's phone rang. "Where the hell is the weather service?" It was the guy responsible for seaborne shipments of fuel to PGE's power plant in SLO. There was urgency in his voice. It seems that the shipping group at PGE's shipments planned fuel deliveries using the weather service originally designed by and for wind surfers and stashed under a developer's desk alongside discarded papers and old shoes.

Welcome to the world of distributed objects. A developer writes an object that does something interesting and makes it available via a network. Users and other developers find that object and put it to work. Creativity yields value, often unexpectedly. Distributed object systems promise an expanding range of software resources for all kinds of applications. The promise depends on developers being able to add new objects to networks with the ease of adding a new Web site to the World Wide Web. Users should be able just as easily to plug into new functionality.

Which brings us to the problem of COM and CORBA—and the valuable insights and advice of authors Michael Rosen and David Curtis. CORBA and COM are competing standards for distributed object systems, COM and CORBA don't work very well together, but developers will be forced to make COM work with CORBA in most projects. This situation exists because Microsoft's Windows dominates desktop environments, while no single standard dominates server environments. COM is the standard developers use to build client-side objects in Windows. CORBA is the most popular standard among developers of server objects, primarily those working in Unix with C++. That's right, the COM and CORBA interworking problem is just another dimension of the divide between Windows and Unix.

The Windows-Unix chasm isn't going away. Microsoft is selling copies of Windows at the same rate as PC makers are selling their wares. That means during the last six months of 1998 alone, users installed 40 million new copies of Windows, give or take a couple of million. (At the beginning of 1998, there were already 200 million copies of Windows in use.) Every one of these new units bundles COM, and most of them are used to run Excel, Word, and other applications based on COM. Unix is growing as a server operating environment at a strong rate, as well. The installed base is much smaller than the Windows base, but Unix remains a central element in the architectures of most corporations. CORBA is one of the most popular methods for development of applications for Unix servers (although CORBA is also available on other server platforms). As Unix grows in importance, CORBA use will also continue to grow.

In the best of all possible worlds, developers will be able to use COM objects as clients that call CORBA services with complete transparency. The shipping manager at PGE would be able to access the weather server from Excel, pumping current and forecast values into his plans, even if the service is implemented as a collection of CORBA objects running on an HP-UX server. As Rosen and Curtis point out, COM is a good basis for client objects, having been designed to support compound documents that provide sophisticated user interface behavior. CORBA, on the other hand, was designed to create server objects that are shared by many users over long periods of time.

These differences in heritage and intent yield technical differences that are truly nasty for developers to mediate. You'll find all of these differences described in these pages—along with programming approaches that bridge the COM-CORBA divide. Rosen and Curtis accomplish this feat in spite of the underlying diversity of Microsoft's COM architecture. They describe both interworking between CORBA and COM, as well as interworking between CORBA and Automation, a special set of interfaces important in Visual Basic programming.

Mike Rosen and David Curtis provide important insights for the VB programmer who has realized that Microsoft's attempts to take COM to the server have a long way to go to efficacy. It also gives C++ developers predisposed to pure CORBA architectures the insights they need to meet Windows half-way in their projects. Lastly, the book should be required reading for any development team evaluating one of the COM-CORBA bridging products emerging on the market today. Most COM-CORBA bridging products implement the Object Management Group's COM/CORBA Interworking standard, after a fashion. However, a look at the newsgroup discussions of these products reveals that developers are struggling with them. Several leading products are in transition. Most are nowhere near as transparent as developers want them to be. In *Integrating CORBA and COM Applications,* development groups will find the knowledge they need to navigate the many choices among bridging products, along with a chapter devoted entirely to the ins and outs of developing applications using COM-CORBA bridges.

People are excited about the promise of distributed object technology. Much of the discussion in the industry, however, ignores the vision of a transparent object network that PGE stumbled upon way back when. Most of the talk is about which standard—COM, CORBA, and now, Java—will push the others off of the scene. We should know better by now. The only constant in software is diversity. COM, CORBA, and Java will all contribute to networks of distributed objects now and in the future. Yes, diversity is messy, and interferes with the creation of "standard" objects that everyone can easily use. So be it. Developers have always had to create great applications in spite of messy diversity. With *Integrating CORBA and COM Applications,* authors Rosen and Curtis have given developers the guide they need to create value in spite of the vagaries of COM-CORBA interworking.

—John R. Rymer, President
Upstream Consulting

Acknowledgments

An endeavor as involved as writing a book cannot be done alone, but requires help and support from many directions. I'd like to thank all my colleagues who provided encouragement and reviewed materials. In particular, I'd like to thank Dan Foody of Visual Edge Software who answered numerous questions and provided material for the section on bi-directional integration. I'd like to thank all my friends who didn't give up on me during the year that I worked exclusively on the book and was "no fun". Most importantly, I'd like to thank my wife Tamar for her constant support and encouragement and for setting an example of what you can achieve when you apply yourself.

—Mike Rosen

There are too many people to thank properly in a finite space, so I can only skim along the top of the ocean of indebtedness. Thanks to Richard Soley for patience with me when I disappeared from sight, to Andrew Watson for keeping my spirits up; to the many people in the OMG community who contributed in one way or another (some without even knowing it): Jeff Mischkinsky, Carol Burt, and Dave Frankel, to name but a few. Thanks to all of the fine people who contributed to the COM-CORBA Interworking specification, which was one of very few enjoyable collaborative standards-writing projects I have ever participated in. Finally, untold gratitude to my wife Mona and my sons Tim and Aaron for their understanding and support.

—David Curtis

Integrating CORBA® and COM Applications

1 *Introduction*

CORBA and COM have both emerged as important technologies for building modern distributed object and client/server systems. In this book we show how these two technologies can work together to build useful systems efficiently, by exploiting their complementary strengths to accomplish together what neither could do (or do as well) separately. In doing so, we will make some value judgments about the relative suitability of each technology for given tasks based on our engineering experience, sound reasoning, and objective observations. Our intent is not to assault either camp, but to show how and why they can and should coexist not only peacefully, but also symbiotically. Both of this book's authors were key contributors to the OMG's COM/CORBA Interworking Specification and have designed, built, and used interworking bridge products. We believe our extensive experience in designing and using CORBA and COM applications will help you make the most of these technologies.

Overview of the Book and the Technology

In many respects, CORBA and COM are perceived to be competing technologies. There is some justification for this. Both offer some notion of standard interfaces for objects or components; both support remote access to their respective objects. There are, however, major differences in their design centers and evolutionary paths that determine their suitability for different tasks. COM (Component Object Model) (and OLE, or Object Linking and Embedding) was designed as a technology for managing compound documents, emphasizing document linking and embedding and event management, and was designed for propagating state changes to multiple views of a document. In doing so, it also needed to support

1

windowing functions for displaying visual presentations, negotiating for display real estate between applications and mechanisms for user-input like drag-and-drop, cut and paste, and so on. Subsequent generations of COM technology evolved to support packaged software components (VBX's, OCX's, or OLE controls) that have made a major impact on visual programming in such environments as Visual Basic (VB), PowerBuilder, and Delphi.

The world in which COM/OLE evolved was a single-user, single-machine environment, that is, the Windows desktop platform. Many of the features of OLE, such as visual rendering, make the most sense in, and take advantage of, this single-machine environment. Even with the recent additions of distribution technology (DCOM/ActiveX) and migration to more sophisticated platforms (Windows NT and UNIX), ActiveX's single-machine, presentation-oriented genealogy remains evident in its organization, features, programming interfaces, and restrictions. Together, these strongly influence its suitability for various roles in complex enterprise software systems.

In contrast, CORBA (Common Object Request Broker Architecture) technology was designed from the outset as a distributed object infrastructure whose goals were interoperability and integration in distributed systems. It evolved within a heterogeneous multiplatform, multilanguage world and is offered by a variety of different vendors. CORBA is an open standard that defines interfaces and interoperability protocols, but does not specify implementation details or trade-offs. As such, different vendor's implementations are focused on different utilization characteristics such as real-time, work group, or very large-scale enterprise applications. However, CORBA is not an application or programming environment or a mechanism for implementing user interfaces. As is the case with COM, CORBA's design and heritage determine the roles it can competently play in software systems.

One of the primary theses of this book may be summed up in this way:

• •

COM's strengths best cast it for the role of a component-oriented programming model for managing presentation and user interaction. CORBA's strengths best suit it to the roles of distributed infrastructure and integration medium. As such, these technologies are complementary, and together they constitute a powerful tool kit for building complex enterprise applications. (See Figure 1.1.)

In this book we hope to show you how to use these technologies together to build successful enterprise applications by letting each one play its strong suit. In

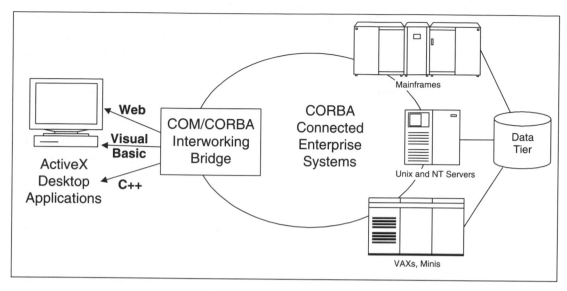

Figure 1.1 *CORBA and COM complement each other in the enterprise.*

doing so, we will examine in detail the rationale for our thesis, considering design alternatives and exploring the operational envelopes of the technologies, to see how they fit together and where boundaries should be drawn.

Who Should Read This Book

This book is a guidebook for real programmers and software architects (not to be confused with programmers). We will present the CORBA and COM technologies by way of application scenarios, for which we will provide solutions in the form of sample code and running programs. We want to provide you with a "nuts and bolts" view of useful, real-world design and programming techniques. About half of the book is dedicated to programming techniques and examples within which we have covered all of the basic interworking programming problems and many of the more esoteric cases that you will encounter when building an application. Our goal for this half of the book is as follows:

• •

When you are presented with interworking progamming problems, you will be able to relate them to programming tasks presented in our examples, and you will understand the issues involved in writing the code to solve the problem.

However, we do not intend for this to be a "cookbook" of canned design patterns or only a catalog of solutions to specific programming problems that you can cut and paste into your applications. It is more important to us that you gain an understanding of the architectural principles involved in the design decisions you will face when you build applications with these technologies. Our goal is the following:

• •

When you are presented with problems unlike any of the examples presented in this book, you will nevertheless be well-equipped to tackle them with confidence in your design judgment regarding where to use which technology, and how to make them work together.

These assumptions dictate the programming environments and languages we use in the book. COM presents two different programming paradigms, Automation and COM (also called Vtable or custom) interfaces. This book will focus mostly on Automation and ActiveX interfaces rather than the low-level COM interfaces, since Automation and Automation-based environments constitute the vast majority of programming activities on the desktop. COM programming is also covered, though not in as much detail. We do specifically highlight and provide examples where COM is a superior implementation choice over Automation. Desktop client programs will be constructed in environments—such as Visual Basic and Visual C++—that you are most likely to be using already, based on your decision to use COM and ActiveX. Distributed services will be constructed in CORBA in a variety of environments, using more than one ORB (Object Request Broker) product, and different CORBA/ActiveX interworking products, and in languages suited to a server environment—specifically, C++ and Java. However, this is not a book on CORBA programming. In general, nothing special has been done to the CORBA servers for them to work with ActiveX clients. In these cases, we provide the server code on our Web site, but do not describe its implementation in the book. When we have specifically done something different to work in the CORBA/COM interworking environment, we do include the CORBA code and describe what we have done and why.

These assumptions also bound the topics covered in this book and the approaches taken to solve problems. We assume that you have decided to use COM/ActiveX and CORBA technologies from the outset, and we will concentrate on showing how this is done. We will not spend much energy on justifying that decision for you, or examining alternative technologies for solving the same problems, although it should be noted that at least one very viable alternative exists. Many architects and developers are choosing to build distributed client-server applications using Java as their desktop client medium, and CORBA as their distribution medium. Java and CORBA together present a powerful combination for cross-platform, highly portable client/server development, and are particularly well suited for Internet- and Web-oriented environments. For an excellent discussion of using these technologies together, see *Client/Server Programming with Java and CORBA*, by Robert Orfali and Dan Harkey (John Wiley & Sons, 1998).

A detailed discussion of the relative merits of these approaches is not the goal of this book, but a brief examination is warranted. Technology decisions are usually motivated by a combination of hardware and software choices. For COM/ActiveX technology, PC desktop machines either already exist throughout an enterprise or are readily available through a variety of low-cost suppliers. There is a wide variety of off-the-shelf components (ActiveX controls) available combined with powerful, easy to use, programming environments such as Visual Basic, Visual C++, and Delphi. These tools are well suited to developing user interface applications and also provide the opportunity for close integration with ubiquitous applications, such as Microsoft Office. At present, and for the foreseeable future, the use of ActiveX carries with it the implicit assumption that you will be using the Wintel platform as your desktop machine. Decisions to use Java are often motivated by a need to run in a multiplatform client environment or on low-cost/low-management NC display systems and the need to eliminate costs for installing and maintaining client software configurations. Java provides a programming environment which can easily exploit and integrate with Web-based technology, and the general sense of hipness associated with being a Java programmer.

How This Book Is Organized

Much of the book is appropriate for technically literate non-programmers, such as product managers, MIS managers, and technical marketing people who need to understand the implications of this technology and how it applies to their environments. Chapter 2 provides an overview of the process of developing a Visual Basic client for a CORBA server, and Chapter 3 covers the details of the interworking architecture. Chapter 11 discusses architectural, technology, and design considerations for COM/CORBA applications. Many of the chapters are targeted specifically at programmers who want to understand how to build applications that use components from both technologies, and to understand the motivation for the interworking's design decisions. Chapters 4 through 6 give detailed programming examples for interface and datatype mappings. Chapters 7, 8, and 9 combine architectural discussion on object model differences with programming examples showing how these are resolved. Chapter 10 gives several examples of building reusable ActiveX controls for CORBA objects. The layout of the book is organized in a logical order for those who want to learn both the architectural and programming details of COM/CORBA interworking and would thus read all of the chapters. Let's look at them in a little more detail.

Chapter 2: COM and CORBA Together: A Simple Example provides a quick overview of the mechanics of object model interoperability and transparency. We develop a simple example of a CORBA object presenting an Automation interface to a Visual Basic client. The example is presented as an overview without delving into detail or hard technical issues. It walks through the steps of developing the Visual Basic application and invoking the CORBA object from Visual Basic, tracing through the interaction between the client application and the remote CORBA server as a precursor to the rest of the book.

Chapter 3: Interworking Architecture discusses the basic correspondence between elements of both object models; object references, typing systems, interface composition, and invocation semantics, initially emphasizing the commonality at an abstract level. Next, we discuss the differences; lifecycle, inheritance, type systems, and interface standards, especially from the perspective of programming style and usage models, each serving its intended purposes admirably. This discussion of differences provides a technical basis for understanding the details of the interworking architecture in the following chapters.

Chapter 4: Basic Mappings describes in detail the mapping between Automation and CORBA for simple datatypes. This is presented as a Visual Basic programming example that illustrates the mappings and usage, intermixed with discussion of practical aspects during usage; what works, what doesn't. We cover mapping of interfaces and invocations, naming conventions applied to the mappings, and the whole range of scalar and simple datatypes.

Chapter 5: Complex Datatypes continues with the detailed description of the mappings, but deals with the complex CORBA datatypes such as structures, unions, arrays, sequences, and anys. This is illustrated with a Visual Basic programming example that simulates an employee 401(k) investment plan interface.

Chapter 6: COM Data Type Mappings provides a discussion and introduction to the differences between integrating CORBA with Automation and CORBA with COM. It describes the CORBA/COM mapping and illustrates the mapping and differences by reimplementing the examples from Chapters 4 and 5, this time using the COM mappings in C++.

Chapter 7: Integrating COM and CORBA covers common patterns of usage in COM and CORBA, showing how they integrate. It describes how and why different specific features of the object models are mutually useful concentrating on the areas of object creation, factories, life cycle, binding, object references, and identity. Visual Basic programming examples illustrate this usage and integration.

Chapter 8: Exceptions continues the previous chapter's comparison of object models by examining the exception handling mechanism of each. The concepts are illustrated with programming examples in Visual Basic and C++.

Chapter 9: Bidirectional Integration explains the motivation and architecture for mapping both from COM to CORBA and from CORBA to COM (reverse mapping). It provides details of the mappings and programming examples of reverse mapping and callbacks. We show programming examples of how to tie these callbacks into the native COM event mechanism and how to call a COM object from a CORBA client.

Chapter 10: Building an ActiveX Control provides practical advice and examples for using ActiveX components in a mixed environment. We describe how CORBA objects can present ActiveX interfaces, and present detailed examples of programs that do so for different uses. One example shows how to write a control in Visual Basic and emphasizes a COM-centric approach, where a CORBA object is being designed or adapted to an ActiveX interface with the typical ActiveX style and usage in mind (i.e., get CORBA to conform to ActiveX's view). Another Visual Basic example describes how a particular CORBA design pattern, a server providing notification to a client, can be best expressed as ActiveX controls, and how to structure the interfaces so that this works well. The last example, in C++ using MFC, uses another design pattern, to show how to take advantage of the superior COM mappings for complex datatypes when constructing an ActiveX control. We also discuss the architectural issue of using these ActiveX controls in a Web-based application.

Chapter 11: Using COM/CORBA Bridges in Distributed Systems offers more detail about what each technology brings to the enterprise. We present discussion and advice on how to incorporate CORBA and COM/ActiveX together into robust distributed object systems, how to determine bridge location in a distributed system, and practical issues of architecture, development, and deployment.

Chapter12: Conclusions and Futures is our glimpse into the future. We describe current trends and directions of evolution of COM/CORBA integration.

Tools You Will Need

You will not need any tools to get a basic understanding of the interworking architecture. However, many readers will want to try the programming examples. Most of our examples are written in Visual Basic version 5. Some examples are written in Visual C++ using MFC. In either case, the examples will work on both Windows NT 4.0 or Windows95. That covers the clients. The interworking bridges that we use are BEA Systems Inc.'s ObjectBroker Desktop Connection version 1.0, Visual Edge Software Ltd.'s Object Bridge and BEA Systems Inc.'s Iceberg ActiveX client. The servers are written using BEA Systems Inc.'s ObjectBroker version 3.0 in C++ and BEA Systems Inc.'s Iceberg Object System in C++. (Links to these companies are provided on our Web site.)

What's on the Web Site

All of the example code in the book is available on our Web site: www.wiley.com /compbooks/rosen. This includes all of the Visual Basic and Visual C++ client examples, all of the servers, and all of the other code fragments throughout the book. The code is available as either one big zip file or as individual zip files by chapter. We have links to the companies that provide the interworking bridges and the CORBA server ORBs that we used during development of the examples. We also have links to sites with useful information on CORBA, COM, ActiveX, and distributed object systems.

Summary

Both CORBA and COM technologies will be used to build enterprise applications. The most successful applications will be those that harness the complementary strengths of each technology. These applications will gain competitive advantage from using the best of each technology over a "one or the other" approach. They will enjoy the benefits of a mature, robust, CORBA-based distribution infrastructure operating in a heterogeneous, multiplatform environment. They will also enjoy the benefits of the Windows desktop, such as powerful user interface development tools like Visual Basic, integration with standard applications like Excel, and low cost, commodity hardware. This book will show you how to build these applications. Let's get started by looking at the simple Visual Basic application example in Chapter 2.

2 COM and CORBA Together: A Simple Example

This chapter introduces the basic concepts, development, and programming tasks involved in getting COM and CORBA to work together. They are introduced together in the context of implementing a simple Automation-based Visual Basic client that accesses a CORBA server. An overview is presented here to give you the big picture. We will step through the process of translating a CORBA object into a COM object and integrating this new object into a Visual Basic project. From Visual Basic, we will create an instance of the object and invoke methods on it. This chapter's overview of the entire process will give you the context to understand the concepts, mappings, development, and programming tasks that are presented in detail in the rest of the book.

The goal of the example in this chapter and of this book is to explain how to write Automation (or COM or ActiveX) clients to CORBA services, not to teach CORBA or ActiveX programming. A basic assumption is that the interface to the checking account referred to in the example in this chapter has already been defined in terms of CORBA Interface Definition Language (IDL). Throughout this book we assume that the interfaces to the remote objects are described in IDL and that the reader is somewhat familiar with IDL. There are many texts available on IDL if you need more information (see our "Recommended Reading" list). We will also not spend much time describing the implementation of the CORBA server, except where specific steps have been taken in the server to accommodate the COM object model. Each example is provided with a working CORBA server.

Let's look at a bank or financial services company where customers have different types of accounts such as checking, savings, loans, IRAs, and the like. There are several different types of people who need information about these accounts: tellers, customer service reps, sales reps, and, of course, the customer. The bank needs to present the account information to each different user in a format that is appropriate for that information consumer—as in our example here through a custom Visual Basic application designed for a bank teller. The bank would probably have several different applications, each of which interacts with account information in potentially different ways. There is also a lot of similarity in these interactions, suggesting the possibility of reuse via a component-based development approach—a major goal of the ActiveX architecture. Before delving into the details of ActiveX controls, we will examine the underlying COM architecture, the components of a control, and how they relate to CORBA objects.

In our simplified Visual Basic example shown in Figure 2.1, we will develop a user interface for a bank teller who deals with checking accounts. The first step the teller must perform is to get the account associated with a customer by supplying the account number. Once the teller has the account, the customer will be able to deposit and withdraw funds from the accounts and get the account information.

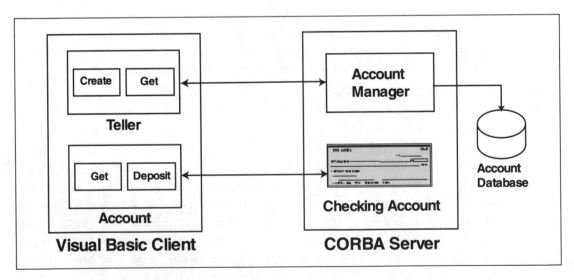

Figure 2.1 *The simple bank teller example.*

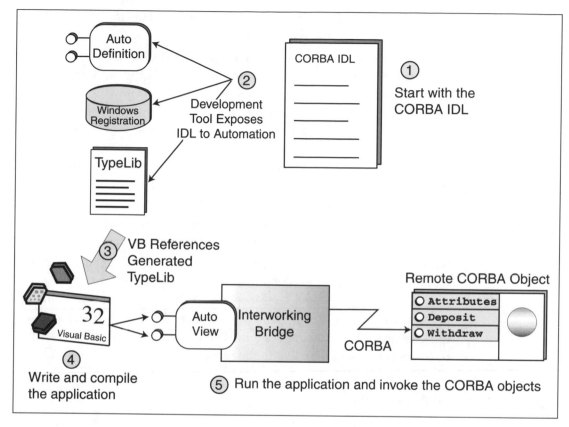

Figure 2.2 *Process overview.*

Developing the Client: From IDL to Visual Basic Application

Figure 2.2 shows the steps you go through to create an Automation client for a CORBA object. Let's get an overview of these steps now and then go into more detail as we go through the process of developing the client.

1. **Start with the CORBA IDL.** We assume that you start with the IDL and that it was probably provided to you by the server developer. If you are also the server developer, it shouldn't be too hard to get the IDL.

2. **Expose the IDL to Automation.** There are two distinct sets of processes involved in developing and using an Automation client: the development process and the run-time process. In the development process, we expose the CORBA IDL to Automation by using a development tool that gener-

ates the variety of things needed by Automation. This tool is provided as part of the interworking bridge product.

3. **Include the Automation Views in Visual Basic.** One of the things generated during the development process is the OLE Type Library (typelib). The typelib contains a description of all of the interfaces for every CORBA object contained in the library. For each interface, the properties and method signatures are described, including the data types of all parameters. Visual Basic needs this information in order to invoke methods on the objects, so you must tell Visual Basic to include the typelib in your project.

4. **Write the Visual Basic client.** This is the step where you create a custom visual presentation, or GUI, for the CORBA object and tie the GUI to the object's methods and properties. After compiling the code, you create an executable file for the client.

5. **Run the client.** The final step is running the client application. The COM/CORBA interworking bridge goes through a series of steps to connect the Visual Basic application to the CORBA object in a way that appears natural to the Visual Basic programmer. Thankfully, these steps are transparent to the client application but are covered briefly in this chapter to give a better understanding of the process.

Development Time

Before a CORBA object can be used in an Automation application, the CORBA definition of that object must be mapped to an equivalent Automation object definition. The mapping, which is described in the next four chapters, will do the following:

- Translate CORBA attributes to Automation properties.
- Translate CORBA operations to Automation methods.
- Translate CORBA data types to Automation data types.
- Generate COM interface IDs and program IDs.

The new, generated definition of the Automation object can be represented as a Microsoft IDL or ODL (Object Definition Language) file and as a typelib. The new mapped object is called an *Automation view of a CORBA target object*, or Automation view for short. As with all COM objects, this object requires several unique identifiers such as the class ID, an interface ID for each interface, and a program ID. The development tool generates these identifiers based on a deterministic algorithm and then registers the IDs in the Window's system registry. While the

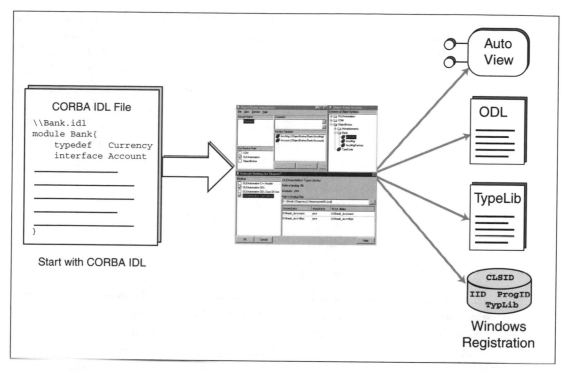

Figure 2.3 *The development process.*

development tool generates the class and definitions for the Automation view object, it does not generate an instance of a view object. Rather, the instance is created dynamically at run time (Figure 2.3).

NOTE Microsoft IDL will eventually replace ODL, but as of this writing most tools and environments are still using the ODL file.

Naming Conventions

Before we can use the Automation View from Visual Basic, we first need to review some of the naming conventions used when mapping CORBA to Automation. CORBA uses the *module* keyword in IDL to provide a unique scope for the names of interfaces described within that module. In other words, the interface "Account," defined in the "Bank" module is different than the interface "Account," defined within the "Credit" module. Because Microsoft ODL does not support the same type of name scoping, but we want to preserve the uniqueness, the COM/CORBA mapping defines a naming convention that appends the module name with the interface name. The combined name is then preceded with *DI* (for Dual Interface), yielding the Automation view interface name as *DImodule_interface*. For our example interface Account in module Bank, the name is "DIBank_Account." Following the same convention, symbolic references to the interface ID are created as "IID_DIBank_Account." If you are familiar with Microsoft ODL format, you may want to take a look at the files created by the development tool to see how the CORBA IDL file has been mapped to ODL.

The CORBA IDL

The bank IDL shown in Listing 2.1 describes a simple bank account object that has three attributes—name, account number, and balance—and two operations—Deposit and Withdraw. The values of funds (the balance) is returned as a user-defined type, Currency, which is defined as a float. The Deposit and Withdraw operations also return the new balance after either crediting or debiting the account. You get an account object by asking the bank account manager to either create a new account or get an existing account. It is assumed that there is only one bank and that you get a new instance of the bank account manager object from a simple factory.

All of the example code in this book is available at our Web site—www.wiley.com/compbooks/rosen—individually or as one zip file. If you copy the entire zip file and expand it, the CORBA IDL file will be in the directory "\Chapter2\Server\Bank.idl."

Exposing the IDL to Automation

Now that we have the IDL file and we know what's going to be generated from it, how does the development process work? Vendors have taken a different approach with their development tools, including command line APIs (Application Programs Interfaces), GUI APIs, and integration with an Integrated Development Environment (IDE). We will use a variety of them throughout this book. A link to each product used is available on our Web site.

Development tools typically allow you to specify several parameters:

The input—either from a IDL file or from a CORBA repository.

The type of mapping—either OLE Automation, COM, or both.

Listing 2.1 Bank CORBA Interface Definition Language (IDL).

```
Module Bank
{
  typedef float   Currency;

  interface Account {
    readonly  attribute  Currency   balance;
    readonly  attribute  string     name;
    readonly  attribute  long        number;

    Currency  Deposit     (in Currency  amount);
    Currency  Withdraw    (in Currency  amount);
  };

  interface AcctMgr {
    Account   createAccount  (in string    name,
                              in Currency  balance);
    Account   getAccount     (in long      number);
  };

  interface AcctMgrFactory {
    AcctMgr   create_object ();
  };

};
```

The type of output—such as header files, MIDL, ODL, and typelibs as well as what directory to write the resultant files to.

For this example, we will use a generic exposure mechanism common to many products. Many interworking bridge products will also provide a different, "value-added" interface for exposure. (1) To expose the IDL, we have first loaded it into the CORBA Interface Repository using the normal utilities provided by the CORBA product. In many business environments, this step will be done for you by the CORBA server developer. We browsed the interfaces in the repository and selected the two that we wanted to expose for this example, Account and Ac-ctMgr. (2) For Visual Basic, we want to use Automation Interfaces, so we select OLE Automation in the "Use Service From" box. (3) For the output, we want to generate an ODL file and a type library, so we select these and provide a directory

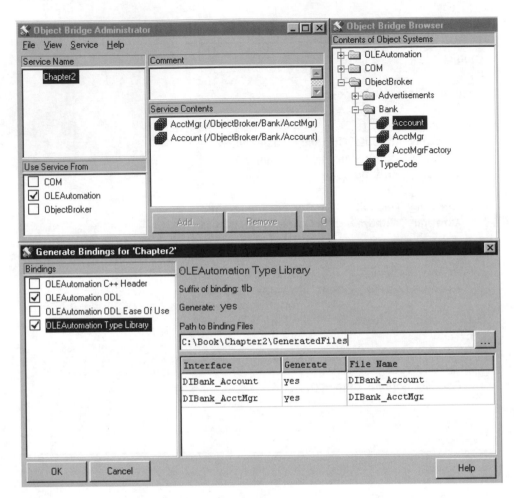

Figure 2.4 *Exposing the IDL to Automation.*

path for the generated files. After making the appropriate selections, we click on "OK." This generates the typelib, ODL file, Automation view definitions, and IDs and registers them in the Windows system registry. When finished, exit the development tool (Figure 2.4).

Including the Automation Views in Visual Basic

Now that we have generated a type library to describe the Automation view object, we need to tell Visual Basic to use it. This is done by including a reference into the project, as follows:

1. In Visual Basic, select the Project menu and choose References.. This brings up a dialog box listing "Available References" or type libraries that Visual Basic knows about.

2. Select Browse, which brings up the familiar File Open dialog box. Find the type library files that were created while exposing IDL to Automation in step 2 of Figure 2.2, Process overview.

3. Choose Open. Notice that "DIBank_Account" now appears in the list of available references and is checked.

NOTE Throughout this book, we will be using Visual Basic version 5.0, which differs slightly from version 4.0 in some areas, such as the inclusion of references. We will describe only the version 5.0 mechanisms.

Now let's see what Visual Basic knows about the DIBank_Account object. This is done using the Object Browser as shown in Figure 2.5.

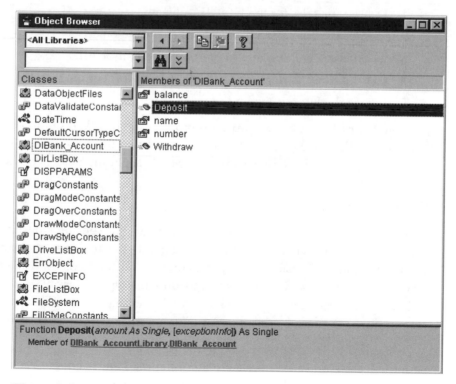

Figure 2.5 *An Automation View definition seen with VB Object Browser.*

1. In Visual Basic, select the View menu and choose Object Browser.

2. In the left pane, scroll down the list of classes until you find "DIBank_Account."

3. Select "DIBank_Account." In the right pane, you will see the properties and methods of the Automation view object.

4. In the right pane, select the Deposit method. The method signature appears in the bottom pane of the browser. Here you can see the CORBA method Deposit, which takes an amount as input and returns the new balance. In CORBA, the data type for these parameters is Currency, which we defined as a float. Notice that this has been translated to the Automation data type Single.

Writing the Visual Basic Client

Now we are finally ready to write the Visual Basic client application. In this very simple example we are going to do the following:

1. Declare variables for the CORBA objects.

2. Create an instance of a bank account manager object.

3. Ask the account manager to return an account object.

4. Get the name, balance, and account number properties.

5. Invoke the Deposit method.

The Visual Basic example project is provided on our Web site in the directory "\Chapter2\VBClient\Teller.vbp." It consists of two forms: a Teller form and an Account form. Figure 2.6 shows the Visual Basic application.

Declare Variables

In Visual Basic, as with most programming languages, you must declare variables before you can use them. This is, therefore, a good place to discuss the naming convention used in the Visual Basic examples throughout this book. Variable names are preceded by a few lowercase letters that identify the type of variable and then a descriptive name that starts with a capital letter. For example, a text box that holds the account number would be called txtAcctNum; a teller object would be objTeller.

We need to declare variables for the Account Manager (AcctMgr) and Account objects. Rather than declare them using the Dim statement each place they are needed, we will declare them as Public so that we can share these objects be-

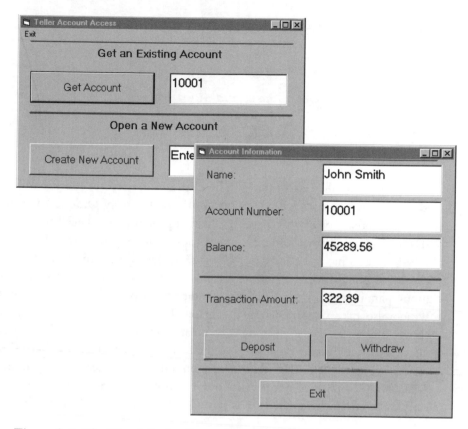

Figure 2.6 *The Visual Basic teller application.*

tween different routines and forms. When declaring an object variable in Visual Basic, you can use the generic *Object* type or specify a particular type. Aside from the obvious compile-time type checking you get, we will see in Chapter 3 another advantage to declaring an object as a type. Objects in Visual Basic, also called "user-defined types," are identified by their interface, so here we will use the Automation form of the CORBA interface name created using the *DImodule_interface* naming convention. Listing 2.2 shows the declaration of the variable in the module "modPublic.bas."

Create the Account Manager Object

In any object-based system, you invoke a method on an object to do work or to create other objects. One common problem shared by all object systems is where to get the first object from. In COM and Automation, objects are created by other

Listing 2.2 Declaring CORBA objects as public variables.

```
' modPublic.bas

' Declare the Account Manager and Account objects here.
Public objAcctMgr As DIBank_AcctMgr
Public objAccount As DIBank_Account
```

special objects called *class factories*. The class factories create specific objects and are identified by the class ID (a 128-bit GUID or Globally Unique Identifier) of the class they create or by the friendlier, textual program ID. Recall that both of these IDs are generated by the development tool while exposing the IDL. Like COM, CORBA also has the concept of object factories. These simple CORBA factories can be mapped directly to COM class factories. (COM class factories do not allow input parameters for the creation of objects, so only CORBA simple factories, which also take no parameters, are mapped to COM class factories.) Listing 2.3 shows the Visual Basic code used to create the AcctMgr object using the COM class factory. In Visual Basic, we use the program ID to identify the COM class to create. This is the ID that was generated by the development tool as *CORBA.OLE.module_interface*. In our example, we create the account manager only once when the application is started in the Form_Load subroutine.

Get an Account Object from the Account Manager

Now that we have our initial Bank object (the account manager), we can get account objects from it using the getAccount method. This method takes the account number as input and returns an account object. This is an action that the teller will be performing repeatedly, so we want it to be easy. When the teller enters the account number and presses Enter, we will invoke the getAccount method and activate the Account form. The CORBA object requires that the account number be passed as a long, but the Visual Basic form will have it as a text string, so we use the convenient CLng, convert to long, function to convert the account number text to a long. Listing 2.3 also shows the code to invoke the getAccount method on the Account Manager object.

Get the Account Properties

The teller has entered an account number that causes an account object to be returned from the bank. When the account is returned, we will bring up a new

Listing 2.3 Creating objects.

```
' frmTeller — code for Teller form

Private Sub Form_Load()
    ' Create an instance of an Account Manager
    ' Do this once, on form load
    Set objAcctMgr = CreateObject("CORBA.OLE.Bank_AcctMgr")
End Sub


Private Sub btnGet_Click()
    ' Ask the bank to return an account object
    Set objAccount = objAcctMgr.getAccount(CLng(txtAcctNum))
End Sub
```

form that displays all of the attributes of the account and allows the teller to deposit or withdraw funds. Recall that CORBA attributes get mapped to Automation properties, each with a *propget* accessor function. We will use these to read the account attributes, as shown in Listing 2.4.

Listing 2.4 Using the account object.

```
' frmAccount — Account information form

Private Sub Form_Load()
    ' Get and display the Account's properties
    txtName    = objAccount.Name
    txtAcctNum = objAccount.Number
    txtBalance = objAccount.balance
End Sub


Private Sub btnDeposit_Click()
    ' Deposit money and display the new balance
    Dim newBalance As Single
    NewBalance = objAccount.Deposit (CSng(txtXactAmount))
    txtBalance = newBalance
End Sub
```

Invoke Account Methods

Invoking the Deposit method on the account object is just as easy. The example we've presented illustrates how the Visual Basic programmer has been able to interact with the CORBA object in a way that is natural to the programmer and native to the COM object system. No knowledge of CORBA is required to use the objects from desktop applications; only the CORBA IDL is required for the purposes of development. When deploying the application, the necessary Automation view definitions, IDs, and registry entries can be distributed and installed with the application. Now let's take a quick look at what happens at run time to provide the object model transparency.

Running the Client

Figure 2.7 illustrates the main steps that take place at run time.

1. **CreateObject**. The Visual Basic application calls CreateObject, specifying the generated program ID CORBA.OLE.Bank_AcctMgr, that corresponds to the CORBA factory. Windows looks up the class ID associated with the program ID and then looks up what server, executable, or DLL is associated with the class ID.

2. **Get the DLL.** The COM/CORBA bridge DLL is the server for this class ID, and it is loaded into the client process. The CreateInstance method is invoked on the COM class factory implemented by the bridge DLL.

3. **Create the CORBA object**. The bridge DLL, acting as a CORBA client, invokes the create_object method on the CORBA AcctMgrFactory object, which returns an object reference to a CORBA AcctMgr Object.

4. **Create the Automation View**. The bridge DLL knows that it cannot return a CORBA object reference to an Automation client. It looks in its repository for the Automation CLSID that was associated with this CORBA object during the development process and dynamically creates the Automation view for the CORBA target object. An interface pointer to the AcctMgr view object is returned to the Visual Basic program.

5. **Invoke an Automation method**. The Visual Basic application invokes a method, such as getAccount, on the view object. The bridge DLL translates the Automation methods, properties, and data types to the corresponding CORBA call and invokes the method on the CORBA object. This may be accomplished statically by linking against compiled stubs or dynamically at run time, depending on how the interworking bridge is im-

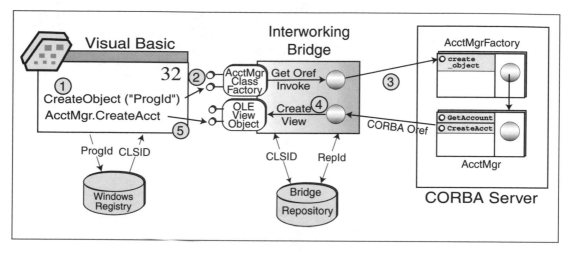

Figure 2.7 *Run-time processes.*

plemented. The resulting status and arguments are then translated to Automation types and returned to the Visual Basic application.

Building and Testing the Example

We have provided a working sample client and server on our Web site, www.wiley .com/compbooks/rosen. The Visual Basic client project is in the directory "\Chapter2\VBClient." The CORBA server is in the directory "\Chapter2 \Server." Both are provided with source and procedures for building the executables. Depending on the version of operating system, compiler, COM/CORBA bridge, and the like on your system, you may need to modify them slightly. Instructions on how to build and run the example are provided in the readme.txt file in the "\Chapter2" directory.

This chapter has presented an overview of the process of mapping CORBA to COM and building client applications. The next several chapters examine the mappings in more detail. Chapter 3 presents an architectural view of the mappings; Chapters 4 and 5 give detailed programming examples of how to use simple and complex CORBA data types from Visual Basic; and Chapter 6 deals with writing C++ COM clients for CORBA objects. We will continue to use programming examples to explain the concepts of object creation, life cycle, and references in Chapter 7, exceptions in Chapter 8, and bidirectional applications in Chapter 9. Chapter 10 will tie many of these topics together with several examples of writing ActiveX controls for CORBA objects, so let's get on with it.

3 *Interworking Architecture*

This chapter discusses architectural issues you will face when using CORBA and COM technologies together—specifically when using a COM/CORBA bridging solution. By *architectural issue* (in this context) we mean the underlying structural mechanisms and capabilities of the two object systems, how they correspond to each other, how they differ from each other, and the problems involved in trying to map the two models together.

An understanding of these issues is vital to the successful use of this technology. The goal of bridging technology is to make the fact that you are using two different object systems as transparent as possible—to create the illusion for COM programmers that the CORBA objects they are using are in fact COM objects, and vice versa. While this illusion is critical to providing straightforward, natural programming models, it is not a perfect illusion. There are some differences between COM and CORBA that cannot be masked or accommodated mechanically, and therefore designers and programmers must take them explicitly into account when building systems that use both technologies together. An appreciation of the architectural issues also makes it easier to understand why the specific programming techniques presented in later chapters are necessary and how they can be employed most effectively.

As we stated in Chapter 1, our discussion in this book will focus primarily on Automation interfaces since that is the area of interest for most users of the technology. It is, however, impossible to describe Automation interfaces without beginning with the COM foundation. Many Automation features are the same as COM's, and others are layered on top of COM features.

Mapping between Object Models

The example used in Chapter 2 illustrates the goal of providing a mapping between object models—to allow clients in one object system to access objects in a different object system but to do so in such a way that the client sees the object in terms of its own system. In Chapter 2, the bank teller client was written in Visual Basic (VB), whose native object model is Automation. The bank object was built with CORBA technology. The interworking solution product automatically converted the bank's IDL interface into a corresponding Automation, or `IDispatch` interface and dynamically built an Automation object that converted invocations on the `IDispatch` interface into invocations on a CORBA object. The teller client is essentially unaware that the bank is anything other than an Automation object.

The most important word in the previous paragraph is *corresponding*: "converted the bank's IDL interface into a *corresponding* `IDispatch` interface." That word begs an interesting question: how does an IDL interface correspond to, or *map* to, a COM interface, or vice versa? The answer (or answers) to that question and its implications for the programmer are at the heart of this chapter and much of the rest of this book.

Becoming Familiar with the Terminology

We need to introduce some basic terms and concepts here that will be used in the following discussion as well as present the symbology that will be used in most of the figures:

Interworking. *Interworking* is the term coined to describe the process by which two object models cooperate, each object system allowing the other to have access to its own objects. *Interoperability* is another word already in existence that means roughly the same thing. Unfortunately, this word had already become heavily overloaded in the context of ORBs, so the authors of the COM /CORBA Interworking Specification decided to coin a new word, *interworking*, thereby accepting the karmic debt that such behavior necessarily entails.

Interworking Specification. The Interworking Specification is an OMG specification (i.e., a document) that defines the mapping between the COM and CORBA object models and the requirements that must be met by specific bridging products to be considered compliant with the specification. The Interworking Specification is the reference that defines the rules for how COM and CORBA cooperate.

Bridging product. Bridging products are specific commercially available software products that implement the Interworking Specification. There are several such products on the market at the time of this writing, supplied by ORB vendors.

Views and Bridges

For a CORBA object to present itself to a Visual Basic (VB) client as if it were an Automation object, there must actually be an Automation object whose job it is to accept invocations and convert them into invocations on the CORBA object. This object is a type of proxy in that it stands in for the real object, creating the illusion that the CORBA object is actually an Automation object. This role is similar to the role played by a COM proxy, except that the proxy's job in this case is not just to convey the invocation across process boundaries; it also translates and conveys the invocation from one object system to another. To avoid confusion with normal COM proxies (and other uses of the heavily overloaded word *proxy*), objects that serve to map interfaces between object systems are called *views* in the COM/CORBA Interworking Specification. Thus, an Automation object that presents a mapped CORBA IDL interface to VB clients is called an Automation view of a CORBA object, as shown in Figure 3.1. Conversely, a CORBA object that presents a mapped Automation interface to CORBA clients is called a CORBA view of an Automation object, as shown in Figure 3.2.

Superficially, what a view does is fairly obvious—it converts any **in** parameters of the invocation to appropriate similar datatypes in the target object system (the

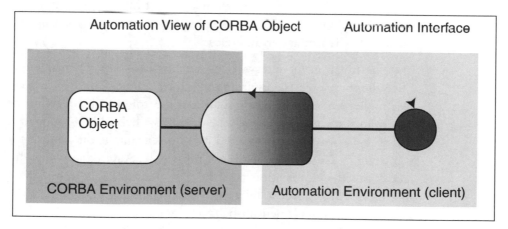

Figure 3.1 *Automation view of CORBA object.*

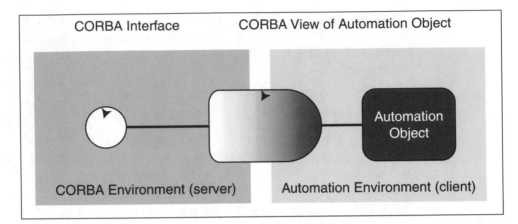

CORBA Interface   CORBA View of Automation Object

Automation
Object

CORBA Environment (server)   Automation Environment (client)

Figure 3.2 *CORBA view of Automation object.*

system in which the actual object being invoked lives), invokes the method in the target object, and converts **out** parameters and return values from the target system's types to the calling system's types and returns them to the calling client.

Notation Conventions

Many descriptions of object systems have adopted the convention of using circles to denote object interfaces or object references and rectangles with rounded corners to represent the actual object implementation. This notation is used in particular when diagramming systems such as COM and CORBA, where making a distinction between an object interface(s) and its implementation is vital and where the object implementation may be physically separated from clients using its interfaces.

The notation for interworking systems has some peculiar requirements since the view objects are playing two roles simultaneously—the role of object implementation in one system and the role of object reference in the other. To show this, a view will be drawn as a hybrid of a rounded rectangle and a circle (see Figures 3.1 and 3.2). In this example, the Automation client is invoking a CORBA target object through an Automation view of that object. From the Automation side, the view looks like an object that presents interfaces. It is, in fact, a fully functional, righteous Automation object that just happens to implement its behavior by invoking a CORBA object. From the CORBA side, it appears to be a client holding an object reference, so the CORBA side of the view is drawn as a half-circle.

Note that this code lives simultaneously in both object systems—it provides an Automation interface, but internally it invokes operations on a CORBA object. As such, it is part of a *bridge* between the two systems. We'll use the term *bridge* in this book to describe software components that implement the mapping between object systems. One important characteristic of the software that constitutes the bridge is that it generally lives in both object worlds simultaneously, just as a physical bridge must touch both sides of the chasm it spans. The bridge includes not only the view objects themselves but all of the supporting mechanics.

Interworking Object Model

The notion of a correspondence or mapping between OLE and CORBA implies that there is some common conceptual view shared by both object systems of what an object is and how you interact with it. This common view provides the basis for mapping between elements in the systems. Figure 3.3 illustrates the structure of that common view, which we will call the *interworking object model*. The interwork-

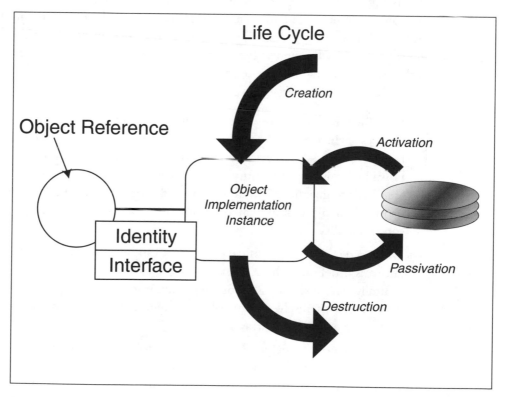

Figure 3.3 *Interworking object model.*

ing object model is an abstract description of the basic concepts shared by both OLE and CORBA—a metamodel, if you will, that can be used to describe the essential elements of either system. The interworking model also serves as a convenient vehicle for comparing the two object systems. The interworking object model has the following elements: interfaces, object references, and object identity and life cycle.

Examining Interfaces

An object is a discrete unit of functionality that presents itself through a well-defined interface described in terms of a well-known, fully described set of interface semantics. Interfaces may be composed by combining or extending other interfaces according to a set of composition rules. For the purposes of the interworking object model, the term *interface* (singular) may be used to denote the collection of all of the interfaces that an object provides. Interfaces are typically described in a specialized language and can be represented in a repository or library.

As illustrated in Figure 3.3, interfaces are a property of both the object and the object reference. The interface characterizes what the object is and does from the client's perspective. An object reference presents the interface to the client, and the object itself supports the interface by providing concrete implementations of the operations that constitute the interface. Our examination will focus on the following aspects of interfaces:

Interface identity. Programs must have a means for identifying specific interfaces, primarily to determine whether a particular object supports the interface they need. Object systems have mechanisms for naming interfaces and possibly for assigning identity values. These mechanisms are less human-readable but are guaranteed to be unique and more amenable to the kind of mechanical manipulation that programs use to determine compatibility and substitutability.

Data types. The range of data types that can be passed as parameters to operations is a defining characteristic of particular object systems. Object systems typically have a set of base types (e.g., numeric types, strings, etc.) that are not fully objects themselves. Some object systems have more complex user-defined types such as structs or arrays.

Interface composition. Generally, object systems provide a mechanism for defining new interfaces in terms of existing interfaces, such as an inheritance mechanism. The specific rules for how interfaces are combined and/or extended constitute the object system's interface composition mechanism.

Requests. The primary purpose of an interface is to make certain operations or methods available to clients. Even though the general notion of object methods is well established, the details of how operations are defined may vary significantly between object models. Such details may include how errors are reported or whether specialized operation forms such as properties or attributes are supported. In addition to the form that operations take, the semantics and behavior of requests at run time must be considered.

Parameters. The description of a request includes a list of parameters that are passed between the client (the caller) and the object (the callee). Important considerations include how parameters are distinguished (e.g., by name or by order), whether optional parameters are allowed, and parameter directionality.

Exceptions. Object systems usually have mechanisms for indicating whether an error occurred during a request and for describing the nature of the error. Some object systems allow users to define their own exception types.

Object References

A client program interacts with a target object by means of an *object reference*. When writing a client program, the reference generally takes the form of a programming object, such as a pointer to a class type in C++ or a value of Object type in Java. From a programming perspective, the object reference acts as a local proxy for the remote object. As such, it presents the object's interface to the client. From the point of view of the overall system, an object reference is an information model that encapsulates the identity of the target object, along with information about the object's location. Precisely what it denotes and how it may be used is an important consideration when mapping between object systems.

Object Identity and Life Cycle

Each request targets a specific object instance, which is denoted by the identity encapsulated in the object reference used to make the request. Precise definitions of object identity are difficult to arrive at and are the subject of considerable debate. In general, your intuitive notion is probably reasonably useful—individual object instances are distinguishable from one another in some scope. In object systems, you can meaningfully discuss a particular object, as distinguished from other objects. In general, there is some behavioral consistency or notion of continuity among a series of requests on the same object reference. In most simple applications objects, object identity is associated with a particular collection of state information encapsulated by the object. The information used to denote a particular instance may or may not be exposed to clients; it may be hidden in the reference.

Object life cycle characterizes how objects are created and destroyed and a great deal of what happens in between. Of particular interest is whether an object model supports transparently persistent objects and, if so, how. In some object systems, a client doesn't need to be concerned about whether the object of interest is currently active (i.e., loaded into a running process) or not. When the client uses the object reference, the object system may automatically activate the object by starting a server and causing the server to load the particular object's state, unbeknownst to the client. Other object systems make clients responsible for explicitly activating the object and doing whatever is necessary to keep the object active as long as they want to use it.

Life-cycle issues are inextricably tied to object identity and object reference concepts. Interworking between COM and CORBA poses interesting challenges in this area, as their life cycle and object identity models are very different.

Describing CORBA with the Interworking Object Model

In CORBA, the interworking object model is mapped to the CORBA object model described in the OMG's *Object Management Architecture Guide* and implemented by ORBs. The details of that model are contained in the CORBA specification. The following summary maps elements of the CORBA object model onto the interworking object model described in the previous section.

Interfaces

In CORBA, interfaces are described in OMG IDL (Interface Definition Language). IDL is a simple declarative language for describing interfaces; it is not a programming language. Full descriptions of CORBA interfaces are also stored in the Interface Repository, which is itself a CORBA object. The Interface Repository gives programs run-time access to information about interfaces in a structured form.

NOTE Unfortunately, a number of languages called IDL are extant in the world, most of which do very similar things. Whenever the (unqualified) acronym *IDL* is used in this book, we're referring to OMG IDL used for CORBA systems. As luck would have it, the corresponding language in COM is called MIDL (Microsoft Interface Definition Language), so there shouldn't be any confusion between the two.

Interface Identity

Each CORBA interface is identified by a repository ID, a unique string that can be used as a key for locating the interface in the repository and to identify the interface for purposes of determining equivalence. Repository IDs can take a variety of forms. The default form is derived from the fully scoped name of the interface. GUIDs can also be used.

Data Typing

IDL data types include the common set of primitives: signed and unsigned integers, floating point numbers, characters and strings, boolean, and an uninterpreted octet type. The CORBA typing system also includes a number of constructed types: structs, unions, enum types, variable-length sequences, and multidimensional arrays. It also includes definitions for exception types (structurally identical to struct types) used to indicate abnormal termination status of operations.

IDL also includes a base type called **any**, which is capable of holding a value of any data type that can be expressed in IDL. An **any** value includes a **TypeCode**, which completely describes the type of the value that the **any** holds.

CORBA also defines a set of *pseudointerfaces* that provide standard APIs for accessing the basic capabilities of the ORB itself. For many of these interfaces, it is not entirely appropriate that they be expressed directly in IDL and implemented as righteous CORBA objects. Usually, this is because they are local, that is, they only make sense within the context of the process in which they are created and being used. The pseudointerfaces are described in PIDL (Pseudo-IDL), which, roughly speaking, means, "IDL that doesn't actually have to compile successfully." PIDL is used as an imprecise descriptive mechanism for the fixed ORB APIs. Individual language mappings define the actual working interfaces for pseudo-objects. The ORB interface and the **TypeCode** interface are prominent examples of pseudointerfaces.

The **CORBA::Object** pseudointerface is unique and particularly important. This pseudointerface is available on all CORBA objects. It is not entirely accurate to say that it is a base interface for all CORBA interfaces since it isn't really an interface, but that is a good practical approximation. In the language mappings to most object-oriented programming languages, there is a class (or interface) at the language level for **CORBA::Object**, and the classes for regular CORBA interfaces do, in fact, derive from it. The operations defined on **CORBA::Object** generally involve interactions with the object reference or the ORB and not the actual object itself.

Interface Composition

IDL interfaces may be combined and extended through a relatively straightforward inheritance mechanism, which is quite similar to C++ inheritance and Java interface inheritance. When an interface is derived from a base interface, the derived interface implicitly includes all of the elements (operations, data types, etc.) from the base interface. IDL supports multiple inheritance, so an interface may be derived from more than one base interface. The most important characteristic of CORBA interface inheritance is that it defines *substitutability*—that is, an object reference supporting a derived interface may be substituted (e.g., as a parameter in an operation) for any of its base interface types.

Requests

A CORBA request is relatively straightforward. A request is a two-way exchange (actually including the request and corresponding reply). The outgoing request encapsulates the operation name, the identity of the target object, and a set of parameters. Some of the parameters are explicitly declared in the operation, and others are implicit, depending on the context in which the request is made. The reply encapsulates either the set of parameters returned by the object or an exception that indicates the failure of the request. There is a special kind of CORBA request called **oneway**. A **oneway** request must not have any parameters that return from the object. When a **oneway** request is made, the client is not required to wait for a response, which means that the client may not be notified of a request failure.

Parameters

As just mentioned, CORBA requests include both the parameters declared in the operation and (potentially) some implicit parameters. IDL requires that the directionality of parameters be explicitly declared. Parameters may be **in** (flow from client to object), **out** (flow from object to client), or **inout** (flow in both directions). The operation result, if there is one, is essentially a distinguished **out** parameter. CORBA has another separately declared quasi parameter called *context*. The utility of context parameters is questionable when interoperability between ORBs is an important consideration, and their use has been discouraged. For the purposes of interworking, request context can be thought of simply as an **in** parameter structured as a sequence of name-value string pairs. CORBA requests may also include implicit service context information. Service context may be used, for example, to carry information about transactional scopes, security, and other object services.

Exceptions

Exceptions are effectively a type of parameter, though they are not declared in the parameter list as such, and they are only raised if the operation fails. They are, however, transmitted as part of the reply and constitute a part of the operation's signature, so we treat them as parameters. CORBA exceptions come in two distinct flavors—system exceptions, which can be raised by any operation, and user exceptions, which must be explicitly declared in a **raises** clause in the operation definition. System exceptions all share the same structure, which includes completion status, a major code, and a minor code. Completion status is an enum type with the possible values **YES, NO**, and **MAYBE**, which indicate whether the operation completed successfully (to the best of the ORB's knowledge). Exception major codes are defined in the CORBA specification. They describe the general type of error that occurred, encoded as an unsigned 32-bit integer. Minor codes have the same structure but are defined differently by each ORB implementation. They generally include a more specific, detailed indication of the error.

Object References

CORBA object references differ significantly from references in other distributed object systems, particularly COM. The details of CORBA object references and their architectural implications are covered more thoroughly later in the chapter. The most important points are that CORBA references (generally) denote abstract, long-lived objects and that any given reference is immutable in that it reliably denotes throughout that object's lifetime, regardless of the object's location or activation state. Any actions necessary to find the object, activate it, bind to it, and so on, are transparent to the client using the reference. The client simply makes the invocation on the reference, and the ORB does the rest. Another important characteristic of CORBA references is that they can be converted into strings, stored indefinitely, converted back into object references, and used to make requests. If the target object has not been permanently destroyed, the request will execute properly.

Object Identity and Life Cycle

In general, a CORBA object's identity is associated with a particular abstract world entity (such as a person, an account, and so on). Generally, the identified object encapsulates a state, and it may have a long lifetime, implying that the state is likely to be persistent. The abstract object may, over the course of its lifetime, be implemented by a series of several different transient programming objects (e.g., instances of C++ classes), which can be created and destroyed (loading and storing their state) as needed to satisfy requests from clients. CORBA object references encapsulate these permanent, immutable identities, giving them the characteristics described in the preceding section.

CORBA objects are usually created by factories, but there is no single standard factory interface that is common to all object types. CORBA objects must be explicitly destroyed, either through the generic **CosLifeCycle::LifeCycleObject** interface (specifically, the **remove()** operation) or though some application-specific interface that destroys objects of a particular type.

Describing COM and Automation with the Interworking Object Model

In OLE, the interworking object model maps to an architectural abstraction known as the Component Object Model (COM). Another distinct object model, originally known as OLE Automation, is constructed on top of the COM. Automation is best thought of as a distinct object model built on top of the COM. They share many common features but differ in important respects, such as interface structure and data typing. These differences necessitate different treatments for the purposes of interworking between object models. When discussing Automation, it is important to understand the context in which the discussion is taking place. Many programming environments that are based on Automation present their own idiosyncratic views of the object model. The most precise and thorough view of Automation can be gained by studying the COM interfaces that implement the Automation model, particularly the IDispatch interface. On the other hand, the programming model presented by Visual Basic is, for practical purposes, the definition of Automation for most of the world. Though other programming environments based on Automation may present slightly different views, the popularity of Visual Basic and its close association with the origins and implementation of Automation make it the definitive expression of Automation functionality. The programming examples in this book that involve Automation will use Visual Basic, for purely practical reasons. In this section, however, we will focus on the underlying mechanics of the object model.

Problems with COM Terminology

The world of COM is changing rapidly. While writing this section, it was a constant struggle to make sure the presentation was consistent with the current "politically correct" COM terminology and concepts. For a time it appeared as though everything was supposed to be called ActiveX, but that point of view seems to have faded in popularity. The main problem is in differentiating between COM, OLE, and Automation. We have tried to adopt definitions that are at least consistent, if not universally accepted. In general, things are described in terms of COM and Automation. By COM we mean the basic framework upon which the rest of the OLE tower is built, primarily including the binary interface standard and the basic mechanisms supported by IUnknown—the model of interface composition and navigation and the reference-counting mechanism. By Automation, we refer to interfaces that are provided through the IDispatch COM interface. (This includes dual interfaces.) Occasionally we use the term *OLE* as a rubric to encompass COM and everything built on top of it, including Automation.

Even more troublesome was deciding how to present specific COM and Automation interfaces in examples and how to delimit the general discussion of precisely what the interworking described here applies to. Specifically, is there a formal (or even semiformal) specification that constitutes the authoritative model for what COM and Automation objects can be? There are three candidates: ODL processed by the MKTYPLIB utility, IDL (or ODL or MIDL?) processed by the MIDL compiler, or the information model defined by the structure of type library itself. Fortunately, these three have been converging and are very close to being equivalent for practical purposes. The MIDL compiler now generates type libraries and accepts (with a few minor exceptions) all of the ODL syntax that used to be processed by MKTYPLIB. The use of MKTYPLIB has been increasingly discouraged. We still can't tell what we're supposed to call the text that is processed with the MIDL compiler; the current MSDN documentation seems to use ODL, IDL, and MIDL almost interchangeably. For the purposes of this discussion, it therefore seemed best to call the descriptive language MIDL (to differentiate it from OMG IDL) and to use the syntax that the MIDL compiler defines for objects, that is, when the keyword object appears in the header. Long-time users of OLE will probably think of this as ODL.

Interfaces

The main pillar of COM is its mechanism for interface management. COM is a binary interface standard that defines how interfaces are expressed and invoked in terms of memory organization and instruction execution. At this low level, a COM interface consists of a vector of function pointers, each of which corresponds to one of the interface's methods (this is equivalent to a C++ Vtbl, for those readers familiar with C++). All interfaces share three fundamental methods—QueryInterface(), AddRef(), and Release(). The AddRef() and Release() methods are concerned with reference counting and resource management, which are unimportant in the immediate discussion. These methods constitute the interface IUnknown, from which all other COM interfaces are derived. Understanding QueryInterface() is the key to understanding the COM interface structure. It is described later in this chapter, in the section on "Interface Composition."

COM interfaces are statically typed because of their binary structure. A particular method is invoked through one of the function pointers in the Vtbl. The identity of the method is associated with its position in the Vtbl. In general, clients must be compiled with an interface's header file in order to be able to use it.

COM interfaces are generally defined in MIDL (Microsoft Interface Definition Language). MIDL is comparable to OMG IDL, with similar expressive capability. COM interface descriptions can also be stored in type libraries that contain structured information available to programs at run time.

> **N**OTE Until recently, there were two different interface languages for COM and OLE objects. COM used MIDL (though it was somewhat different from the current MIDL), and OLE objects used ODL (Object Definition Language). In Microsoft Developer Studio 97 these have been coalesced into a single, expanded MIDL. As a historical note, MIDL has its roots in DCE IDL, which is used to defined interfaces for DCE RPC.

The Automation interface structure is designed specifically to allow clients with no compile-time knowledge of their structure to use interfaces. In many ways, it is similar to the CORBA Dynamic Invocation Interface (DII). An Automation object is actually a COM object that supports a particular interface called IDispatch. The IDispatch interface has a method called Invoke, which can be used to invoke any Automation method. IDispatch::Invoke takes as parameters (among other things) the identity of the Automation operation to be invoked and a parameter (of Invoke) that holds a list of parameters for the Automation method. This parameter list is an array of type `VARIANT`. `VARIANT` is, in essence, a tagged union of a fixed set of data types. It is similar to the **any** type in CORBA but less capable in that it cannot describe user-defined types like structs. `IDispatch::Invoke()` is a generic meta-method, if you will, which can be used to invoke any Automation method. The parameters to the `IDispatch::Invoke()` method itself are a generic, one-size-fits-all-methods style. The `IDispatch` interface also provides a run-time description of the Automation interface's methods and properties, in the form of a type library.

Automation interfaces distinguish between methods and properties. Properties are really a shorthand mechanism for defining a common form of method access for an encapsulated value. A property definition results in the definition of two methods—a *get* method and a *set* method, or in the case of readonly properties, a single *set* method. Though this has important implications for Automation programming environments, from the perspective of describing interworking, these are indistinguishable from methods in general.

Interface Identity

COM and Automation interfaces are identified with GUIDs (Globally Unique Identifiers). A GUID is a 128-bit binary string that is generated in such a way as to virtually guarantee uniqueness. Although it is impossible to guarantee uniqueness absolutely, the probability against two GUIDs being independently created with the same value is astronomical.

Data Typing

MIDL data types available for use in COM interfaces include a set of base primitives (character and string types, signed and unsigned integer types of different sizes, floating point numeric types, Boolean, and an uninterpreted byte type). In addition, MIDL supports struct, union, enum, and arrays. MIDL also supports pointer types, which allow the creation of types that can express linked data structures such as trees.

Automation interfaces differ in some important ways from COM interfaces. From an interworking point of view, the most significant differences are in the data typing system. As described previously in the section named "Interfaces", parameters for Automation operations must all be types that can be held in a `VARIANT`.

Although a VARIANT can hold a wide variety of types (including the usual set of base types, arrays, a set of predefined pointer types, and other useful types such as DATE and CURRENCY), the range of types is fixed. A VARIANT cannot hold, for example, a user–defined struct (as such).

Interface Composition

An individual COM interface may be extended with single inheritance. Multiple COM interfaces on single COM object are composed through a mechanism called *aggregation*. Aggregation is quite different from inheritance, particularly in that it does not define any explicit structural relationships between the interfaces being aggregated. The unit of interface composition in COM is the *component*. A component is not an interface type but an implementation of a well-defined set of functionality. A component provides this functionality through a set of interfaces. The QueryInterface() operation shared by all interfaces allows a client to navigate between the interfaces that belong to a component. Each COM interface is identified by a GUID. A client that holds an interface pointer for a particular component can find out if that component supports another interface (and thus a certain set of capabilities) by invoking QueryInterface() on the current interface pointer, with the desired interface's ID (the interface's GUID) as a parameter. If the object supports the requested interface, QueryInterface() will return a pointer to that interface; otherwise it returns a null pointer. A full discussion of COM's aggregation mechanism is beyond the scope of this book. For the purposes of COM/CORBA interworking, the important thing to note is that COM components support a set of disjoint interfaces and a run-time mechanism to navigate between them. In general, each individual interface is a flat collection of methods.

A program that uses Automation objects is usually referred to as an *Automation controller*. Until recently, most Automation controllers (such as programming environments like Visual Basic and Delphi or applications like Microsoft Office) did not support the notion of multiple IDispatch interfaces on a single object. Thus, for some time Automation interfaces were, in effect, flat collections of operations and properties with no composition mechanism. As the use of Automation evolved, the need to support the same kind of multiple interface management that COM offers became evident. The current version of Automation supports the ability to differentiate between different IDispatch interfaces and navigate between them on a single object. More advanced Automation controllers such as Visual Basic version 5.0 expose this capability to users.

The composition of Automation interfaces is roughly equivalent to that of COM and is built on top of the COM aggregation mechanism. A single automation interface comprises a set of properties and operations. A component may support multiple, distinct Automation interfaces, which can be navigated through calls to `QueryInterface()`. One important difference is that all Automation interfaces are of type `IDispatch`, so they are all structurally identical and could all potentially be returned by a call to `QueryInterface()` requesting an `IDispatch` interface. Automation allows different dispatch interfaces to have their own unique Interface IDs, even though they are all structurally identical at the COM level. Any component supporting multiple Automation interfaces must define one that is the default, which will be returned if a client simply requests the `IDispatch` interface with `QueryInterface()`.

Requests

Method invocations in COM and Automation are conceptually straightforward. They include the identity of the operation and a set of parameters. The corresponding reply contains the return parameters, a status value of type `HRESULT` (see the next section named "Exceptions" later in this chapter). In COM interfaces, the method is implicitly identified by an offset in a table of function pointers. In Automation interfaces, the method is explicitly identified in the call to `IDispatch::Invoke()`. COM and Automation requests are synchronous request/reply interactions.

Parameters

Much like CORBA, COM and Automation support three modes of parameter directionality: `[in]`, `[out]`, and `[in,out]`. They also allow a distinguished return value parameter to be defined for an operation. This is not declared as the actual function return value but in the parameter list. All COM methods return a datum of type `HRESULT` as the function return value, which provides limited information about the call's completion status.

As described earlier, the parameters of Automation methods must be able to be encoded as `VARIANT`s. This is a fairly serious constraint for many purposes, particularly interworking with object systems that support user-defined data types. The result of an Automation method is returned as a separate output parameter of `IDispatch::Invoke()`, also encoded as a `VARIANT`. Languages built on top of Automation usually present the result more naturally, as the value returned by the method.

Exceptions

The error-handling mechanisms of COM and Automation are a bit of a Rube Goldberg contraption. All COM methods (at the binary interface level) return a value of type HRESULT. An HRESULT is a 32-bit value that contains a hodge-podge of information. The highest-order bit indicates whether the invocation succeeded or failed. The next fifteen bits identify (in very vague terms) the *facility* (such as Windows, storage, or RPC) that was the source of the error. In most cases, this field holds the value FACILITY_ITF, indicating that the error is specific to the particular interface that generated it. The low-order sixteen bits hold a value that identifies the specific error that occurred. The meaning of the value is relative to the facility and interface that generated the error. The values are not unique across all interfaces. For most objects, the implementer chooses the error codes that the object's interface will generate and determines what they mean. Just to confuse issues more, the HRESULT is overloaded so as to be able to return Boolean values unrelated to errors.

This is a relatively impoverished mechanism, capable of expressing only very general information. Many OLE interfaces, including Automation interfaces, required a richer structure. Consequently, another mechanism was introduced, referred to as either EXCEPINFO or error objects, alternatively. An OLE error object is a COM interface that encapsulates a struct of type EXCEPINFO, so these two names (error objects and EXCEPINFO) are different presentations of the same information. An EXCEPINFO struct contains the following useful information:

- A string describing the source of the error.
- A string describing the error itself.
- A string identifying a help file.
- A numeric value that identifies a topic inside the help file.

This structure is not user-extensible, but it conveys more information than the SCODE. The information it contains is generally intended for human consumption, not for programming utility (unless you count the dubious practice of encoding programmatically useful information in a string and passing it as the error description, to be parsed by the receiver of the exception).

Although error objects evolved in the context of Automation, they can be used by any COM object, though a non-Automation object must do extra work to use them. Automation objects return an EXCEPINFO struct as an output parameter of IDispatch::Invoke(), so the error object is explicitly associated with a particular invocation. In methods of interfaces other than IDispatch, there is generally no parameter for error information. This forces COM to awkwardly transfer error information from the object back to the caller. Before returning, the object's method creates an error object and calls a global function, `SetErrorInfo()`, passing it the error object. The error object is stored in static memory (i.e., not on the stack) local to the current thread. When the method generating the error returns, it sets the `HRESULT` value to an appropriate error code. To retrieve the error object, the client must first ask the object whether it supports this error mechanism through an interface named `ISupportErrorInfo`. If the object does in fact support error objects, then the client can retrieve the error object by calling another global function, `GetErrorInfo()`, which returns the current contents of the thread-local error object. This procedure allows the client to ensure that the object it just invoked is the actual source of the error object it retrieves. Because error objects are not passed on the stack (as a parameter), the current value returned by `GetErrorInfo()` may have been generated by a previous invocation. Thread-local storage is used (as opposed to global storage) to prevent multithreaded programs from overwriting each others' error objects.

The following discussions of object references, object identity and life cycle, and implementation apply equally to COM and Automation. Automation does not change these aspects of the COM model.

Object References

Since COM is a binary interface standard, a reference to a COM object takes the form of an interface pointer, the memory address of a table of function pointers. The pointer may in fact be the address of an object (e.g., an instance of a C++ class) that lives in the same address space as the caller, in which case the table of function pointers contains the addresses of the actual methods of the object itself. In cases where the target object is in another process or on another machine, the interface pointer is the address of a proxy object whose methods will marshal the request and send it to the target. More important than the form of reference is what the reference denotes. A COM interface pointer denotes the transient programming object that lives at a particular address in memory at a point in time. The interface pointer does not encapsulate any long-term, persistent identity of the target object and cannot be used to automatically activate the object. COM references (interface pointers) cannot exist for inactive objects; the concept is meaningless in COM.

Another important aspect of the COM model is its reference-counting mechanism. Every time a copy of an interface pointer is made, the client using the copy is responsible for calling the `AddRef()` method inherited by all COM interfaces from the `IUnknown` interface. This informs the object implementation that another client is holding a reference and ostensibly using the object. When the client is finished using the reference, it should call the Release method, again notifying the target object that one less reference is in use. The target object has the option of keeping track of how many references are extant and deleting itself when there are no more active clients. This behavior is closely linked to the fact that COM references denote transient objects and do not encapsulate the permanent identity of long-lived objects associated with a particular state.

COM offers another mechanism that can be thought of as a kind of object reference, called a *moniker*. In simple terms, monikers do encapsulate (conceptually) permanent object identities, in the form of the class ID (the identifier for a component type that defines the behavior of the object) and some information that identifies a particular state, such as a file name or URL. The moniker itself is not the object reference, in that you cannot invoke the object's methods directly through the moniker. Monikers are themselves COM objects, with interfaces of their own (in particular, the `IMoniker` interface). You must first bind the moniker, an operation that activates the conceptual object by creating a transient instance of the class and loading it with the identified state, producing an interface pointer. Monikers offer many of the properties associated with permanent object identities but are not entirely equivalent. For example, once a moniker is bound and an interface pointer is created, it may not be possible to retrieve the moniker (i.e., the permanent identity) from the interface pointer (or any other interface supported by the object). The moniker is not inherently encapsulated by the reference. This is particularly important to note since clients and objects pass references between themselves in terms of reference pointers. If client A binds a moniker and passes the resulting interface pointer to client B, client B does not inherently have any way of knowing the object's permanent identity (i.e., obtaining the moniker). Thus, client B can't store the reference and use it later (in a different process) to activate the object.

Object Identity and Life Cycle

Some of the important aspects of COM object identity were discussed in the preceding section "Object References." In general, the COM model separates the identities of the active object instance and the associated state (if any). A single COM component instance may, over its lifetime, hold several distinct identifiable persistent states, such as a single running instance of Microsoft Word that loads and stores several different documents. As described earlier, monikers offer a model that corresponds more closely to the conventional notion of object identity, that is, an encapsulation of behavior and state. However, monikers have some limitations, noted previously, and they are not the uniform coin of the COM realm; interface pointers are.

The life cycle of the transient COM object is controlled by the reference-counting mechanism. When all of the extant interface pointers are released by the clients that hold them, the COM object (in most cases) is destroyed. The life cycle of the storage (which may be considered part of the conceptual object) is not determined or controlled by the COM model. In most cases, some application or user interface deletes the storage as an intentional act.

To a great extent, the conceptual identity of an object from the client's perspective is reflected in how the client initially obtains the reference to the object. A COM program typically locates or creates an object in one of the following ways:

- It creates an "empty" instance of the class by invoking the class factory and subsequently loads some state into it.
- It obtains an interface pointer to an already active object from some directory-like service, such as the registry or a distributed directory.
- It binds a moniker.

COM objects (i.e., instances of COM classes) are normally created using class factories. Each COM class is expected to provide a standard factory and place that factory in the system registry using the class ID as the key. Clients can either look up the factory in the registry and invoke it directly or call the global function `CoCreateInstance()`, which simply does the lookup and factory invocation for you. The standard class factory doesn't provide any way to initialize the object being created with a specified state since there are no parameters for this in the creation method. To the client that creates objects in this way, the conceptual identity of the object is a combination of two separate things—the transient instance of the COM class created by the factory and the state that was explicitly loaded into it.

NOTE Many adherents of object orientation complain that this separation of state from object identity violates the principle of encapsulation. The complaint is justified. Strict observance of encapsulation has proved in practice to be an invaluable discipline, often yielding benefits unforeseen at the time of original design. Its absence in COM is the source of many shortcomings.

The second approach (publishing an object in a registry or directory service) is useful when an object needs to be available under a well-known name. In these cases, the client's conceptual view of the object's identity is the name (or other key value) used to look up the object in the service. For example, in most object-oriented business systems there are well-known objects that embody major services or subsystems, such as inventory or personnel. These service-level objects manage smaller objects, such as individual inventory items or employees, and provide access to them. Service objects of this kind are expected to be constantly available and are generally *singleton objects*, in the sense that a business has one inventory or one personnel department. As such, their life cycle is quite different from lower-level objects. Clients would not, for instance, create an empty inventory object and load its state from a file. In reality, it is likely to be implemented as an object that acts as a front end for an online database. Such objects are usually created as part of the system's initialization process and are kept alive until the system shuts down (intentionally or otherwise). Even then, when the system is restarted the new object created to provide inventory services is the same object conceptually; clients obtain it from the registry or directory with the same name, and it is expected to have the same state it had when it shut down.

Implementing a service object of this type in COM usually requires some bending of the rules. For example, their implementations may choose to ignore reference counting and remain alive until some explicit management action is taken (such as shutdown). Their factories may be hidden from clients since there is no need to create them dynamically. Another approach commonly taken for singleton objects in COM is to provide a factory that doesn't really create the object in question; it simply keeps track of it and returns the same object to all clients when they ask to "create" it. This allows clients to use the factory as, in essence, a directory. This is the approach taken in the bank example in Chapter 2. The account manager object (AcctMgr) is obtained by calling the VB function `CreateObject()`, which ends up invoking the class factory. Conceptually, there is really only one account manager, and it is shared by all clients. The `IAcctMgr` class factory simply returns that shared object.

This example also illustrates how the standard COM life cycle mechanism is often subverted in another way. The account manager object is the vehicle through which individual accounts are created and located; a class factory for Account is not provided or used. This technique allows (indeed, forces) the client to establish an initial state and permanent identity at the time of creation, by giving the `createAccount()` operation parameters for the account name and balance. It also acts as a class-specific directory by providing access to account objects.

Mapping from CORBA to COM/Automation

Once the object models are characterized in terms of this model, correspondences between elements in the different object models become clearer. Many of the basic mappings are obvious. Others have subtle but troublesome aspects. The following sections describe the mapping in general terms and point out important architectural considerations. Later chapters will cover the mechanics in detail and provide programming examples.

Interfaces

Mapping a CORBA interface into a COM or Automation interface is one of the more mechanically complex problems faced by interworking solutions, though in concept it is straightforward. It was important to the authors of the Interworking Specification that the COM interfaces produced by different mapping products from the same CORBA interface be identical to ensure substitutability and interoperability between implementations. This requirement drives much of the resulting complexity.

Identity

Mapping interfaces between COM and CORBA entails creating an association between a CORBA repository ID and a COM interface ID. CORBA repository IDs don't have a prescribed form, so valid COM interface IDs (i.e., GUIDs) must be created for the mapped COM and Automation interfaces. To guarantee interoperability between mapping solutions, all products must generate the same COM interface ID for any given CORBA interface. The prescribed method involves a complex hashing function of the CORBA interface's repository ID that produces most of the 128 bits required for a GUID. High-order bits have particular assigned values to differentiate between the COM, Automation, and dual interfaces that are mapped from the same CORBA interface. The important aspect for users of bridging products is that any CORBA interface will result in the same COM interface ID when it is mapped with various products or at different times with the same product, but the probability of collision (i.e., two different CORBA interfaces producing the same interface ID when mapped) is extremely low.

> **N**OTE If one million distinct repository IDs are mapped, the probability of a collision occurring is less that 10^{-23}.

The names of mapped interfaces in COM are formed by concatenating the character *I*; the names of any enclosing modules from left to right, separated by underscore characters ("_"); and the name of the IDL interface. Dispatch interfaces use a leading *D* instead of the *I*, and dual interfaces use a leading *DI*. Thus, an IDL interface named

```
module A {
    module B {
        interface foo { ...
    }
}
```

would have the following names when mapped to the various OLE interfaces:

```
IA_B_foo  // custom COM interface
DA_B_foo  // dispatch interface
DIA_B_foo // dual interface
```

Similarly, the interface ID name is formed by prepending the mapped interface name with "IID_", as in

```
IID_IA_B_foo  // custom COM interface
IID_DA_B_foo  // dispatch interface
IID_DIA_B_foo // dual interface
```

Data Typing

For COM interfaces, almost all of the CORBA IDL data types map to nearly identical MIDL data types, including structs and unions. The details of the specific low-level data type mappings are covered in Chapters 4 and 5. The only CORBA base type that does not have a natural mapping is **any**. The limitations on Automation data types are somewhat more troublesome. Almost all of the base types map directly, but complex user-defined types have no direct mapping.

The only reasonable alternative in cases like these is to map the complex CORBA data types into native object types (i.e., interfaces) in COM and Automation. This is a common phenomenon when mapping between different object systems. Most object models (such as object-oriented programming languages) differentiate between object types and nonobject data types, though the point at which they draw the line between the two varies widely. When object system A has a nonobject data type that doesn't map naturally into object system B, it typically gets mapped as an object in B since the **Object** type in most systems is by far the most versatile. Consequently, the CORBA **any** type gets mapped into a native object interface in COM and a dispatch interface in Automation. Additionally, CORBA struct and union types are mapped into dispatch interfaces in Automation.

The mappings for CORBA **any** are fixed since the **any** type is not user-definable or -extendable. These mappings are presented in detail in Chapter 5. In Automation, a CORBA struct maps into a dispatch interface with properties that correspond to the struct members. A union maps into a similar dispatch interface with the addition of a discriminator to indicate the type currently held by the union and, thus, which member property has a valid value.

The Interworking Specification defines a base interface for all of the dispatch interfaces that represent CORBA nonobject types, called `DIForeignComplexType`. This interface originally contained methods to return the CORBA repository ID of the original type and to clone the object. For various reasons, the latest revision of the Interworking Specification deprecated these methods and moved them to a separate utility interface called `DIObjectInfo`. As a result, the `DIForeignComplexType` is, for practical purposes, an empty rubric and acts as a placeholder base interface for all of the specific interfaces that map complex CORBA types. Similarly, there are type-empty placeholder interfaces that both derive from `DIForeignComplexType`—`DICORBAStruct` and `DICORBAUnion`. All of the specific Automation interfaces that are mappings of CORBA structs derive from `DICORBAStruct`; likewise for unions and the `DICORBAUnion` interface. All of these interfaces that are derived from `DIForeignComplexType` represent objects to the automation programmer, and are generically referred to as *Helper Objects*.

Using Mapped Complex Types Using Automation objects (and, in the case of **any**, a COM object) to represent CORBA nonobject types causes some problems that complicate the mapping architecturally:

Efficiency. In some cases, accessing struct members through calls to `IDispatch::Invoke()` has orders-of-magnitude more overhead than a simple struct access in C or C++.

Semantics. When a struct is passed as a parameter in CORBA invocations it is passed *by value*, that is, an independent copy is made and passed from the caller to the object (or from the object back to the caller in the case of **out** parameters). When an `IDispatch` pointer is passed as a parameter in Automation, the object is being passed by reference—the caller and the callee share the same copy of the struct being represented. If one of them changes values in the struct, the other will see those changes. Note that this change in parameter-passing semantics occurs only after a CORBA struct is passed through the bridge and converted into an Automation object. The bridge creates the new Automation object and copies the struct values into it, then passes it to the Automation object or client involved in the exchange. Any modifications made on the Automation side will not affect the original CORBA struct. However, if the Automation pseudostruct is passed around between several Automation objects after crossing the bridge, they will all share the same physical object.

This does not pose significant problems for programmers on either side of the bridge. COM/Automation programmers expect objects to behave this way (i.e., pass by reference) on their side of the bridge, and CORBA programmers expect structs to act as they do on the CORBA side. The main possibility for confusion for a naïve programmer occurs at the boundary between the two object systems. For example, an Automation client that is using a CORBA object with a struct parameter will see the parameter as an object (an `IDispatch` pointer). The programmer might assume that the CORBA object that is the target of the invocation will share the Automation pseudostruct object that it sends it, since that is generally the way it would work in COM, but it does not. The bridge will create a new struct on the CORBA side and copy the values from the Automation pseudostruct into it. Whether this constitutes a problem or not depends on the assumptions made by the programmer regarding the behavior of the target object and its effects on the parameter.

Life cycle. In most object systems, the life cycle of object types is quite different from the life cycle of nonobject types. For example, in C++, a struct can be declared in the scope of a method, where it will live on the stack and be destroyed when it goes out of scope at the time the method returns. Objects, on the other hand, are generally created by factories and must be explicitly destroyed or released. The responsibilities associated with objects are more complex, and the system must provide more wherewithal (such as factories) to support their existence. To accommodate this difference, COM/CORBA bridges provide special factory mechanisms to support Automation objects that represent complex CORBA types. The programming details will be presented fully in Chapter 5, but we will describe their general structure here.

First, understand the requirement for this factory. When the structs are return values or **out** parameters, the bridge will automatically create instances of the Automation pseudostruct object and pass it to the Automation client that made the invocation. When an Automation client is making an invocation with an **in** parameter of a struct type, the client has to be able to produce an instance of the pseudostruct object type and initialize its member values.

Bridges supply a factory object that supports the `DICORBAFactoryEx` interface. This factory is used to create instances of Automation objects that map to complex CORBA types. You may ask, "Why not just use normal COM class factories?" While using class factories is the natural way for creating most objects in COM and Automation applications, doing so requires that all of the types be available in the registry and that they have known interface IDs or ProgIDs. Doing this for all CORBA complex types could prove burdensome and would also introduce programming inconvenience. The `DICORBAFactoryEx` interface allows clients to create instances of pseudostructs by knowing only the name of the struct type. The `DICORBAFactoryEx` interface has two methods, `CreateType()` and `CreateTypeByID()`.

The `CreateType()` method is generally the most useful. You invoke it with two parameters—the name of the struct or union you want to create and the interface pointer of an Automation view that represents a CORBA object. The interface of the CORBA object associated with the second parameter defines the IDL name scope within which the name will be resolved. In most cases, IDL struct types used as parameters are defined in the scope of the interface where they are used or in the scope of an enclosing module. This means that you will almost always invoke `CreateType()` with the interface pointer of the view that you will be invoking with the struct you create.

The second method on `DICORBAFactoryEx`, `CreateTypeByID()`, does the same thing, but it uses the repository ID of the CORBA struct or union type instead of the name. While generally less convenient, it is useful (even necessary) in some cases. It may seem curious that this method requires a scoping object since repository IDs aren't scoped by modules or interfaces. They are, however, scoped by the interface repository in which they are defined. There is not necessarily a single repository associated with the bridge, but an object does unambiguously identify a particular repository with which it is associated. Though this could theoretically be any object that shares the appropriate repository, there is no way to know with absolute certainty that objects share an interface repository. It is most reliable to use the object that will be the target of the request in which you're going to pass the type you are creating.

Once a pseudostruct or pseudounion is created, it follows the same life cycle rules as any Automation object, based on COM's reference-counting mechanism. Chapter 5 will present detailed programming examples showing how to use `DICORBAFactoryEx`.

Interface Composition

In general, inheritance mechanisms such as CORBA's are used for two distinct purposes—to extend and to combine. Extending an interface by adding some new methods is a natural use of single inheritance. It can be used to achieve a variety of goals, such as defining a new, but backward-compatible version of an interface or for specializing a generic interface. Multiple inheritance, on the other hand, is typically used to combine independent interfaces into a composite, or to *mix in*, as many object-oriented models describe the process. For example, you may have an application-specific object to which you want to add a new generic capability, such as the ability to be printed. You could use multiple inheritance to add an interface for printing to the object.

COM makes a clear distinction between these two uses by providing two distinct mechanisms to support them. A COM interface may be extended through single inheritance. Combining interfaces is done through the aggregation mechanism. Ideally, a CORBA interface graph could be partitioned into distinct subgraphs that expressed the intended use of inheritance, either for extension of combination, and these linear subgraphs could be mapped directly into a set of COM interfaces that could then be aggregated. Unfortunately, it is impossible to tell from the structure of a CORBA interface what the intentions of the author(s) were, that is, whether a given base interface is being extended or mixed in. This forced the Interworking Specification's authors to adopt a less satisfactory, but still workable solution.

The Interworking Specification defines a process for partitioning a CORBA inheritance graph into a set of COM interfaces, while attempting to preserve single inheritance relationships. The rules are relatively straightforward:

- Each CORBA IDL interface that does not have a parent is mapped to a COM interface deriving directly from `IUnknown`.
- Each CORBA IDL interface that inherits from a single parent is mapped to a COM interface that derives from the mapping for the parent interface.
- Each CORBA IDL interface that inherits from multiple parent interfaces is mapped to a COM interface that derives directly from `IUnknown`.

Figure 3.4 shows a sample CORBA interface inheritance graph and the resulting mapped COM interfaces. The important result from the user's perspective is that each distinct CORBA interface in the graph has a corresponding COM interface, so a client can call `QueryInterface()` to access any of these inherited interfaces, whether they are singly inherited or not. Whenever a single inheritance

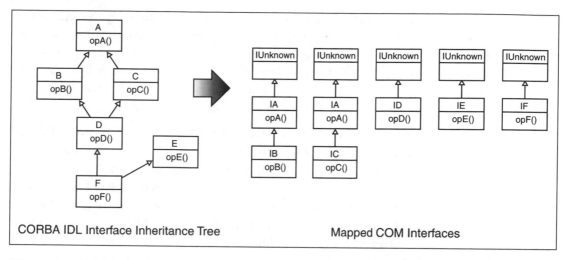

Figure 3.4 *CORBA inheritance mapped to COM.*

relationship exists, the resulting COM interfaces preserve it. This may not be exactly the effect that the original designer of the CORBA interface in question intended, but it serves to expose all of the original interfaces and operations in a predictable, usable manner.

The order of methods in a COM interface is important because the methods determine the order of function pointers in the binary interface's vtable. To ensure interoperability between different bridging solutions, all compliant bridge products must map the operations of a particular CORBA interface in the same order. The Interworking Specification achieves this by sorting the names of the operations and the attributes and placing the attributes before the operations. The resulting order corresponds to the order in which the methods will appear in the mapped COM interface.

CORBA inheritance maps differently to Automation than it does to COM. In past versions of COM and OLE, there was only one interface ID for all Automation interfaces—IDispatch. There was no way to QueryInterface() for different Automation interfaces, so an object that supported Automation was forced to put all of its operations in a single, flat interface. As of VB version 4.0, an object can support multiple, distinct dispatch interfaces. A VB programmer can't call QueryInterface() directly but can achieve the same effect by declaring typed object variables (described in VB as *early binding*). Unfortunately, not all Automation controllers support this capability, and they can only use a single Automation interface on an object. Therefore, the transformation for CORBA inheritance to COM just described won't work in practice for Automation. To work with all controllers, there must be a single Automation interface that supports all of the operations in the CORBA interface inheritance graph. The method for doing this is a bit complicated, but a detailed understanding of it is not necessary to use the mapped interfaces. We will present a brief summary here.

The operations and attributes in each CORBA interface are ordered in the same way as when they are mapped to COM interfaces. The base interfaces for each interface are also ordered by sorting in the same manner. The resulting inheritance graph can be drawn with the sorted base interfaces ordered from left to right. Figure 3.5 shows such a graph. It is important that the same graph be produced by all mapping solution products for reasons of portability and interoperability. This ordered graph can be thought of as the canonical form of a CORBA inheritance hierarchy.

The graph is flattened by following the leftmost path, using single inheritance to combine the interfaces. When an interface with multiple base interfaces is encountered, the attributes and operations from non-leftmost base interfaces are copied onto the end of the interface that inherits them in the order of their appearance from left to right. The result is a flat (linear) interface containing all of the operations defined in the CORBA inheritance graph. There is one problem with the

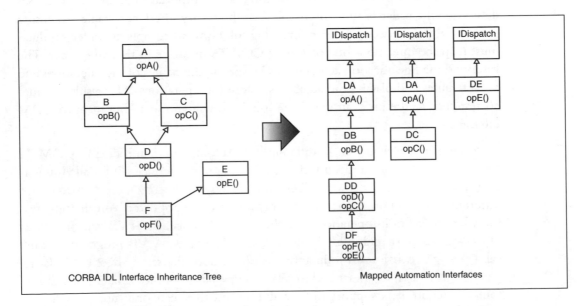

Figure 3.5 CORBA inheritance mapped to Automation.

result—the interfaces whose operations were copied into their child interface (i.e, multiple-inherited base interfaces) have lost their identities. A client would not be able to `QueryInterface()` for these dispatch interfaces (such as the interfaces DC and DE in Figure 3.5). To solve this problem, all of the non-leftmost interfaces are also supplied as separate dispatch interfaces derived directly from `IDispatch`. A component supporting all of these dispatch interfaces can successfully respond to `QueryInterface()` calls on any of the mapped interfaces from the entire CORBA inheritance hierarchy. At the same time, an automation controller that does not support querying for multiple dispatch interfaces has access to all of the operation in the entire hierarchy on the single flattened interface. This all-inclusive interface is the primary Automation interface for the Automation View object and will be returned to any client querying for the `IDispatch` interface.

The methods on an Automation interface do not need to be ordered since `IDispatch::Invoke()` uses an explicit identity to indicate the method rather than the position. However, the Automation mapping of CORBA interfaces can also be used to build dual interfaces, which support direct invocation through a function table as well as indirect invocation through `IDispatch::Invoke()`. Consequently, the Automation mapping specifies a complete ordering of all attributes and operations in essentially the same way that it does for COM.

Requests

Each CORBA request maps directly onto a corresponding COM or Automation request. With the exception of **oneway** operations in CORBA, the request/reply interactions between client and object in both object models are essentially identical. COM does not support an equivalent to CORBA **oneway** semantics. CORBA **oneway** operations simply map onto COM operations with no output parameters.

COM does not support a dynamic invocation mode. The CORBA DII- and DSI-related pseudointerfaces such as **Request** and **NVList** are not mapped. As a side effect, this avoids the problem of mapping deferred synchronous requests into COM. They simply do not map, nor do any of the CORBA pseudo-object types that exist solely to support the dynamic invocation interfaces, such as **Request** and **NVList**.

NOTE It can be argued, of course, that Automation is the equivalent of a DII for COM. This is not correct, however, in that Automation is in many ways a different model and in particular cannot support all of the capabilities of COM.

Parameters

Mapping a CORBA operation's parameter list to COM and Automation is straightforward. The IDL parameter passing modes **in**, **out**, and **inout** map directly to MIDL/ODL [in], [out], and [in, out]. The order of the parameters in the COM/Automation parameter list are the same as in IDL, with the following additions:

- The return value of the IDL operation (if any) maps to a MIDL/ODL [retval, out] parameter that appears after the declared parameters. The return value of the MIDL/ODL operation is always HRESULT.

- If the IDL operation in question has a raises clause (i.e., it specifies user exceptions that may be raised), a parameter is added to the end of the COM operation's parameter list to return exceptions.

Exceptions

The COM and Automation mappings for CORBA exceptions are different and, unfortunately, complicated. There are two distinct subproblems addressed by the mappings—*mapping system exceptions* and *mapping user exceptions*. Ideally, the system exceptions (at least) would map into the "natural" COM and Automation error mechanisms, SCODE for COM and EXCEPINFO for Automation. The Interworking Specification attempts to do this as much as possible, but it must enhance these mechanisms in order to supply the full information model of CORBA system exceptions.

System Exceptions Mapping into COM The COM HRESULT is used to convey as much CORBA exception information as it can, which happens to be the completion code and the system exception major ID. To do this, the Interworking Specification defines a (rather large) set of HRESULT constants. For each CORBA system exception, there are three exception constants, corresponding to the three possible completion code values (**YES**, **NO**, and **MAYBE**). For example, for the CORBA **BAD_PARAM** system exception, there are three HRESULT error codes—ITF_E_BAD_PARAM_YES, ITF_E_BAD_PARAM_NO, and ITF_E _BAD_PARAM_MAYBE. The same bits are used for each system to represent the completion code for each system exception, so the completion code can be examined independently of the system exception major code.

While this information is adequate for many purposes, some applications need the rest of the information in the system exception, such as the minor code. The

Interworking Specification uses standard OLE error objects to achieve this. All COM views must support the `ISupportErrorInfo` interface (and the related interfaces and functionality). The view uses this mechanism to return the following additional information in the `EXCEPINFO` structure:

- The name of the CORBA interface and operation that generated the error in the error source string
- The exception repository ID, minor code, and completion status in the description string

The contents of the remaining fields (help file name and help context ID) are unspecified, so any bridge product is free to use them as it wants. Note that bridging products are required to support the `ISupportErrorInfo` interface on all COM views; they are not required to actually support error objects themselves. If not, the `ISupportErrorInfo` interface must so indicate. In some cases, constraints on client applications and platforms may be so stringent that the bridge needs to eliminate as many nonessential run-time features as possible. Hence, support for some features such as error objects is optional in the Interworking Specification.

User Exceptions in COM   When the IDL operation being mapped into COM includes user-defined exceptions in a **raises** clause, the bridging product generates a set of interface-specific data types to support them. The individual exceptions are mapped to COM structs. For each CORBA interface that includes user exceptions, a COM interface is generated that acts as a union of all of the exception types used in the interface. This interface has accessor methods for each exception struct type, but it actually holds only one at a time. It accommodates the need for polymorphism without creating a separate interface for each exception type. Finally, another struct type is generated that is the actual parameter type in the method signature. This struct contains a flag indicating error status, the repository ID of the exception that occurred, and a pointer to the exception interface though which the actual exception struct can be obtained. This struct appears as the method's last parameter. The caller can choose to pass a null pointer in this parameter, indicating a lack of interest in the details of the user exception details. If the caller passes a non-null pointer, the COM view will return the appropriate struct. Figure 3.6 illustrates the organization of user-defined exceptions in COM views.

The COM mapping of CORBA exceptions is admittedly complicated. It is a good example of the kind of compromise necessary when mapping disparate ob-

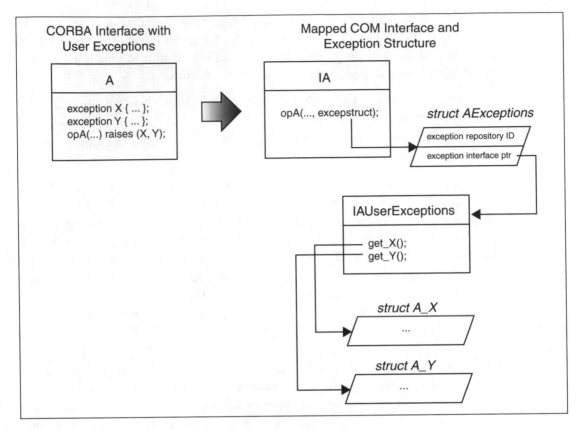

Figure 3.6 CORBA exception handling in COM views.

ject systems. The cleanest organization might have been to unify system and user exceptions into a single, straightforward mechanism, but that would have made exception handling for COM views of CORBA objects completely foreign to COM programmers, even in the simple case of system exceptions. The alternative chosen in the Interworking Specification allows system exceptions to be mapped in terms of standard COM mechanisms (HRESULT and EXCEPINFO) while user exceptions (for which there is no analog in COM) map differently. Making the programming model natural for COM programmers was deemed more important than providing the most elegant possible organization.

Exceptions in Automation CORBA exception handling in Automation is slightly less complicated than in COM, although the programmer using the interface has a few options for the way in which exceptions should be reported and chooses from among them by passing or not passing certain parameters in the invocation. Both CORBA system and user exceptions map to dispatch interfaces that derive from the interface `DIForeignException`, which in turn derives from `DIForeignComplexType`, the same base interface used by structs and unions. `DIForeignException` has readonly properties that contain the exception major code (**NO_EXCEPTION**, **SYSTEM_EXCEPTION**, or **USER_EXCEPTION**) and the name of the exception if one is raised. User exceptions are derived from the interface `DICORBAUserException`, which is an empty base interface deriving from `DIForeignException`. The specific user exception dispatch interfaces are essentially the same as pseudostructs, with properties that map one to one to the members of the CORBA IDL exception. System exceptions are expressed by the fixed interface `DICORBASystemException`, which also derives from `DIForeignException`. `DICORBASystemException` has properties containing the ORB-specific exception minor code and the completion status of the operation. The exception objects that support these interfaces are called *pseudoexceptions*.

If you want to use this straightforward mechanism, you simply supply an optional exception parameter in the method invocation. If an exception occurs, the view will fill in this parameter with the dispatch interface pointer of the pseudoexception. The view also sets the HRESULT to S_FALSE. It does not, however, set the severity bit in the HRESULT, which prevents the Automation controller's error-trapping mechanisms (such as VB's error traps) from being fired. This is important to understand. Standard error-trapping mechanisms don't know about CORBA exceptions and would not be able to recognize or use the CORBA pseudoexceptions. If you use this mechanism to get access to the detailed CORBA exception information, you must check the status of the exception parameter after the invocation. If no exception occurred, the view will return a pseudoexception of type `DIForeignException` whose major code is NO_EXCEPTION.

Alternatively, you may choose to use the standard Automation exception mechanism by omitting the optional pseudoexception parameter and passing an EXCEPINFO to IDispatch::Invoke(). If an exception occurs, the invocation will return an HRESULT value of DISP_E_EXCEPTION and fill in the EXCEPINFO structure with the interface name, operation name, and the CORBA repository ID of the exception. This exception will trigger the error-trapping mechanism of the Automation controller. Note that this approach prevents you from accessing the actual contents of any CORBA user exception.

Object References

To a COM or Automation programmer, a CORBA object reference takes the form of an interface pointer to the corresponding COM and Automation view, as you would naturally expect. Because COM interface pointers are inherently transient, COM programmers would not normally write programs that depended on CORBA's persistent reference behavior. For example, CORBA programs may convert object references to strings, store them indefinitely, and subsequently retrieve them, converting them back to references. COM programmers, on the other hand, typically obtain an interface pointer (and thus the associated object) through a factory, the registry, or by binding a moniker every time the object in question is needed. They cannot simply store the reference and retrieve it for later use.

Since CORBA reference behavior is a superset of COM's, a COM programmer using a CORBA object mapped through a COM View will (in general) not experience the potential loss of function as long as the programmer only expects the usual COM behaviors for object references (interface pointers). In cases where COM and Automation programmers are explicitly aware that they are using a mapped CORBA object and want to have access to the richer behavior of CORBA references, the Interworking Specification provides a useful mechanism that still does not entirely depart from general COM practice. A COM or Automation view may optionally make the encapsulated CORBA reference available to the COM client in the form of a moniker.

COM and Automation Views may optionally support an interface called `IMonikerProvider`. This interface, if available, will return a custom moniker that encapsulates the CORBA object reference in string form. Since this string is in a standard interoperable form for object references, monikers of this type that are created by one bridging product can be bound and used by any other compliant bridge. Using this mechanism, COM programs can store references to CORBA objects in structured storage (e.g., a compound document with a link that is actually a reference to a CORBA object) to be retrieved later and bound. CORBA reference semantics guarantee that if the object has not been explicitly destroyed, binding and using this moniker will cause the object to be automatically activated if necessary. This is an extremely convenient and powerful feature that extends some of the superior scalability of CORBA systems into COM by providing an efficient mechanism for resource management in servers (transparent passivation and activation) without requiring reference counts and keep-alive ping messages on the network.

Object Identity and Life Cycle

The most significant architectural differences between CORBA and COM object models lie in their notions of object identity and life cycle. The differences may be summarized as described in the following paragraphs.

A COM object reference (i.e., interface pointer) denotes a particular in-memory instantiation of a programming object in a particular process. In contrast, a CORBA reference denotes a conceptual object that may be implemented over the course of its lifetime by several distinct programming objects in different processes. The conceptual object may passivate itself by storing its state and deleting the current programming object that embodies it. When a client invokes an operation on one of the object's references, the ORB will take whatever steps are necessary to activate the object, possibly including the creation of an appropriate server process. This process is completely transparent to the client.

The lifetime of a COM object is bounded by the lifetimes of its clients and ultimately by the lifetime of the process in which it exists. When no more clients are attached to an object, it is destroyed. The lifetime of a CORBA object is disassociated from its clients. It must be explicitly destroyed. To a great extent, this reflects the differences between the evolutionary trajectories of COM and CORBA—COM emerged from the swamp of local compound documents, while CORBA climbed out of the ocean of distributed objects.

The identity of a COM object is, in general, not associated with a particular state. A COM object may, over the course of its lifetime, load and store several distinct, identifiable states. Object identities (memory addresses of programming objects) are managed separately from state identities (usually file names). Client programs are usually responsible for explicitly managing state and its association with COM objects. In contrast, CORBA objects are usually associated with particular states throughout their lifetimes. This association is often implicit from the client's perspective since the CORBA object may completely encapsulate its state. Clients do not usually have any notion of state with a separate identity, apart from the object that encapsulates it.

These differences primarily affect the way clients locate or create objects through the bridge and the way in which the bridge manages the life cycle of the views that expose objects between object systems. COM and Automation clients can access CORBA objects in a number of ways, which are described in the following sections.

Mapping CORBA Factories into COM Class Factories

A bridging product may allow a CORBA factory to be encapsulated by a COM class factory, which is placed in the registry in the standard way. The Interworking Specification defines a CORBA IDL interface called **SimpleFactory** with a parameterless create operation. If the bridging product supports this mechanism, an application can expose a CORBA **SimpleFactory** for a given object type through a class factory. Since CORBA implementation types don't have explicit identities, a COM class ID must be assigned to the class factory. When a COM client invokes the class factory associated with this class ID, the class factory invokes the encapsulated CORBA **SimpleFactory** and creates a view for the new CORBA object returned by the **SimpleFactory**.

Registering COM Views of CORBA Objects in the Active Object Registry

Alternatively, the bridge may allow existing CORBA objects to be bound to COM views and exposed through the COM active object registry. This allows clients to access these views though `GetActiveObject()` or `GetObject()`. This is an optional behavior for bridging products. If supported, the specific manner in which a CORBA object is bound to a view and placed in the registry is defined by the product.

Using Monikers and the IMonikerProvider Interface

As mentioned in the previous "Object References" section, a bridge product may provide support for the `IMonikerProvider` interface. If so, clients can ask any view object for its `IMonikerProvider` interface with `QueryInterface()`. If the view returns a non-null interface pointer, the client can invoke the moniker provider interface to obtain a moniker that encapsulates the actual CORBA object reference for the target object. The resulting moniker can be stored and subsequently loaded and bound. This is a custom moniker type implemented by the bridge. Binding the moniker will invoke the internals of the bridge, which will convert the string back into a CORBA object reference and create a COM view that encapsulates that reference.

Using the CORBA Factory

The resources associated with the COM registry are limited. In some applications, very large numbers of objects may need to be exposed through the bridge. To avoid overloading the registry, the bridges support an interface called ICOR-

BAFactory (DICORBAFactory for Automation clients). This interface has methods GetObject() and CreateObject() that appear to be very similar to the VB functions of the same names. These methods take string parameters that are names with a syntax almost identical to COM ProgIDs—a sequence of identifiers separated by periods. The CORBA Factory (which is actually a component of the bridge itself) maps these names into some namespace managed by the bridge. In most cases, this is implemented with the CORBA Naming Service. By not specifying the implementation, the interworking architecture opens the door for a variety of possible implementations, from very simple, lightweight directories to large-scale distributed, replicated, fault-tolerant directory systems. The details of how objects are mapped through the CORBA Factory interface are product-specific. The bridge creates views as necessary for objects as they request access through the CORBA Factory.

Support for the first three mechanisms (factory mapping, active object registry, and IMonikerProvider) is optional; they may not be available in all products. However, all compliant bridge products must support the ICORBAFactory interface. Other required objects are exposed through the CORBA factory at well-known, standard names. While the other methods are slightly more natural to COM programmers, using the CORBA factory for locating specific objects and services will be the only reliably portable method. Depending on the implementation, it is also likely to be distributed, more reliable, and more scalable.

Destroying the CORBA Object from a COM Client

Once a CORBA object is bound to a view by any of the mechanisms just described, the life cycle of the view is unrelated to the life cycle of the CORBA object. Specifically, when the reference count for the COM view goes to zero, the view itself will be destroyed, but not the CORBA object. If the target object supports the CORBA **LifeCycleObject** interface, the object COM view will support the mapped version of this interface, **ICosLifeCycle_LifeCycleObject**. A COM client can use the remove() method on this interface to explicitly delete the target object.

In many cases, CORBA applications provide application-specific life cycle operations, including destroying objects. The bank example in Chapter 2 illustrates a common approach. The **AcctMgr** interface acts as a factory for **Account** objects. In a more complete rendering of the application, it might also provide an operation for destroying accounts. This example illustrates the essential difference between the life cycles of CORBA and COM objects and the ways they interact. A

CORBA **Account** object, once created, exists until it is explicitly destroyed. This statement only applies to the conceptual Account object, not to a particular programming object that implements the account at some point in time. The server that implements the object manages its own resources internally by storing object states and deleting their in-memory instantiations as necessary. Since object activation is automatic in CORBA, the client doesn't need to be aware of the object's activation state, and the object doesn't need to keep track of all the current clients that hold references. Since COM objects are transient instantiations, the life cycles of view objects are independent of the target CORBA objects they represent. When a COM client "locates" an existing CORBA object through one of the mechanisms just described, the bridge creates a new view that represents the object temporarily until the view's reference count goes to zero. This relationship between the life cycles of views and objects works quite well in practice. It provides a simple, intuitive model for thinking about object life cycles at the application level.

What's Next?

This chapter has provided a conceptual discussion of the architectural issues you will face when building systems with CORBA and COM. Some of the differences you must deal with introduce slightly cumbersome interfaces, such as the COM mapping of CORBA exceptions. Though annoying, these are differences of detail, not essence. The most important differences are in the areas of identity and life cycle. These differences are fundamental, though they do not introduce any particularly complex interfaces. They affect the basic behavior of objects and the concept of what it means to be an object. Bridging products do as much as possible to mask these differences, but ultimately you will be responsible for understanding and accommodating the subtle differences, particularly if you are implementing a CORBA object that you want to expose to COM and Automation clients through a bridge. You should now have a good foundation for proceeding to the following chapters, which will present the details of the programming models you will use.

4 *Basic Mappings*

This chapter will present a detailed look at how to map basic data types from CORBA to Automation, with emphasis placed on a programming example in Visual Basic. Before starting the example we will discuss the details of how interfaces are mapped. These details will be illustrated in a simple example that uses each of the basic data types. We will describe the CORBA IDL for the example and the ODL that is generated from the interworking bridge development tool and explain the organization of our Visual Basic project. We will then present a section for each data type that explains the details of using it in Visual Basic.

Mapping Interfaces and Invocations

In this chapter, we discuss the Visual Basic implementation, but we will not cover the implementation of the CORBA server. As is the case with all of the examples in this book, the code is available at our Web site—www.wiley.com/compbooks /rosen—in the directory "\Chapter4\VisualBasic and \Chapter4\Server." A

A Note on Terminology

We will use the term *Automation* to mean the functions available through the `IDispatch` interface as well as dual interfaces. When we refer to *COM*, we generally mean the COM object model that applies to both COM Vtable and Automation interfaces. Typically, we will use the term *COM Interface* when we mean only the COM Vtable interfaces.

CORBA interface can be mapped to a Automation interface, a Dual interface, or a COM interface. For Automation views, most bridging products map to a Dual interface rather than to an Automation interface, so this is the example that we will use here. Recall the naming conventions from Chapter 3. An interface with one operation described in CORBA IDL as

```
//IDL
module Chapter4 {
    interface foo {
        returntype      opername  (in intype inparam,
                                    out outtype outparam);
};
```

would have the following name and ODL signature when mapped to the Dual interface:

```
interface DIChapter4_foo : IDispatch
    {
    HRESULT opername(
              [in] intype inparam,
              [out] outtype outparam,
              [in,out,optional] VARIANT* exceptionInfo,
              [out,retval] returntype* returnValue);

};
```

Let's examine the details of the mapping. First notice that the CORBA operation name, *opername*, maps directly to the Automation method name without modification. The input and output parameters of the CORBA method also map directly to input and output parameters in the Automation method, again without modification to the name or data types.

NOTE Basic data types map directly. We will see in the next chapter how constructed CORBA data types are mapped.

The next argument in the signature is the optional exceptionInfo. You may recall from Chapter 3 that all CORBA operations have implicit exception information. When this is mapped to Automation, the exception information is made available as an additional parameter in the method signature. However, since most Automation programmers will not want to bother with this parameter, it is made optional. We will deal with exceptions in more detail in Chapter 8. Finally, notice that the CORBA return parameter, *returntype,* is the last parameter in the Automation signature. By definition, all COM methods return an HRESULT, therefore, there can be no return parameters. Thus, the CORBA return parameter is mapped as the last parameter in the Automation method signature.

CORBA attributes are mapped to COM properties in a similar way. For each CORBA attribute, a propput and propget method is added to the Automation interface. For CORBA readonly attributes, only a propget method is added. Listing 4.1 shows the CORBA IDL for the examples used throughout this chapter. Listing 4.2 shows the corresponding ODL generated by the bridge product. Examine these listings for more examples of operation and attribute mappings.

Using the Basic Data Types

The mappings for the basic data types are shown in Table 4.1. In most cases, the mappings are straightforward. There are a few exceptions where there are differences between Win16 and Win32 platforms. For example, Win32 platforms have the concept of an 8-bit unsigned integer, called an *unsigned char.* However, there is

Table 4.1 Basic Data Type Mappings

CORBA TYPE	AUTOMATION TYPE	DESCRIPTION OF AUTOMATION TYPE
boolean	VARIANT_BOOL	True = –1, False = 0
char	short	16-bit unsigned integer
char	unsigned char★	8-bit unsigned integer
double	double	64-bit IEEE floating point number
float	float	32-bit IEEE floating point number
long	long	32-bit signed integer
octet	short	16-bit unsigned integer
octet	unsigned char★	8-bit unsigned integer
short	short	16-bit unsigned integer
unsigned long	long	32-bit signed integer
unsigned short	long	32-bit signed integer
string	BSTR	Length-prefixed string. Prefix is an integer.
bounded string	BSTR	Length-prefixed string. Prefix is an integer
wstring	BSTR	Length-prefixed string. Prefix is an integer.

★Only available on Win32 platform.

no equivalent to this on Win16 platforms. This left the interworking architecture with a choice, either to have the same mapping on all Win platforms or to map the CORBA 8-bit data types to 8-bit types on Win32 platforms and have a different mapping on Win16 platforms. It was decided to go with the different mappings for several reasons. First, it is more accurate to map 8-bit types to 8-bit types, and, second, Win16 platforms are quickly being replaced by Win32, so it didn't make sense to use an inferior mapping when the platform requiring it is going away. (In fact, many bridging products don't even support the Win16 platform.)

A Basic Data Type Example

The example presented in this section illustrates the basic data types in a Visual Basic program, including their use in properties and methods as input, output, and **inout** parameters. The emphasis of the example is to show how to use all of the different basic data types. Instead of developing an especially contrived scenario for this, we chose not to have any real scenario associated with the example. In this example, there are two interfaces, one for the scalar data types and one for strings. The CORBA IDL file for the interfaces is shown in Listing 4.1. The Basic-Types interface has three attributes and three methods with boring but descriptive names, each of which uses different data types in different ways. For example, the indoublefloat method has two input parameters, a double and a float. It returns a long. The StringTypes interface has one method.

The ODL file corresponding to the CORBA IDL is shown in Listings 4.2 and 4.3. The ODL for the StringTypes interface is shown in Listing 4.3 as a separate file because most bridge products have chosen to create a separate ODL file for each CORBA interface. We will refer back to these listings during our discussion and examples of the basic data types.

All of the methods and attributes from both interfaces are included in a single Visual Basic form as shown in Figure 4.1. A button to invoke the method, titled "Invoke method," is included in the left-most column. Any input parameters are provided using text boxes in the "Input Parameters" column. Output parameters are displayed in text boxes in the "Output Parameters" column, and return parameters are displayed in text boxes in the "Return Parameters" column. This layout makes it easy to see what the input, output, and return parameters are for each of the different methods. There is a separate Visual Basic routine for every method. Each routine is discussed in the following sections and is accompanied by a listing of the Visual Basic code.

Listing 4.1 Chapter 4 CORBA IDL file.

```
module Chapter4
{
        constlong  Authors = 3;
        enumcolor {red, green, blue};

        interface BasicTypes
        {
                attribute              boolean      boolType;
                readonly attribute     char         charType;
                attribute              color        theColor;

                long  indoublefloat       (in    double       doubleType,
                                           in     float        floatType);

                boolean     outoctetshort (out    octet        octetType,
                                           out    short        shortType);

                unsigned long    uTypes   (in     unsigned short  ushortType,
                                           in      unsigned long   ulongType);

        }; //end of interface BasicTypes

        interface StringTypes
        {
                string        inoutstrings    (inout string       boundedString<10>);

        }; //end of interface StringTypes
}; //end of module Chapter4
```

Listing 4.2 DIChapter4_BasicTypes.odl file.

```
[
    helpstring("DIChapter4_BasicTypes Library"),
    version(1.0),
    uuid(efe9a338-a978-471d-1d77-c68d5d9b02c8)
]
library DIChapter4_BasicTypesLibrary
{

    typedef enum Chapter4_color
```

(continues)

Listing 4.2 DIChapter4_BasicTypes.odl file. (*Continued*)

```
{
        red = 1,
        green = 2,
        blue = 3
} Chapter4_color;

[
        odl,
        dual, oleautomation,
        version(0.0),
        uuid(e25a3f47-4e7c-77fb-1de1-c74d8cec4a85)
]
interface DIChapter4_BasicTypes : IDispatch
{
        [ id(7)]
        HRESULT indoublefloat(
                [in] double doubleType,
                [in] float floatType,
                [in,out,optional] VARIANT* exceptionInfo,
                [out,retval] long* returnValue);

        [ id(8)]
        HRESULT outoctetshort(
                [out] unsigned char* octetType,
                [out] short* shortType,
                [in,out,optional] VARIANT* exceptionInfo,
                [out,retval] boolean* returnValue);

        [ id(9)]
        HRESULT uTypes(
                [in] long ushortType,
                [in] long ulongType,
                [in,out,optional] VARIANT* exceptionInfo,
                [out,retval] long* returnValue);

        [ id(10), propget]
        HRESULT boolType([out,retval] boolean* returnValue);
        [ id(10), propput]
        HRESULT boolType([in] boolean Value);
```

Listing 4.2 DIChapter4_BasicTypes.odl file. (*Continued*)

```
            [ id(12), propget]
            HRESULT charType([out,retval] short* returnValue);

            [ id(13), propget]
            HRESULT theColor([out,retval] Chapter4_color* returnValue);
            [ id(13), propput]
            HRESULT theColor([in] Chapter4_color Value);


        };
};
```

Listing 4.3 DIChapter4_String.odl file.

```
[
    helpstring("DIChapter4_StringTypes Library"),
    version(1.0),
    uuid(879ff7ac-7919-93f1 1d56-524650e3ddc9)
]
library DIChapter4_StringTypesLibrary
{

    [
        odl,
        dual, oleautomation,
        version(0.0),
        uuid(869a7900-bae1 104f-1dcd-d542507fcc54)
    ]
    interface DIChapter4_StringTypes : IDispatch
    {
        [ id(7)]
        HRESULT inoutstrings(
            [in,out] BSTR* boundedString,
            [in,out,optional] VARIANT* exceptionInfo,
            [out,retval] BSTR* returnValue);

    };
};
```

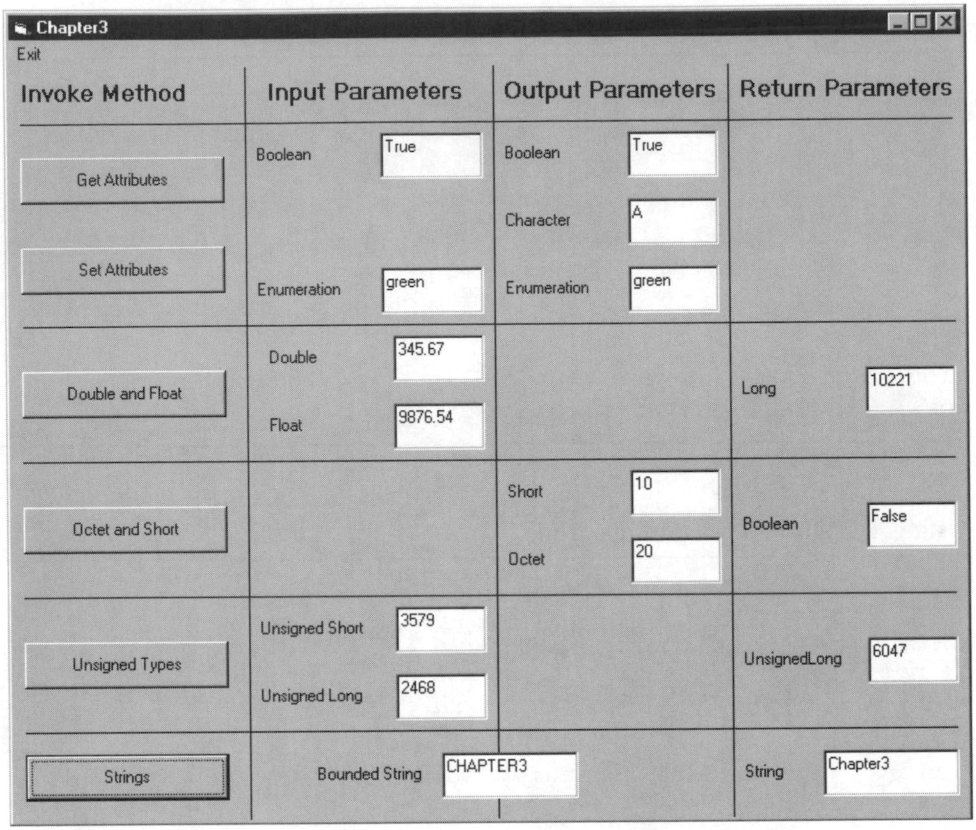

Chapter3   _ □ ✕

Exit

Invoke Method	Input Parameters	Output Parameters	Return Parameters
Get Attributes	Boolean `True`	Boolean `True`	
		Character `A`	
Set Attributes	Enumeration `green`	Enumeration `green`	
Double and Float	Double `345.67`		Long `10221`
	Float `9876.54`		
Octet and Short		Short `10`	Boolean `False`
		Octet `20`	
Unsigned Types	Unsigned Short `3579`		UnsignedLong `6047`
	Unsigned Long `2468`		
Strings	Bounded String `CHAPTER3`		String `Chapter3`

Figure 4.1 _Chapter 4 Visual Basic application._

Before we go into the details of the methods, let's discuss the setup code for the example shown in Listing 4.4. As we did in the basic example in Chapter 2, we are going to explicitly declare typed variables for each interface. The CORBA IDL for this example has a module of "Chapter4" and an interface called `Basic-Types`. The Dual interface name generated for this is `DIChapter4_Basic-Types`, so we will declare our local object _objBasicType_ as an object of this interface. Similarly for strings, we declare a local object _objStringType_ as `DIChapter4_StringTypes`. Next, we have some common subroutines that will get us an instance of the Automation views of the CORBA target objects, one called GetBasicType and the other GetStringType.

Each method in the Visual Basic application that uses one of these objects calls the common subroutine. The first time the subroutine is called, the view is created and a flag is set indicating that the object exists. Subsequent invocations simply return

Listing 4.4 Example program setup code.

```
' Public object variables for the Automation Views of the
' CORBA interfaces
Public objBasicType As DIChapter4_BasicTypes
Public objStringType As DIChapter4_StringTypes

Private Sub GetBasicType()
    ' Subroutine to get the DIChapter4_BasicTypes object.

    ' If we've already gotten the object, don't get it again.
    If gotBasicType = False Then
        ' Use the custom "Namespace" moniker to get the object
        ' based on its entry in the CORBA namespace.
        Set objBasicType = GetObject
                ("@ObjectBroker.Bridge\Advertisements\BasicType")
        gotBasicType = True
    End If
End Sub

Private Sub GetStringType()
    ' Subroutine to get the DIChapter4_StringTypes object.

    ' If we've already gotten the object, don't get it again.
    If gotStringType = False Then
        ' Use the custom "Namespace" moniker to get the object
        ' based on its entry in the CORBA namespace.
        Set objStringType = GetObject
                ("@ObjectBroker.Bridge\Advertisements\StringType")
        gotStringType = True
    End If
End Sub
```

without creating another instance of the view object. This example uses a custom namespace moniker to reference the CORBA object. Creating instances of objects is discussed in detail in Chapter 6, but it's appropriate here to give a description of the namespace moniker. You may have used the Visual Basic function `GetObject` before, which requires you to pass in a descriptor. Actually, the descriptor that you pass in is a type of moniker, where a file moniker is the default type.

The Microsoft convention for specifying a custom moniker is to preface the string with the "@" symbol followed by the program ID of the moniker implementation. So "@ObjectBroker.Bridge" indicates to the system that this is a custom moniker with a program ID of ObjectBroker.Bridge. The system looks up the program ID in the system registry, loads the DLL associated with it, and passes the remainder of the string to the `ParseDisplayName` interface implemented by that DLL. A namespace moniker accepts the name of the object in a hierarchical CORBA namespace. In this case, the naming context is Advertisements, and the name of the object in that context is BasicType, so the entire string passed to GetObject is "@ObjectBroker.Bridge\Advertisements\BasicType." The CORBA server for the "Chapter4" example writes this name to the namespace when it initializes.

Working with boolean, enum, and char

The CORBA `BasicTypes` interface has three attributes: **boolType**, which is a boolean; **charType**, which is a char; and **theColor**, which is an enum. In this section we will deal with each of these data types. Recall that CORBA attributes map to Automation properties, with a propput and propget method created for each read/write attribute and a propget method created for readonly attributes. If you look at the generated ODL file for `DIChapter4_BasicTypes` in Listing 4.2, you will see that only a propget method exists for the readonly attribute char-Type, whereas the other attributes have both propget and propset methods.

Let's look at the Visual Basic code for handling CORBA attributes, shown in Listing 4.5. First we declare local variables for the data types used in the routine. The first data type in the routine is a boolean. In CORBA, the values of a boolean

Naming Conventions Used in Our Example

Local variables are declared for each of the data types at the beginning of each routine. The variable name contains text of the CORBA data type in the original CORBA operation. The type of the variable is the corresponding Automation type. So, by simply looking at the declaration, you can see what the data type mapping is. For example, "Dim charType As Byte" tells us that the original CORBA data type is char and that it gets mapped to a Byte in Visual Basic. Components of the Visual Basic form have descriptive names that are prefixed with the type of control on the form, so txtAttBoolean is a text box that will display the Boolean attribute.

Listing 4.5 Boolean, enum, char handling.

```
Private Sub cmdGetAtt_Click(Index As Integer)
    ' Get the BasicType object attributes

    ' Declare local variables for the CORBA datatypes
    ' CORBA::boolean -> Boolean, CORBA::char -> Byte,
    ' CORBA::enum -> enum
    Dim boolType As Boolean
    Dim charType As Byte
    Dim enumType As Chapter4_color

    ' Handy-dandy array to print out colors
    Dim ColorValues(1 To 3) As String
    ColorValues(1) = "red"
    ColorValues(2) = "green"
    ColorValues(3) = "blue"

    GetBasicType      ' Get the DIChapter4_BasicTypes object

    ' Get and write out the boolean
    boolType = objBasicType.boolType
    txtAttBoolean = boolToText(boolType)

    ' Get and write out the character
    charType = objBasicType.charType
    txtChar.text = Chr(charType)

    ' Get and write out the enum
    enumType = objBasicType.theColor
    txtEnum.text = ColorValues(enumType)
End Sub
```

are True = 1, False = 0. In Automation, the values are True = -1, False = 0. The bridge will automatically convert these values for you. Good programming technique would suggest that you always use "True" and "False" rather than numeric values when assigning or comparing booleans.

The next data type in this routine, enumType, is a CORBA enum that gets mapped to an enumeration in Visual Basic. The name of the enumeration is derived from the CORBA IDL based on the module name and the enum name, such as module_enum. In our example, the enum is named "color" and the module is "Chapter4," so the Visual Basic enumeration becomes "Chapter4_color." We will want to print the color as text, rather than the integer value of the enumeration, so we create a simple table, `ColorValues`, to translate the integer to text.

The last data type in this routine is a CORBA char, which is an unsigned 8-bit value. On Win32 platforms, this gets translated to an unsigned char, which is also an 8-bit value. Unfortunately, there is no equivalent data type on Win16 platforms, so there it gets translated to a short.

Now that we have local variables for all of the data types, we get the `objBasicType` view object using the `GetBasicType` routine discussed in the previous section. Finally, we assign the values of the attributes to our local variables as you would with any Automation object, such as `boolType = objBasicType.boolType`. The example code also lets you set the attributes. Because setting attributes is so much like getting them, we don't include the code listing in the book.

Working with Long, Double, and Float

The handling of long, double, and float data types is quite straightforward since there is a one-to-one mapping between these types in CORBA and Automation. Listing 4.6 shows the Visual Basic code used in our example. The structure of this routine is similar to the boolean, enum, and char routine described in the last section. Notice that although the actual data type is an IEEE float, in Visual Basic a float is declared as a "Single" as in the example `Dim floatType As Single`. The routine will execute the `indoublefloat` method, so the first thing it does is get a value for the double and float from text box controls on the Visual Basic form. The common routine `GetBasicType` is used to get the `objBasicType` view object, and then the method is invoked. The `indoublefloat` method simply takes two input parameters, a double and a float, adds them together and returns them as a long (no overflow checking is done). The returned value is then displayed on the form in a text box.

Working with Octet and Short

The CORBA octet data type is an unsigned 8-bit value. Sequences of octets are frequently used to pass opaque data. For Win32 platforms, this translates to an un-

Listing 4.6 Long, double, and float handling.

```
Private Sub cmdDoubleFloat_Click(Index As Integer)
    ' Invoke the indoublefloat operation

    ' Declare local variables for the CORBA datatypes
    ' CORBA::double -> Double, CORBA::float -> Single,
    ' CORBA::long -> Long
    Dim doubleType As Double
    Dim floatType As Single
    Dim longResult As Long

    ' Verify that all the input parameters are supplied.
    ' No type or range checking is done.
    If txtDouble.text = Empty Then
        MsgBox "You must supply an amount for Double"
        Exit Sub
    End If
    If txtFloat.text = Empty Then
        MsgBox "You must supply an amount for Float"
        Exit Sub
    End If

    GetBasicType     ' Get the DIChapter4_BasicTypes object

    ' Get the input parameters
    doubleType = CDbl(txtDouble)
    floatType = CSng(txtFloat)

    ' Invoke the inDoubleFloat method and write the output
    ' to the form
    longResult = objBasicType.indoublefloat(doubleType, floatType)
    txtDFLong = CStr(longResult)
```

signed char. As with the CORBA char data type, there is no equivalent on Win16 platforms, so there it is translated to a short. The Visual Basic code for handling octet and shorts in our example is shown in Listing 4.7. The structure of this routine should look familiar by now. Again, notice that although the actual data type

Listing 4.7 Octet and short handling.

```
Private Sub cmdOctetShort_Click(Index As Integer)
    ' Invoke the outoctetshort operation

    ' Declare local variables for the CORBA datatypes
    ' CORBA::short -> Integer, CORBA::octet -> Byte
    Dim shortType As Integer
    Dim octetType As Byte
    Dim boolResult As Boolean

    GetBasicType    ' Get the DIChapter4_BasicTypes object

    ' Invoke the method and display the results
    result = objBasicType.outoctetshort(octetType, shortType)
    txtOctet.text = CStr(octetType)
    txtShort.text = CStr(shortType)
    txtOSBoolean.text = boolToText(boolResult)
```

is an unsigned char, in Visual Basic it is declared as "Byte" as in the example `Dim octetType As Byte`. Also, in Visual Basic an Integer is a 16-bit value, so a short is declared as an Integer as in `Dim shortType as Integer`. You can always refer to the generated ODL file to see what the Automation data type is. The routine will execute the `outoctetshort` method, which fills in two output parameters, an octet and a short, and returns a boolean. The server always returns the same values when this method is invoked.

Working with Unsigned Types

If you thought the data type handling was starting to get monotonous, unsigned data types should provide some variety. CORBA has both signed and unsigned data types, but Automation has only signed types. This gives rise to some interesting overflow conditions when mapping from one model to the other, as we will see in our examples. The Visual Basic code for handling unsigned types is shown in Listing 4.8. The interworking architecture recognizes that these overflow conditions exist, and it requires bridge products to be able to detect them and return an error when they occur. Thus, the first thing we do in our unsigned types routine is declare an error handler that will display an error in a message box. As usual, we declare local variables. Notice that both the CORBA unsigned long and unsigned short map to an Automation long data type. This routine will invoke the utypes method, which takes two input parameters—an unsigned short and an unsigned long—and returns an unsigned long. This method signature was designed to illustrate the three different overflow conditions that can arise using unsigned types.

Converting Automation Long to CORBA Unsigned Long

The first overflow condition can occur when converting an automation long to a CORBA unsigned long, as is the case for the ulong input parameter in this example. An unsigned number can contain only positive values. Thus, if the value of the input parameter is negative, an overflow condition will occur.

Demoting Automation Long to CORBA Unsigned Short

The second overflow condition is similar to the first, except that the CORBA data type is a short rather than a long. Again, if the value of the input parameter for the ushort is negative, an overflow condition will occur. You can try this out using the example client and server provided on our Web site. Enter a negative number for either of the input parameters, and the bridge will signal a DISP_E_OVERFLOW error.

Demoting CORBA Unsigned Long to Automation Long

The last overflow condition can occur when converting a CORBA unsigned long to an Automation long. An unsigned long can contain a positive value of up to 2e31; however, a signed long can only contain a positive value of up to 2e30. This overflow condition can occur when a CORBA unsigned long is an output or return parameter. You can also try this out using the example client and server provided on our Web site. The server will check for a special case value of 1234 for the ulong input parameter. If 1234 is specified, the server will return an unsigned long value that will cause an overflow condition.

If no overflow conditions occur, the method will add the two input parameters together and return the sum. If an overflow condition does occur, the bridge will return an HRESULT value of DISP_E_OVERFLOW, which is a hex value of 0x8002000A. Visual Basic puts the HRESULT into the OLE error object in the Err.Number property, which displays it as an ugly negative number. This is the number that you see in the select statement in the error handler in Listing 4.8.

Listing 4.8 Unsigned long and short handling.

```
Private Sub cmdUTypes_Click(Index As Integer)
    ' Invoke the uTypes operation

    ' Declare an error handler for overflow condition
    On Error GoTo errorHandler

    ' Declare local variables for the CORBA datatypes
    ' CORBA::ulong -> Long, CORBA::ushort -> Long
    Dim ulongType As Long
    Dim uShortType As Long
    Dim ulongResult As Long

    ' Verify that a short and a long have been entered for input
    If txtInUShort.text = Empty Then
        MsgBox "You must supply an amount for Unsigned Short"
        Exit Sub
    End If
    If txtInULong.text = Empty Then
        MsgBox "You must supply an amount for Unsigned Long"
        Exit Sub
    End If

    GetBasicType      ' Get the DIChapter4_BasicTypes object

    ' Get the input values
    ulongType = CLng(txtInULong)
    uShortType = CLng(txtInUShort)

    ' Invoke the utypes operation and display the returned result
    ulongResult = objBasicType.uTypes(uShortType, ulongType)
    txtOutULong = CStr(ulongResult)
    Exit Sub
```

Listing 4.8 Unsigned long and short handling. (*Continued*)

```
errorHandler:
    ' Two different overflow conditions can result from this
    ' invocation:
    '  1) A negative number can be entered for input. Since the
    '      original CORBA datatype is unsigned, negative numbers
    '      are not allowed. If a negative number is entered for
    '      either the uShort or uLong input parameters, a
    '      DISP_E_OVERFLOW error will be flagged
    '
    '  2) The returned long result can be greater than 2e30.
    '      Since the original CORBA datatype is unsigned, the
    '      maximum value of the CORBA ulong can be greater than
    '      the maximum value of a Long in VB. If this occurs, a
    '      DISP_E_OVERFLOW error will be flagged
    Select Case Err.Number
        Case -2147352566 'DISP_E_OVERFLOW
            Errmsg = Err.Source & " reported error:
            DISP_E_Overflow" _
            &_vbCrLf & "ObjectSystem Interworking Error: "_
            & Err.Description & vbCrLf _
            & "Cannot convert a negative number to an unsigned
               CORBA type"
        Case Else
            ' General purpose error handling
            Errmsg = Str(Err.Number) & vbCrLf & Err.Source _
            & vbCrLf & Err.Description
    End Select

    ' Display the error in a message box and continue
    MsgBox Errmsg
    Err.Clear
    Resume Next
End Sub
```

Working with Strings

The last data types covered in this chapter are strings. CORBA has two varieties of strings, bounded and unbounded. A bounded string is just a string with a maximum length. Automation has its own string type called a *BSTR*, which is a string prefixed with an integer length. There is no equivalent to the bounded string. Again, there is the possibility of an overflow condition, which we will illustrate in the example in Listing 4.9. The Visual Basic code for handling strings is shown in Listing 4.9. As in the unsigned types routine, the first thing we do is to declare an error handler to catch the overflow condition. Next we declare local variables for the strings. Notice that both the CORBA string and the CORBA bounded string map to a Visual Basic String as in `Dim boundedString As String`. Visual Basic hides the complexities of the Automation BSTR type from the programmer. This routine also demonstrates the use of the **inout** parameter type, which we have not yet used in our example. An **inout** parameter allows you to provide value on input and get a different value after executing the method. The `inoutstrings` method will take a string as input and change that value to all-capital letters. The original input string will be returned as the return parameter. Like all the other routines, we use a common subroutine to get the Automation View object. This time, we want `objStringType`, so we use the `GetStringType` routine. Once we have the object, we use the following code to invoke the method: `resultString = objStringType.inout-strings(boundedString)`. The CORBA IDL limits the bounded string to a maximum of ten characters. There is no way to indicate this in either Visual Basic or the ODL file. However, the bridge keeps track of this, and if you try to enter a string that has more than ten characters, the bridge will return a DISP_E_OVERFLOW error.

Wide Character Support

Microsoft supports the use of Unicode strings. On Win32 platforms, BSTRs are Unicode, so CORBA strings, which are not wide characters, always map to a Unicode string on Win32 platforms. The OMG has approved an extension to IDL that adds the wstring or wide string type. At the time of this writing, most IDL compilers did not yet support the wstring type so we could not include it in the example. However, since it also maps to a BSTR, it is handled just like the other string types in Visual Basic.

Listing 4.9 String handling.

```
Private Sub cmdStrings_Click(Index As Integer)
    ' Invoke the inoutstrings operation

    ' Declare an error handler for overflow condition
    On Error GoTo errorHandler

    ' Declare local variables for the CORBA datatypes
    ' CORBA::string -> String, CORBA::string<n> -> String
    Dim resultString As String
    Dim boundedString As String

    ' Verify that a string has been entered for input
    If txtBString.text = Empty Then
        MsgBox "You must supply a string for Bounded String"
        Exit Sub
    End If

    GetStringType    ' Get the DIChapter4_BasicTypes object

    ' Get the input string
    boundedString = txtBString.text

    ' Invoke the inoutstrings method and display the new values
    ' The original input string will be returned in the outString
    ' parameter. The input string (inout) will be changed to all
    ' upper case and returned.
    resultString = objStringType.inoutstrings(boundedString)
    txtBString.text = boundedString
    txtRetString.text = resultString
    Exit Sub


errorHandler:
    ' The boundedString is limited to 12 characters by the CORBA
    ' IDL. Attempting to pass a string of more than 12 characters
    ' will result in data overflow error.
```

(continues)

Listing 4.9 String handling. (*Continued*)

```
    ' The error handler catches that error and displays all
    ' of the available error info from the OLE error object.

Select Case Err.Number
    Case -2147352566 'DISP_E_OVERFLOW
        Errmsg = Err.Source & " reported error:
        DISP_E_Overflow" _
        vbCrLf & "ObjectSystem Interworking Error: "_
        & Err.Description & vbCrLf _
        & "Input String is longer than maximum of CORBA
        Bounded String"

    Case -2147216872 'ITF_E_DATA_CONVERSION_YES
    ' Some bridges return this error rather than
    ' DISP_E_OVERFLOW
        Errmsg = Err.Source & " error is:
        ITF_E_DATA_CONVERSION_YES"_
        & vbCrLf & "ObjectSystem Interworking Error: " _
        & Err.Description & vbCrLf _
        & "Input String is longer than maximum of CORBA
        Bounded String"
    Case Else
    ' General purpose error handling
        Errmsg = Str(Err.Number) & vbCrLf & Err.Source &
        vbCrLf & Err.Description
End Select

    ' Display the error in a message box and continue
    MsgBox Errmsg
    Err.Clear
    Resume Next

End Sub
```

Wrapping Up

In this chapter we have seen how all of the basic data types map from CORBA to Automation and how to use these data types from Visual Basic. We have seen how accessing CORBA attributes is no different than using properties in Visual Basic. We have learned how to invoke CORBA operations, which is just like invoking any other method in Visual Basic. We have also considered some of the potential overflow conditions that can occur because of mismatches in the data types supported in the two object systems. In the next chapter, we will look at the more complex, constructed data types supported by CORBA, such as structs and unions.

5 *Complex Data Types*

This chapter continues with the detailed description of the mappings from CORBA to Automation. First we will discuss the challenges of mapping complex CORBA data types to Automation and describe the helper objects that are used to facilitate that mapping. An example program will then be introduced that will use all of the different data types. In subsequent sections of the chapter the details of each mapping will then be described and illustrated with Visual Basic programming examples.

CORBA was designed to facilitate efficient networked communications between clients and servers. Typical distributed systems try to minimize the number of network messages required to perform business operations. This usually involves the use of complex or constructed data types that allow a group of information to be combined together and sent in a single network message. Automation was designed to allow for the run-time determination of an object's methods and properties. As such, a much simpler set of data types was required for this task. One challenge met by the COM/CORBA interworking architecture was to map the complex data types used in CORBA to corresponding data types in Automation in a way that would be natural to the Automation programmer but would not lose any information.

The mappings for these complex data types are shown in Table 5.1.

Using Typedefs and Constants

Although *typedefs* and *constants* are not constructed data types themselves, they are frequently used (and in some cases required) in the construction of complex types.

89

Table 5.1 Complex Data Type Mappings

CORBA TYPE	AUTOMATION TYPE	DESCRIPTION OF AUTOMATION TYPE
typedef	alias	An alias with the scoped name
const	alias	An alias with the scoped name
structure	IDispatch	An interface with property accessors for each structure member
sequence	SAFEARRAY	An array with lower and upper bounds
array	SAFEARRAY	An array with lower and upper bounds
union	IDispatch	An interface with property accessors for the union discriminator and members
any	DICORBAAny	A special object
object	IDispatch	An interface to the Automation view

For example, typedefs are needed to define sequences and arrays in CORBA IDL. For this reason, we have chosen to include them in this chapter rather than in the previous chapter on basic data types.

Typedefs—the assignment of names for data types, such as "Currency"—are a common practice in CORBA IDL files. Their use allows an application to change a data type without having to change all of the places that refer to the data type. For example, the following IDL segment defines Currency to be a float and uses Currency in the deposit operation of the account interface. At a later time, Currency could be changed to a double without having to change all of the interface definitions that use the type Currency:

```
//IDL
module Chapter5 {
    typedef    float    Currency;

    interface account {
        const    long    max = 10000;
        deposit    (in    Currency  amount);
    };
};
```

A similar practice is to define constants in CORBA IDL files. When mapping to Automation, an alias is defined for the typedefs and constants. The alias follows the same naming conventions as interfaces, so the alias for the above typedef and

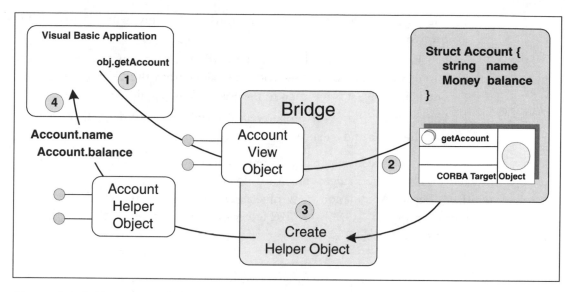

Figure 5.1 *Bridge creates a helper object.*

constant would be "Chapter5_Currency" and "Chapter5_account_max," respectively.

Typedefs and constants can be used in any of the constructed CORBA data types. Now let's see how these constructed types are mapped to Automation.

Helper Objects

CORBA structures and unions cannot be mapped directly since Automation does not support any equivalent data types. Rather, they are mapped to helper interfaces. The objects that implement the helper interfaces are called *helper objects*. Helper objects are pseudo-objects, or objects that are implemented locally in the bridge. Figure 5.1 depicts the basic functioning of the helper objects.

In Figure 5.1, a Visual Basic or any Automation application wants to get account information. To do this, it does the following:

1. It invokes the getAccount method on the Automation Account view object. Account is actually a structure containing a name and a balance contained in a CORBA target object. The request flows from the view object through the bridge and on to the getAccount operation on the remote CORBA object.

2. The object returns the account structure in the reply, which arrives at the interworking bridge.

3. The bridge creates a helper object for the account structure and sets the name and balance properties with the values from the CORBA structure. The helper object is returned to the Visual Basic application.

4. The application uses the property accessor functions of the helper object to read the name and balance.

As just mentioned, helper objects are pseudo-objects, objects that are implemented locally in the bridge; thus, they do not expose the `IForeignObject` interface that all Automation view objects expose. Helper objects derive instead from another special COM/CORBA interworking interface, `DIForeignComplexType`.

```
//ODL
interface DIForeignComplexType : IDispatch
{
    [propget] HRESULT INSTANCE_repositoryID(
                 [out, retval] BSTR* val);
    [propget] HRESULT INSTANCE_clone (
                 [in] Idispatch *pDispatch,
                 [out, retval] Idispatch **val);

}
```

There are two different types of helper objects although their use is exactly the same to the programmer. Each different helper derives from a specific interworking interface, which itself derives from `DIForeignComplexType`. In the case of a CORBA structure, the helper object derives from `DICORBAStruct` and in the case of a CORBA union the helper object derives from `DICORBAUnion`. Neither of these interfaces have methods, so the programmer only sees the methods of the base interface, `DICORBAComplexType`. The specific interworking interfaces are used internally to mark the helper objects as mappings of a CORBA complex type. This information is essential for mapping the type back to CORBA.

Creating Helper Objects

As a programmer you shouldn't have to worry about the mappings from CORBA types nor about how to create the helper objects with the correct mappings. This is something that the system should do for you, and in this case the system component that creates the helper object is the *interworking bridge product*. Let's look at the different scenarios that involve creating helper objects, starting with the scenario in Figure 5.1.

Obtaining the helper object as an out parameter. In this scenario, the helper object is returned after invoking a method on the Automation view object. The system creates the helper object and populates its properties with the member values from the corresponding CORBA constructed type.

Creating the helper object for an in parameter. In this scenario, the programmer needs the helper object as an **in** or **inout** parameter, so he or she must be responsible for creating it. However, the system should still provide the means for that creation. In COM, objects are created using factories so the interworking architecture defines a programming interface to a factory for creating helper objects.

Copying an instance of a helper object. There are frequently programming requirements for making a copy of an object, and its data and programming languages typically support operations for doing this. Although you could create a new instance of the helper using the factory and then manually copy each member value yourself, the interworking architecture defines a method for a helper object to copy or clone itself.

When the helper object is an output parameter, the interworking bridge does all of the work, and there is nothing for the programmer to do. Let's look in detail at the other two cases where the programmer needs to do something to create the helper object.

Creating Helper Objects as an In Parameter

When we pass a helper object as an input, we must first create it. The creation of a helper object is similar to the creation of other Automation objects but different in some important aspects. Although the factory mechanism is similar, the namespace for CORBA complex types is fundamentally different. Complex types can be created either by their typename or by their unique type identifier in the CORBA namespace. Normal Automation objects, and their factories, are registered in the Windows System Registry. Because there could be dozens or even hundreds of the helper objects, it would be an unnecessary management burden to register them all (and maintain the registrations) in the System Registry. Instead, the interworking bridge registers a special factory object, the CORBAFactory, in the Windows System Registry. That factory is then capable of creating the helper objects based upon their names in the CORBA namespace.

We introduced the concepts of the CORBA factory in Chapter 3, and we will go into the details of how it works for creating Automation view objects in the next chapter. The base `DICORBAFactory` interface has an extension to it, the `DICORBAFactoryEx` interface, for creating complex types:

```
//ODL
interface DICORBAFactoryEx : DICORBAFactory
{
    HRESULT CreateType      ([in] IDispatch *scopingObject,
                             [in] BSTR typename,
                             [out, retval] VARIANT *val);
    HRESULT CreateTypeById ([in] IDispatch *scopingObject,
                             [in] BSTR repositoryId,
                             [out, retval] VARIANT *val);
}
```

The `CreateType()` method is used in all but certain exceptional cases, and we demonstrate its use in this chapter's example in the "Creating Helper Objects" section. The first parameter, `scopingObject`, is an interface pointer to the Automation view object that uses the helper object. The view object provides a CORBA naming scope within which the second argument, `typeName`, is resolved.

The second method on `DICORBAFactoryEx`, `CreateTypeByID`, uses the repository ID of the CORBA struct or union type to create the helper object. In CORBA, it is theoretically possible for two different data types to have the same name in a repository but be uniquely identified by their repository ID, which must be different. In this case, it would be necessary to use the `CreateType-ByID` method to create a helper object. In practice, however, no commercial CORBA ORB products allow different structures to have the same scoped name in a repository, and thus the `CreateTypeByID` method gets less use than the Maytag repairman.

Copying an Instance of a Helper Object

It is not uncommon during programming to copy an instance of a helper object. The second method of the `DIForeignComplexType` interface, `INSTANCE_clone`, is intended for this purpose. The method is generic enough to allow cloning of any helper object by passing the pointer to that object as the input parameter. In practice, however, the method is almost exclusively used to copy an instance of itself by passing a null on input. A copy of the helper object is returned with all of the same data values as the original helper object. We show an example of using `INSTANCE_clone` in Listing 5.9, titled "A really complex one."

Obtaining Helper Object Identifiers

Now let's discuss the second method of the `DIForeignComplexType` interface. The authors of the COM/CORBA interworking architecture made a valiant effort to make interworking easy to use. However, until something is actually used, you don't know how easy it will be. The `INSTANCE_repository` method is an example where interworking could have been easier to use. The repositoryID in this method is the CORBA repositoryID string, such as "00492161c961.02.ce.bd.c5.32.00.00.00." Although this is certainly unique and thus unambiguous, it is also ugly and nonintuitive, especially to a Visual Basic programmer. The version 1.1 revision of the interworking architecture addresses this problem. Although the method still exists, the use of `INSTANCE_repositoryID` is deprecated in version 1.1. Instead, a new interface has been added that allows applications to get more useful information about a helper object's CORBA type. The new interface is as follows:

```
//ODL
interface DIObjectInfo : DICORBAFactoryEx
{
  HRESULT type_name    ([in] IDispatch *target,
                        [out, optional] VARIANT *except_obj,
                        [out, retval] BSTR *typeName);
  HRESULT scoped_name  ([in] IDispatch *target,
                        [out, optional] VARIANT *except_obj,
                        [out, retval] BSTR *scopedName);
  HRESULT unique_id    ([in] IDispatch *target,
                        [out, optional] VARIANT *except_obj,
                        [out, retval] BSTR *repositoryID);
}
```

The `DIObjectInfo` interface provides three different methods for getting information about a complex type:

type_name returns a string, such as "Currency"

scoped_name returns the fully scoped string, such as "Chapter5::Currency"

unique_id returns the repository ID, such as "00492161c961.02.ce.bd.c5.32.00.00.00"

Notice that `DIObjectInfo` derives from the `DICORBAFactoryEx` interface. In practice, it is implemented by the CORBA factory object. Thus, when your program gets an instance of the CORBA factory object, it gets the functionality of three interfaces: `DICORBAFactory`, `DICORBAFactoryEx`, and `DIObjectInfo`.

Naming Conventions

The naming conventions for helper objects are the same as for other view components. However, data types can be declared at several different scopes in a CORBA IDL file, as illustrated in the following segment taken from the IDL for this chapter's example:

```
//IDL
module Chapter5 {
    struct itemData
    {
        ...
    };

    interface investor    {
        struct address
        {
            ...
        };
    };
};
```

Because helper objects are local Automation objects and not view objects, they do not have the "DI" prefix. The name is constructed by appending the different scopes together. The name for the helper object for the preceding itemData structure will be `Chapter5_itemData`, whereas the name for the address structure, which is declared within the scope of the investor interface, will be `Chapter5 _investor_address`.

Introducing the Example

It is finally time to examine the use of complex types in a programming example. This section explains the example that will be used throughout the rest of the chapter. Each example of Visual Basic code is contained in the chapter section describing that data type. For this chapter, the example is about choosing investment options for a 401(k) savings plan. As in Chapter 4, the IDL and example is designed

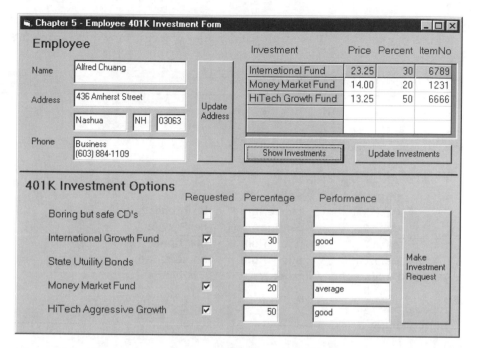

Figure 5.2 *Chapter 5 Visual Basic application.*

primarily to demonstrate the use of the different CORBA data types rather than to be (even remotely) realistic. Figure 5.2 shows the Visual Basic interface for the example. The top left portion of the form displays the investor's name, address, and phone and has a button for updating the address. The right top portion of the form displays the investment name, price, percentage of funds in that investment, and the internal item number, along with buttons to show and update the investment. The bottom of the form lists the five possible investments for this 401(k) plan. For each investment there is a check box, a box for the percentage of funds to invest, and a text box indicating the current performance of that fund. The investor checks the desired investments, assigns a percentage to each, and presses the "Make Investment Request" button. The performance of each investment is returned.

The application is implemented by two CORBA objects, an Investor object and an Order object. The CORBA IDL for the application is shown in Listing 5.1. The Investor object has attributes for the name, fullAddress, and phone number of the investor and methods for updating the address, making an order, or showing the current investments. The corresponding ODL file for the investment Automation view object is shown in Listing 5.2. The Order object has one method for updating the order. We will use the Order object in the last example of the chapter. The ODL for the Order view object is shown in Listing 5.8.

Listing 5.1 Chapter 5 CORBA IDL file.

```
//IDL
module Chapter5{
// Phone number related items
      typedef string<13>  phoneNum;
      typedef string<18>  cellNum;
      union   phoneNumber   switch (long)      {
              case 1:         phoneNum        bizPhone;
              case 2:         cellNum         cellPhone;
              case 3:         phoneNum        faxPhone;
              default:        phoneNum        homePhone;
      }; //end of union phoneNumber

      typedef any     misc;
      struct itemData
      {
              string          name;
              float           price;
              long            quantity;
              long            partNumber;
              misc            miscInfo;
      };
      typedef sequence <itemData> items;

      typedef long      itemArray[3][5];

      interface order
      {
              void            updateOrder     (in      items   theItems);
      }; //end of interface order

      interface investor        {
              // Interface specific definitions
              struct address {
              string    street;
                      string    city;
                      string    state;
                      string    zip;
```

Listing 5.1 Chapter 5 CORBA IDL file. (*Continued*)

```
        };

        // Attributes
        readonly attribute        string    name;
        readonly attribute        address   fullAddress;
        readonly attribute        phoneNumber  primaryPhone;

        // Operations
        void         updateAddress      (in      address    newAddress);
        order        showOrder          (out  itemArray   data,
                                         out   items       theItems);
        order        makeOrder          (inout itemArray    data);
    }; //end of interface investor
}; //end of module Chapter5
```

Listing 5.2 DIChapter5_investor.odl file.

```
[ interface Chapter5_investor_address : DICORBAStruct
  {
    [id(128),propget] HRESULT street([out,retval] BSTR* rtrn);
    [id(128),propput] HRESULT street([in] BSTR valueToPut);

    [id(129),propget] HRESULT city([out,retval] BSTR* rtrn);
    [id(129),propput] HRESULT city([in] BSTR valueToPut);

    [id(130),propget] HRESULT state([out,retval] BSTR* rtrn);
    [id(130),propput] HRESULT state([in] BSTR valueToPut);

    [id(131),propget] HRESULT zip([out,retval] BSTR* rtrn);
    [id(131),propput] HRESULT zip([in] BSTR valueToPut);
  };

#define Chapter5_phoneNum SAFEARRAY(wchar_t)
#define Chapter5_cellNum SAFEARRAY(wchar_t)

  interface Chapter5_phoneNumber : DICORBAUnion
  {
```

(continues)

Listing 5.2 DIChapter5_investor.odl file. (*Continued*)

```
    [id(128),propget] HRESULT UNION_d ([out,retval] long *rtrn);


    [id(129),propget, helpstring("Union item index 1")]
    HRESULT bizPhone([out,retval] BSTR* rtrn);
    [id(129),propput]
    HRESULT bizPhone([in] BSTR valueToPut);


    [id(130),propget, helpstring("Union item index 2")]
    HRESULT cellPhone([out,retval] BSTR* rtrn);
    [id(130),propput]
    HRESULT cellPhone([in] BSTR valueToPut);


    [id(131),propget, helpstring("Union item index 3")]
    HRESULT faxPhone([out,retval] BSTR* rtrn);
    [id(131),propput]
    HRESULT faxPhone([in] BSTR valueToPut);


    [id(132),propget, helpstring("Union default item 0")]
    HRESULT homePhone([out,retval] BSTR* rtrn);
    [id(132),propput]
    HRESULT homePhone([in] BSTR valueToPut);
};

interface DIChapter5_investor : IDispatch
{
  [ id(7)]
  HRESULT makeOrder(
    [in,out] VARIANT* data,
    [in,out,optional] VARIANT* exceptionInfo,
    [out,retval] DIChapter5_order** returnValue);


  [ id(8)]
  HRESULT showOrder(
    [out] VARIANT* data,
    [out] VARIANT* theItems,
    [in,out,optional] VARIANT* exceptionInfo,
    [out,retval] DIChapter5_order** returnValue);
```

Listing 5.2 DIChapter5_investor.odl file. (*Continued*)

```
[ id(9)]
HRESULT updateAddress(
  [in] Chapter5_investor_address* newAddress,
  [in,out,optional] VARIANT* exceptionInfo);


[ id(10), propget]
HRESULT fullAddress([out,retval] Chapter5_investor_address
                                          ** returnValue);
[ id(11), propget]
HRESULT name([out,retval] BSTR* returnValue);


[ id(12), propget]
HRESULT primaryPhone([out,retval] Chapter5_phoneNumber
                                          ** returnValue);
  };
};
```

The relationship between the Visual Basic application and the CORBA server is illustrated in Figure 5.3. The investor address is implemented as a structure. The structure is used to display and update the address. The code for this is demonstrated in the section on "Working with Structures" later in this chapter. Each investment item is a structure. When the showOrder method is invoked, the list of investments is returned as a sequence of items. This is demonstrated in the "Working with Sequences" section later in this chapter. The investment options (requested, percentage, performance) is implemented as an array. The array is used in the showOrder and makeOrder methods. The code for this is demonstrated in the section "Working with Arrays" later in this chapter. The investor phone number is implemented as a union as demonstrated in the section on "Working with Unions" later in this chapter. Finally, the updateOrder method takes a sequence of structures as an input parameter. This is demonstrated in the section "Working with Nested Datatypes" later in this chapter.

As in the previous chapter, we will only discuss the Visual Basic implementation, not the implementation of the CORBA server. And as in Chapter 4, the code is available at our Web site—www.wiley.com/compbooks/rosen—in the directory "\Chapter5\VisualBasic and \Chapter5\Server."

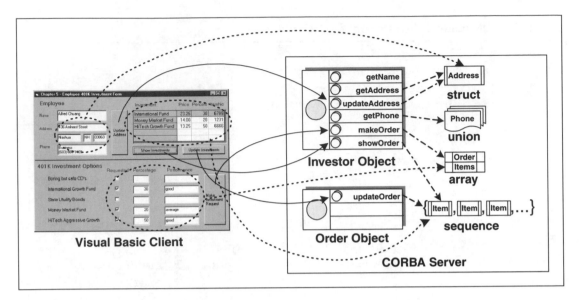

Figure 5.3 *Chapter 5 CORBA server.*

We use the same mechanism that we used in Chapter 4 to get the Investor object; however, the variable declaration and the common subroutine are not shown in the listings this time. We will also use the same variable-naming conventions in this chapter, so the `DIChapter5_investor` object will have a local object for it called *objInvestor*. A new prefix will be introduced for the helper objects. CORBA structs will get the *struc* prefix, for example, *strucAddress*, and unions will get the *union* prefix, for example, *unionPhone*. Now let's look at the code, starting with the simplest case, a structure returned as an **out** parameter.

Working with Structures

The first structure we will look at is the address. Notice that in Listing 5.1, the CORBA IDL defines **address** as a structure containing four strings: street, city, state, and zip. The address is defined within the scope of the `investor` interface and is also an attribute of the `investor` interface called fullAddress.

Examining the ODL for this in Listing 5.2, we see an interface called `Chapter5_investor_address` that derives from `DICORBAStruct`, which, as we discussed earlier, derives from `DICORBAComplexType`. The `Chapter5_investor_address` interface has a `propput` and `propget` method for

NOTE In our example, we would have probably wanted to call this attribute simply "address." However, the IDL compiler would not allow us to have two things with the same name in the same scope, that is, an address structure and an address property. This is common behavior for IDL compilers and one reason that the CORBAFactory CreateTypeByID is not used often.

each of the members of the CORBA structure: street, city, state, and zip. Listing 5.3 shows how we get the address. In our example, we will read the address when the form is loaded. The first thing we need to do in the Form_Load routine is to declare a local variable for the address we will get back. Using our prefix-naming convention, we Dim strAddress As Chapter5_investor_address. Note that since this is a helper object, it does not have the DI prefix. Also, we

Listing 5.3 Structures.

```
Private Sub Form_Load()
    'On form load, we will read the properties of the investor

    'In the CORBA IDL, address is returned as structure called
    '"address". This will be represented in Visual Basic as a
    'helper object.
    'Declare a variable here.
    Dim strucAddress As Chapter5_investor_address   'CORBA::Struct

    'Get the investor object from a subroutine, just like in
    'Chapter 4
    GetInvestor

    'Print the address
    'Address is returned as an object. Each member of the CORBA
    'address structure is a property in the VB address object
    Set strucAddress = objInvestor.fullAddress
    txtStreet = strucAddress.street
    txtCity = strucAddress.city
    txtState = strucAddress.state
    txtZip = strucAddress.zip
```

could have declared it as "object" if we didn't care about the early binding. Now, we use the common subroutine `GetInvestor` to get the `DIChapter5_investor` object. `fullAddress` is an attribute of the investor object, so we simply get it by invoking the property accessor of the view object. Since this returns an object, we must use the Visual Basic `Set` instruction. Finally, we get each member of the structure by using the property accessor method of the helper object and display the returned values in the text boxes of our form. Note that since we did not specify what property of the text box was being used, the default property `text` is used.

In the simple code just presented, the interworking bridge created the helper object and returned it to our Visual Basic application. In the next code segment, shown in Listing 5.4, "Creating helper objects," we will create the helper object and use it as an input parameter. This routine is entered when the "Update Address" button on our form is clicked. We will fill in a new address structure using the values in the text boxes on the form and pass that in to the updateAddress method.

To create the helper object, we first must get an instance of a CORBA factory. We get this just like any other Automation object, by using the Visual Basic `CreateObject` method. Now we will create the helper object using the CORBAFactory's `CreateType` method. The method takes two parameters, first the scoping object, or the object that defines the structure. In our example, that is the investor object. The second parameter is the typeName in the CORBA namespace. This is derived by concatenating the module, interface, and structure names together, or by looking up the names in the CORBA interface repository or the IDL file.

NOTE At the time of this writing, most CORBA repositories and interworking bridge products support the "::" separator. Some also support "." or "\" as separator.

Thus, our code looks like `Set strAddress = CorbaFactory.CreateType(objInvestor, "Chapter5::investor::address")`. Now that we have the helper object, we use its property accessor methods again to set the values. This is done using the information in the Visual Basic form's text boxes as input. Once all the properties are set, we invoke the updateAddress method of the investor object.

Listing 5.4 Creating helper objects.

```
Private Sub cmdUpdate_Click()
    'Update the employee's address

    'Declare variables, including the CorbaFactory
    Dim CorbaFactory As DICORBAFactory
    Dim strucAddress As Chapter5_investor_address    'CORBA::Struct

    'Here, the address structure is an input parameter, so we
    'have to create the helper object for it ourselves. This is
    'done using a special CORBAFactory object. So first we'll
    'need to get the factory.
    Set CorbaFactory = CreateObject("CORBA.Factory")
    'Now, create an instance of the address helper object using
    'the CORBA Factory CreateType routine. There are two inputs:
    '    1) The "Scoping Object", in the case the investor
    '    2) typeName, the CORBA Repository identification of the
    '       object, in this case: Chapter5::investor::address.
    Set strucAddress = CorbaFactory.CreateType(objInvestor, _
                        "Chapter5::investor::address")

    'Set the structure members from the form's text boxes
    strucAddress.street = txtStreet
    strucAddress.city = txtCity
    strucAddress.state = txtState
    strucAddress.zip = txtZip

    'Invoke the updateAddress method passing in the address
    'helper object.
    objInvestor.updateAddress strAddress

End Sub
```

The address was defined within the scope of the investor interface and thus had "investor" as part of its mapped name. In the next section, we will use the itemData structure that is defined at the module level and thus is mapped to a helper object called Chapter5_itemData.

Working with Sequences

Sequences in CORBA IDL map to VARIANTs containing a SAFEARRAY in Automation. *Safearrays* are one- or multidimensional arrays containing elements of any of the basic Automation data types. One of the basic data types is an IDispatch interface pointer, which can point to a helper object. Referring back to the CORBA IDL in Listing 5.1, we can see the **itemData** structure and just below it the definition of the **items** sequence: **typedef sequence <itemData> items**. We also see the use of the **typedef** statement. What this means is that **items** refers to a **sequence** of **itemData** structures. We use the **items** type in the **showOrder** operation of the **investor** interface. In the ODL in Listing 5.2 we can see that the showOrder method of the DIChapter5_investor interface returns this sequence as a VARIANT*. The VARIANT will contain a SAFEARRAY of IDispatch pointers to Chapter5_itemData helper objects for the **itemData** structure. Listing 5.5, on sequences, shows the Visual Basic code for invoking the showOrder method and processing the **out** parameters.

The routine for this part of the example is entered by clicking the Show Order button on the Visual Basic form. The first thing we need to do, as usual, is to declare local variables. The showOrder method has two **out** parameters, an array and a sequence. We will handle the array in the next section, but we must declare it here. We declare two VARIANTs, itemArray to receive the array, and itemDataSequence to receive the sequence. We also declare a helper object strucItemData for the **itemData** structure. Lastly, we declare an object to receive the order that is returned by the showOrder method. This will be important in the complex example at the end of the chapter, but for now we will just ignore it. We invoke the showOrder method specifying the itemArray and itemDataSequence VARIANTs that will get filled in by the interworking bridge. We are going to use a Microsoft FlexGrid control to display the values returned in the sequence, so we do a little control initialization first. With that out of the way, we can get down to the business of taking apart the sequence. To determine how many items were returned we use the UBound method of the SAFEARRAY and then loop through all of them. In the loop, we get the strucItemData helper object from the safearray using Set strucItemData = itemDataSequence(i). Finally, for each **itemData** structure, we extract the values for name, price, quantity, and partNumber and insert them into cells in the FlexGrid.

CORBA IDL supports two types of sequences, bounded and unbounded. The sequence we just used is an unbounded sequence, meaning that there is no limit to

Listing 5.5 Sequences.

```
Private Sub cmdShowOrder_Click()
    'Shows the current order in table format, and updates the
    'display array

    'Declare variants to receive the array and the sequence
    'of orderitems

    'Declare a strOrderItem helper object
    Dim itemArray As Variant                    'CORBA::Array
    Dim itemDataSequence As Variant             'CORBA::Sequence
    Dim strucItemData As Chapter5_itemData      'CORBA::Struct
    Dim objOrder as DIChapter5_order

    'The showOrder method returns an order object and fills in
    'two output parameters, the itemArray and the sequence of
    'itemData
    Set objOrder = objInvestor.showOrder(itemArray,
                                            itemDataSequence)

    'Set up the grid control
    Dim i, j As Integer
    grdOrder.Clear
    grdOrder.formatString = formatString
    j = 0

    'Get the number of items ordered from the upper bound of the
    'array. Display the items by getting the OrderItem helper out
    'of the sequence. Get the Name, partNumber, quantity, and
    'price from the helper object and insert them in the grid
    'control
    NoItems = UBound(itemDataSequence)
    For i = 0 To NoItems
        'Get the next itemData structure from the returned VB array
        Set strucItemData = itemDataSequence(i)
        grdOrder.TextArray(j) = strucItemData.Name
        j = j + 1
```

(continues)

Listing 5.5 Sequences. (*Continued*)

```
        grdOrder.TextArray(j) = CStr(Format(strucItemData.price,
                                      "##.00"))
        j = j + 1
        grdOrder.TextArray(j) = CStr(strucItemData.quantity)
        j = j + 1
        grdOrder.TextArray(j) = CStr(strucItemData.partNumber)
        j = j + 1
    Next

    . . .
```

the number of items that could be returned. However, since our user interface can't display more than five investments, it might have been wise to limit the number of **itemData**s that could be returned. A server might also want to limit the size of a sequence that it will accept as input. This could be done using a bounded sequence. Unfortunately, there is not an equivalent concept in SAFEARRAYs, so the bound cannot be checked at compile time but can only be checked at run time by the interworking bridge. This is similar to the bounded string that we used in the example in Chapter 4. If a bounded sequence is an input parameter and the Automation program attempts to pass in a SAFEARRAY that is longer than the maximum size of the sequence, a run-time DISP_E_OVERFLOW error is raised by the bridge. The code for this is analogous to the bounded string error handling in Listing 4.9, on string handling, and is not repeated here.

Working with Arrays

Our next method, makeOrder, will use an array as an **inout** parameter so we will see both how to construct an array for input and how to receive one on output. In the CORBA IDL, we can see that makeOrder uses **itemArray**, which is defined as a two-dimensional array of longs. In the ODL, the array is passed as a VARIANT*. The routine for arrays in Listing 5.6, on arrays, gets entered when the Make Investment Request button is clicked. We declare three local variables in the routine. First, we declare an array of longs to correspond to the CORBA array: Dim itemArray(0 To 7, 0 To 2) As Long 'CORBA: long itemArray[3][8]. The first thing to notice about this is that dimensions de-

Listing 5.6 Arrays.

```
Private Sub cmdMakeOrder_Click()
    'Make an order for 401(k) investment options

    'Handy array for printing out performance
    Dim InvestStatus(0 To 4) As String
    InvestStatus(0) = ""
    InvestStatus(1) = "poor"
    InvestStatus(2) = "average"
    InvestStatus(3) = "good"
    InvestStatus(4) = "not known"


    'Declare local variables for the CORBA data types
    'CORBA::array[x][y] -> Array[y][x]
    Dim itemArray(0 To 7, 0 To 2) As Long
                                    'CORBA::long itemArray[3][8]
    Dim varArray As Variant
                                    'CORBA::Array
    Dim objOrder As DIChapter5_order

    'Fill in each element of the array from the form's
    'controlArrays of check boxes and text boxes. There are 5 in
    'each array.
    For i = 0 To 4
        If Check(i).Value = Unchecked Then
            'Fill in elements 0 and 1 in row i of array
            itemArray(i, 0) = 0
            itemArray(i, 1) = 0
        Else
            'Fill in elements 0 and 1 in row i of array
            itemArray(i, 0) = 1
            itemArray(i, 1) = CLng(txtPercent(i).Text)
        End If
        'Fill in element 2 of row i, always zero on input
        itemArray(i, 2) = 0
    Next

    'Arrays are passed as variant, so assign ours here
```

(continues)

Listing 5.6 Arrays. (*Continued*)

```
    varArray = itemArray

    'Invoke the makeOrder method
    Set objOrder = objInvestor.makeOrder(varArray)

    'The varArray is an inout parameter so update the form's
    'display based on the returned array. In the returned array,
    'the investment's performance is in the 3rd column of the
    'array
    For i = 0 To 4
        If varArray(i, 0) = 0 Then
            'If element 0 is "off", other fields are blank
            Check(i).Value = Unchecked
            txtPercent(i).Text = ""
            txtPerformance(i).Text = InvestStatus(0)
        Else
            'If element 0 is "on", get percentage from element 1
            'and performance from element 2.
            Check(i).Value = Checked
            txtPercent(i).Text = CStr(varArray(i, 1))
            txtPerformance(i).Text = InvestStatus(varArray(i, 2))
        End If
    Next
End Sub
```

clared in the CORBA IDL from left to right get declared from right to left for the Visual Basic array. The second thing to notice is that the CORBA dimensions are one-based and the Visual Basic dimensions are zero-based (by default, you can, of course, change the default or explicitly declare the base, as we have done here for clarity). The next variable is a VARIANT to contain the array. Lastly, we need an object to accept the **Order** output parameter.

To make the next code clear we need to discuss what the elements of the array mean and how the array is processed on our Visual Basic form. Think of the array as having five rows, each of which have three columns. Each row represents one of the possible 401(k) investments. For each investment, the first column indicates if the investment has been requested (0 = no, 1 = yes). If the investment was requested, the second column indicates what percentage of the total investment should be allocated to this particular investment. These are the only two columns filled in for input. The third column indicating the performance of the particular investment is filled in by the server and returned on output along with the two columns of input.

This might be a good time to remind you that the example isn't intended to be realistic, but it should demonstrate how to use the different CORBA data types from Visual Basic. Anyhow, each column is represented on the Visual Basic form by a Control Array of five controls, one for each investment, or row, in the CORBA array. Using the Control Array allows us to index nicely through things as illustrated by the code that formats the array for input. We loop through the five rows, and if the "Requested" box (Check(i)) is not checked, we set the first column in this row to zero. If the box is checked, we set the first column to one and set the second column to the value in the "Percentage" textbox: (txtPercent(i)).

There is one more step required before we can invoke the method. Recall from the ODL that the array is passed as a VARIANT. In the previous example, on output, the interworking bridge created a SAFEARRAY for the CORBA array and then put the SAFEARRAY in a VARIANT. In this example, we are responsible for creating the input parameter, so we must first create and populate the array and then put the array in a VARIANT as varArray = itemArray. Now we can invoke the makeOrder method passing in the VARIANT. Remember that this is an **inout** parameter, so the same array is going to be returned with more information in it. On output we use the varArray directly, but we could also reassign the varArray back to the itemArray if we wanted.

Working with Object References

The last two examples have shown how an object reference can be returned. In the CORBA IDL, we see that both the **showOrder** and **makeOrder** operations return an **Order** object. In the ODL, this is returned as a DIChapter5_order**. In our examples, we declared a local object objOrder of type DIChapter5_order to receive the returned object. We have also seen throughout our examples that a CORBA return parameter and an **out** parameter are treated exactly the same from Visual Basic. As you would expect, to pass a CORBA object reference as an input we need an instance of a Automation view object. The interworking bridge will automatically translate the COM interface pointer into the CORBA object reference when it is passed, just as it did for the returned Order object. We already know how to create an Automation view of a CORBA object, such as the Investor object, since we've needed this for all of our examples. We will explore more fully the many ways to create view object in Chapter 7, but thus far we have done it using a factory and a custom Moniker. We have not explicitly included an example of an object reference as an **out** parameter or an example of passing one as an **in** parameter because we already know how to do all of this.

There is one interesting aspect of passing object references that we will comment on. As object references are passed back and forth between object systems and are mapped through view objects, the potential exists for view chains to be created. One view would delegate control to another view, which delegates to other views, and so on, so that rather than interacting directly with an object the interaction may be chained through several intermediate, unnecessary views. To deal with this, the architecture defines another special interworking interface that all view objects must implement:

```
//ODL
interface IForeignObject : IUnknown
{
    HRESULT GetForeignReference  (
                            [in] objSystemIds systemIDs,
                            [out] long *systemID,
                            [out] LPSTR *objRef);
    HRESULT GetUniqueId    ([out] LPSTR *id);
}
```

This interface allows the interworking bridge to access object references from foreign object systems that are encapsulated in the view object. It is done in a generic format that allows systems other than COM and CORBA to be included in the interworking. The programmer should not have to worry about potential view chains, and the interface is not generally intended for use by the end user, particularly the Visual Basic programmer. (In fact, there is no Automation version of the interface, only a COM version.) We include the information here for those wise guys who may have figured out that the problem exists and were wondering what the interworking architecture does about it. It should be noted that although all view objects are required to support this interface, an interworking bridge product is not required to use it or to limit the chaining of views (although now that you know about it, you will require it in any product you purchase).

Working with Unions

A *union* is the next CORBA complex type that requires mapping to a helper object. In our example, we have represented the investor's phone number as a union in which there are four possible types of phone numbers: home, business, fax, and cell—each of which may require a different number of digits. The investor has a primary phone number that is one of these four. Looking at the CORBA IDL we can see the declaration of the **phoneNumber** union. In the union, there are four different cases for each of the different types of phone. Each case uses one of two phone number types declared as bounded strings with different numbers of digits. The ODL for the union is slightly different than for the struct helper objects. Notice several things about the helper object `Chapter5_phoneNumber` declared in the ODL file. The naming convention is the same as with structure helper objects, however, the interface derives from `DICORBAUnion` this time. For each case in the CORBA union declaration, there are propput and propget property accessor methods. In addition to these, there is a union discriminator `UNION_d` property. Notice that only a propget method has been generated for the discriminator, that is, you cannot set this value. The union is an **out** parameter in our example, but if the union were an **in** or **inout** parameter the discriminator would have to get set somehow. The interworking bridge product will automatically set the descriminator in the helper object when the value of the union is set programmatically, one less thing for the programmer to worry about or get wrong.

There is a primaryPhone property in the CORBA IDL definition of the investor interface that returns the phoneNumber union. Listing 5.7, on unions, shows the Visual Basic code for reading the phoneNumber. This is also part of the Form_Load routine, so we have already gotten the investor object in Listing 5.3. As usual, we declare a local variable for our union helper object and then read the investor object's primaryPhone property. The union discriminator is returned in the UNION_d property of the union, and we use this for our case statement to determine which type of phone number is the primary phone for the investor. We get the phone number by using the case-specific property accessor of the union helper object. There can always be only one case per union, and for that case we print out the type of phone, a carriage return/line feed, and then the actual phone number.

Working with Anys

This brings us to our final CORBA complex type, the CORBA **any**. What exactly is a CORBA **any**? It is a data type that can contain any OMG IDL data type

Listing 5.7 Unions.

```
   . . .

   'In the CORBA IDL, phone number is returned as a union
   'called phoneNumber. This is represented in Visual Basic as
   'a helper object.
   'Declare a variable here.
   Dim unionPhone As Chapter5_phoneNumber

   'Print the phone number
   'phoneNumber is returned as a union of different phone number
   'types. The union discriminator tells us which one it is.
   unionPhone = objInvestor.primaryPhone
   Select Case unionPhone.UNION_d
       Case 1
       txtPhone = "Business" & vbCrLf & unionPhone.bizPhone

       Case 2
       txtPhone = "Cellular" & vbCrLf & unionPhone.cellPhone

       Case 3
       txtPhone = "Fax" & vbCrLf & unionPhone.faxPhone

       Case Else
       txtPhone = "Home" & vbCrLf & unionPhone.homePhone
     End Select
End Sub
```

including objects, user-defined types, and typecodes. Without these last few types, an **any** could have been mapped directly to a VARIANT. However, there are types that can be expressed in an **any** that cannot be represented in a VARIANT. Thus, the **any** is mapped to another special interworking interface that allows the programmer access to the CORBA typecode information:

```
//ODL
interface DICORBAAny : DIForeignComplexType
{
```

```
    [propget] HRESULT value    (
                    [out, retval] VARIANT *val);
    [propput] HRESULT value    ([in] VARIANT val);
    [propget] HRESULT typeCode (
                    [out, retval] DICORBATypeCode **val);
}
```

The DICORBAAny interface derives from DIForeignComplexType, just like the other helper objects, but extends the interface to support the typecode. There are property accessor methods for getting and setting the value of a CORBA **any** and also for getting the type code. However, since the DICORA-BAny is a case of a helper object, albeit a more complicated case, it can only be created by the interworking bridge. In other words, you cannot create a generic CORBA **any** object and then set its type; you can only create a specific instance of a CORBA **any** that has been defined in your CORBA IDL file, typically as a typedef.

A CORBA typecode has specific information for each of the different CORBA types and is represented in Automation by the DICORBATypeCode interface. Like the DICORBAAny, it is another special case of a helper object and can only be created by the interworking bridge. If the **any** is an **out** parameter, the DICORBATypeCode object is created and set by the bridge when the DICOR-BAAny object is created. If the **any** is an **in** or **inout** parameter, the DICOR-BATypeCode object is created and set when the value of the **any** is set programmatically, much like the way the union discriminator is automatically set by the bridge.

```
//ODL
typedef enum {
     tk_null=0, tk_void, tk_short, tk_long, tk_ushort, tk_ulong,
     tk_float, tk_double, tk_boolean, tk_char, tk_octet, tk_any,
     tk_TypeCode, tk_Principal, tk_objref, tk_struct, tk_union,
     tk_enum, tk_string, tk_sequence, tk_array, tk_alias, tk_except};

interface DICORBATypeCode : DIForeignComplexType
{
     [propget] HRESULT kind     ([out, retval] CORBA_TCKind *val);

// for tk_objref, tk_struct, tk_union, tk_alias, tk_except
     [propget] HRESULT id       ([out, retval] BSTR *val);
```

```
                [propget] HRESULT name        ([out, retval] BSTR *val);

    // for tk_struct, tk_union, tk_enum, tk_except
        [propget] HRESULT member_count  ([out, retval] long *val);
                HRESULT member_name      ([in] long index,
                                          [out, retval] BSTR *val);
                HRESULT member_type      ([in] long index,
                                        [out, retval] DICORBATypeCode **val);
    // tk_union,
                HRESULT member_label    ([in] long index,
                                          [out, retval] VARIANT *val);
        [propget] HRESULT discriminator_type (
                                        [out, retval] IDispatch **val);
        [propget] HRESULT default_index ([out, retval] long *val);

    // for tk_string, tk_array, tk_sequence
        [propget] HRESULT length          ([out, retval] long *val);

    // for tk_array, tk_sequence, tk_alias
        [propget] HRESULT content_type ([out, retval] IDispatch **val);


}
```

As you can see, the CORBA **any** requires a fair amount of complexity and a certain amount of CORBA knowledge. It was not possible to hide this complexity when mapping the **any** to Automation. Unless it is absolutely necessary, we recommend that your application avoid the use of CORBA **any**s when the clients will be Visual Basic or Automation.

Working with Nested Data Types

The final example in this chapter will show how to use a CORBA **any**. However, after making it this far through the book, you would probably find that too simple of an example. Instead, we will illustrate a scenario in which one complex data type is nested, or contained, within another. Our example will be nested three levels deep and will require the creation of a a sequence (level 1) of structs (level 2), each of which contains an **any** (level 3), for input to the updateOrder method. In the process, we will finally demonstrate the last of the helper object creation methods, *cloning*. To get the Order object, we will first invoke the showOrder method on the `Investor` object. One of the things that this returns is a sequence of **itemData** structs. This time, we will look at the value of the **any** in the **itemData** structure, just to show how it's done. We will then clone a new **itemData**, create a new **any** and replace the **any** in the struct with the new one. Finally, we'll use this sequence as input for the `updateOrder` method on the Order object. Listing 5.8, on a DIChapter5_order.odl file, lists the ODL for the order interface and the ODL for the itemData helper object.

Listing 5.8 DIChapter5_order.odl File.

```
interface Chapter5_itemData : DICORBAStruct
{
   [id(128),propget] HRESULT name([out,retval] BSTR* rtrn);
   [id(128),propput] HRESULT name([in] BSTR valueToPut);

   [id(129),propget] HRESULT price([out,retval] float* rtrn);
   [id(129),propput] HRESULT price([in] float valueToPut);

   [id(130),propget] HRESULT quantity([out,retval] long* rtrn);
   [id(130),propput] HRESULT quantity([in] long valueToPut);

   [id(131),propget] HRESULT partNumber([out,retval] long* rtrn);
   [id(131),propput] HRESULT partNumber([in] long valueToPut);

   [id(132),propget] HRESULT miscInfo([out,retval] DICORBAAny**
                                                  rtrn);
   [id(132),propputref] HRESULT miscInfo([in] DICORBAAny*
                                                  valueToPut);
};

interface DIChapter5_order : IDispatch
{
   [ id(7)]
   HRESULT updateOrder(
     [in] VARIANT theItems,
     [in,out,optional] VARIANT* exceptionInfo);

};
};
```

In the CORBA IDL **itemData** is defined as a struct with five elements, the last of which is an **any**. In the ODL, you can see that the last set of properties in the Chapter5_itemData helper object returns a pointer to a DICORBAAny object. Also, remember how sequences are mapped by noticing that the updateOrder method takes theItems, the sequence of CORBA **itemDatas**, as a VARIANT.

This part of the example is started by clicking the Update Order button on the Visual Basic form. The code for the example is in Listing 5.9, "A really complex one." As usual, we declare our local variables. This time we have two sequences, itemDataSequence and newItemDataSeq(). The newItemDataSeq must be declared as an array, thus the () after it, but since we don't know the size yet, we don't specify a dimension. We also declare two new interworking objects. The miscInfo is a DICORBAAny that corresponds to the **miscInfo** member of the **itemData** struct, and miscInfoType is a DICORBATypeCode that contains the CORBA typecode of the item in the **any**. Finally, there is theCOR-BAKind, which is an enumeration of the possible CORBA Type kinds shown in the previous section on **any**. We invoke the showOrder method on the Investor object that returns an Order object, the sequence of itemDatas, and the itemArray (which we don't care about in this example). We do care about the item-DataSequence, which we are going to make a copy of to use as input to the updateOrder method. Whenever you create a SAFEARRAY for a sequence in Automation, you must also set its size. We use the Visual Basic statement ReDim newItemDataSeq(0 To NoItems) to reset the size of the new array to the size of the returned one. Each element of the array is a Chapter5_itemData helper object. The INSTANCE_clone method of the returned helper object is used to create a copy helper object for use in the new sequence. The cloned helper object is a copy of the structure and all of the data of the original helper object.

One of the members of the itemData structure miscInfo is an **any**, so we set our CORBA **any** helper object, anyMiscInfo, from the itemData using the miscInfo property accessor function. Now we can read the value and the typeCode using the anyMiscInfo helper object's property accessors. Once we have the typeCode helper object, we can get the CORBA Type Code Kind enumeration, such as tk_long, from it. We use the CORBAFactory to create a new CORBA **any** helper object. To do this, we declared a typedef "misc" for the **any** in the CORBA IDL. We can now pass in the type name Chapter5::misc to the CreateType method of the factory to create the helper object. Notice that we just reuse the anyMiscInfo object variable. When we reuse an object variable in Visual Basic, the variable is reassigned to the new object and the previous object is released. Now we use the new CORBA **any** and set the value, to, say, 5 in our

Listing 5.9 A really complex one. An input sequence of structures containing an Any.

```
Private Sub cmdUpdateOrder_Click()
    'Update the investor order

    'Declare the variables
    Dim itemArray As Variant              'CORBA::Array
    Dim itemDataSequence As Variant       'CORBA::Sequence
    Dim newItemDataSeq() As Variant       'CORBA::Sequence
    Dim anyValue As Variant
    Dim objOrder As DIChapter5_order
    Dim anyMiscInfo As DICORBAAny         'CORBA::Any
    Dim miscInfoType As DICORBATypeCode   'CORBA::TypeCode
    Dim theCORBAKind As CORBA_TCKind

    'First, get the Order object which is returned from invoking
    'showOrder
    Set objOrder = objInvestor.showOrder(itemArray, itemDataSequence)

    'Now create a new sequence of order items. We're not going to do
    'any fancy processing with the form here. We're just going to update
    'each entry in the list returned from showOrder. First we'll read
    'the value of the miscInfo any. Then we'll update the quantity field
    'in every OrderItem and pass in a new value for the Any.
    NoItems = UBound(itemDataSequence)
    ReDim newItemDataSeq(0 To NoItems)
    For i = 0 To NoItems
        'Rather than use the CORBAFactory to create it, we're going to
        'use the INSTANCE_clone helper function. This copies the
        'structure and all of the values.
        Set newItemDataSeq(i) = itemDataSequence(i).INSTANCE_clone

        'Get the any, its value and typeCode
        Set anyMiscInfo = itemDataSequence(i).miscInfo
        anyValue = anyMiscInfo.value
        Set miscInfoType = anyMiscInfo.typeCode
        theCORBAKind = miscInfoType.kind

        'Now we'll change the quantity
```

(continues)

Listing 5.9 A really complex one. An input sequence of structures containing an any.
(Continued)

```
        newItemDataSeq(i).quantity = CLng(txtPercent(i))


        'Create an Any helper object using the CORBA Factory.
        'When we set the value, the interworking bridge automatically
        'sets the type for us.
        Set anyMiscInfo = CorbaFactory.CreateType(objOrder,
                                        Chapter5::misc)

        anyMiscInfo.value = 5
        Set newItemDataSeq(i).miscInfo = anyMiscInfo
    Next


    'Pass in the constructed sequence in the updateOrder invocation
    objOrder.updateOrder newItemDataSeq


. . .
```

example. The interworking bridge automatically creates a DICORBATypeCode object and sets its kind to tk_long as a result of us setting the value property of the **any**. The new **any** is then inserted into the new itemData struct, and finally the updateOrder method is invoked with the newItemDataSeq. Whew.

This example was designed to use all of the different CORBA complex data types in different ways. A real application would probably be simpler and certainly more straightforward. As you can see, the CORBA data types, except for the **any**, are easy and intuitive to use from Visual Basic. Now that we know how to use all of the data types from Visual Basic, the next chapter will illustrate the use of the COM mappings of CORBA data types from C++ and will allow us to compare the Visual Basic and C++ programs. After looking at the data types, we will then explore other aspects of interworking, starting with finding and creating objects and object life cyle considerations in Chapter 7.

6

COM Data Type Mappings

This chapter describes the CORBA to COM mappings for both the basic and complex data types discussed in the previous two chapters. The COM mappings are most appropriate for C++ or Java programmers and do not use the `IDispatch` interface that is required by Visual Basic and other Automation-based languages. Instead, COM programs link directly against the `Vtable` interfaces of the COM View objects. This has two advantages over the Automation mappings. First, this is a more efficient way to invoke methods because the request parameters are formatted by the compiler, rather than constructed at run time and do not involve several method invocations for discovering, formatting, and invoking the request. Secondly, and more importantly, the complex CORBA data types such as structures and unions map directly to equivalent data types in COM, so no helper objects need to be constructed by the interworking bridge or application program. With the exception of CORBA **anys**, the mappings are direct, intuitive, and easy to use. In this chapter, we will implement a C++ client to illustrate the use of these data types.

Mappings of Interfaces and Invocations

Let's examine how a CORBA interface is mapped to a COM object using the same sample IDL interface as in Chapter 4.

```
//IDL
module Chapter4 {
        interface foo {
                returntype      opername      (in  intype  inparam,
                                                out outtype outparam);
        };
```

121

This would have the following Microsoft IDL definition:

```
interface IChapter4_foo : IUnknown
    {
        HRESULT opername(
            [in]   intype inparam,
            [out] outtype outparam,
            [out] returntype* returnValue);
};
```

and the following C++ definition:

```
DECLARE_INTERFACE_(IChapter4_foo,IUnknown)
{
    STDMETHOD(opername)(THIS_
        intype inparam,
        outtype outparam,
        returntype VBYREF returnValue) PURE;

};
```

The COM interface name is the concatenation of three parts:

1. "I", the standard prefix for all COM interfaces (as compared to DI for the dual Automation interfaces),

2. The CORBA module name scope, and

3. The CORBA interface name, that is, *Imodule_interface* or *IChapter4_foo.*

Notice that the CORBA operation name, *opername*, maps directly to the COM method name without modification. The input and output parameters of the CORBA method also map directly to input and output parameters in the COM method, again without modification to the name or data types. Finally, notice that the CORBA return parameter, *returntype,* is the last parameter in the COM signature. By definition, all COM methods return an HRESULT; therefore, there cannot be any return parameters. Thus, the CORBA return parameter is mapped as the last parameter in the COM method signature and is always passed by reference.

CORBA attributes are mapped to COM properties in a similar manner. For each CORBA attribute, a *_put_attribute* and *_get_attribute* method is added to the COM interface. For CORBA readonly attributes, only a *_get_attribute* method is added.

If you compare this mapping with the Automation mapping from Chapter 4, you will notice that no optional exception argument is added to the COM mapping. The COM mapping can convey any standard CORBA system exception in the COM HRESULT. The CORBA minor code or repository ID can be obtained from the OLE error object if desired, as described in the section "Handling Exceptions in COM" in Chapter 8. However, if the IDL had contained a user exception, an exception parameter would have been added to the COM method signature. The COM C++ header files for the CORBA IDL from Chapters 4 and 5 are shown throughout this chapter. Examine these listings for more examples of interface, operation, attribute, and data type mappings.

Table 6.1 summarizes the CORBA to COM data type mappings. Throughout the remainder of this chapter, we will have a C++ programming example for each of these data types. The example CORBA servers will be exactly the same as those used in Chapters 4 and 5. The client will not have any GUI component but will

Table 6.1 CORBA to COM Data Type Mappings

CORBA TYPE	COM TYPE (MIDL)	DESCRIPTION OF COM TYPE
boolean	bool	8-bit quantity limited to 0 and 1
char	char	8-bit quantity limited to ISO Latin-1 character set
double	double	64-bit IEEE floating point number
float	float	32-bit IEEE floating point number
long	long	32-bit signed integer
octet	byte	8-bit opaque data type. (unsigned char in ODL)
short	short	16-bit unsigned integer
unsigned long	unsigned long	32-bit unsigned integer
unsigned short	unsigned short	16-bit unsigned integer
string	LPSTR	Null terminated 8-bit character string [string,unique] char *
bounded string	13B-2-4 13B-42	
wstring	LPWSTR	Null terminated Unicode string [string,unique] wchar_t *

just run from start to finish, executing each method once. The structure of the C++ code mirrors the structure of the Visual Basic code. First, we will declare local COM variables for the CORBA data types and point out in our comments where those types are different. Then we will invoke the method that uses those types. The names of the local variables in the C++ code are the same as those used in the Visual Basic examples so that it will be easy to understand and to compare the COM and Automation mappings. We will start with the most basic data types, those illustrated by our `BasicTypes` interface from Chapter 4. You might want to go back and review the basic type IDL and processing before getting into the C++ coding example.

Using Basic Data Types

Listing 6.1 shows the C++ header files for the `IChapter4_BasicTypes` interface.

The first operation we will perform in the client is getting the COM interface pointer to the `BasicTypes` object. In our examples in Chapters 4 and 5 as well as in this chapter, we use the namespace moniker to get these objects. In Chapter 7, we will present the details on creating views of CORBA objects as well as several different ways to do it but for now we want to concentrate on the data type handling. Because we will need to get three different view objects throughout the example, `BasicTypes`, `StringTypes`, and `Investor`, we have implemented a generic function, `getInterfacePointer`, that takes a string as input and returns an interface pointer. The routine should be able to handle any type of view object, so it must return the base COM interface, `IUnknown`. We then use the `QueryInterface` method, required on all COM objects, to get the specific interface pointer that we want, in this case, `BasicTypes`. Listing 6.2 shows the C++ client code for the basic types.

Now that we have the interface pointer, we can start with getting and setting the `boolType`, `charType`, and `theColor` attributes. In the .h file we can see that `boolType` and `theColor` both have _get_ and _put_ methods, while `charType`, which is a readonly attribute, has only the _get_ method. We declare local variables for the boolean, char, and enum. Notice that the COM types for these are the same as the CORBA types. We set the attribute as `hr = pBasic-Types->_put_boolType(FALSE);`. Our local variable is `hr` to receive the COM `HRESULT` completion status. In a real application, you would always check the status and perform error handling. However, we have generally left this out of the example here to add clarity and remove clutter.

Listing 6.1 IChapter4_BasicTypes.h.

```
typedef enum Chapter4_color
{
    red = 1,
    green = 2,
    blue = 3
} Chapter4_color;

DECLARE_INTERFACE_(IChapter4_BasicTypes,IUnknown)
{
    STDMETHOD(indoublefloat)(THIS_
            double doubleType,
            float floatType,
            long VBYREF returnValue) PURE;

    STDMETHOD(outoctetshort)(THIS_
            unsigned char VBYREF octetType,
            short VBYREF shortType,
            boolean VBYREF returnValue) PURE;

    STDMETHOD(uTypes)(THIS_
            unsigned short ushortType,
            unsigned long ulongType,
            unsigned long VBYREF returnValue) PURE;

    STDMETHOD(_get_boolType)(THIS_ boolean
                                    VBYREF returnValue) PURE;
    STDMETHOD(_put_boolType)(THIS_ boolean Value) PURE;

    STDMETHOD(_get_charType)(THIS_ char
                                    VBYREF returnValue) PURE;

    STDMETHOD(_get_theColor)(THIS_ Chapter4_color
                                    VBYREF returnValue) PURE;
    STDMETHOD(_put_theColor)(THIS_ Chapter4_color Value) PURE;

};
```

Listing 6.2 Using basic data types.

```
int    BasicTypes()
{
   HRESULT          hr;
   LPCOLESTR        szDisplayName;
   IUnknown         *pUnk;
   IChapter3_BasicTypes  *pBasicTypes;

   // Use our generic function to get an interface pointer.
   szDisplayName = L"BasicType";
   pUnk = getInterfacePointer(szDisplayName);
   if (FAILED(hr = pUnk->QueryInterface(IID_Ichapter4_BasicTypes,
                                (void **) &pBasicTypes)))
   {
        pUnk->Release();
        return 0;
   }
   pUnk->Release();

   //Handy-dandy array to print out colors
   LPSTR          ColorValues[3];
   ColorValues[1] = "red";
   ColorValues[2] = "green";
   ColorValues[3] = "blue";

   // Boolean, Char and Enum Types
   // Declare local variables for the CORBA data types
   // CORBA::boolean -> boolean, CORBA::char -> char
   boolean        boolType;
   char           charType;
   Chapter3_color enumType;

   // Set, get, and write out the boolean.
   // Good programmers should check for and handle any errors.
   // We've left that out for the readability of the example...
   // These are attributes of the CORBA BasicTypes object, thus
   // we use the generated _put and _get routines for them.
   hr = pBasicTypes->_put_boolType(FALSE);
```

COM Data Type Mappings

Listing 6.2 Using basic data types. (*Continued*)

```
hr = pBasicTypes->_get_boolType(&boolType);
cout << "The boolean is: " << boolType << endl;

// Get and write out the character
hr = pBasicTypes->_get_charType(&charType);
cout << "The char is: " << charType << endl;

// Set, get, and write out the enum
hr = pBasicTypes->_put_theColor(red);
hr = pBasicTypes->_get_theColor(&enumType);
cout << "The enum is:" << ColorValues[enumType] << endl;

// Long, Double, and Float Types all map to equivalent types
// Declare local variables for the CORBA data types
// CORBA::double -> double, CORBA::float -> float,
// CORBA::long -> long
// Values are hard-coded for our simple examples.
double    doubleType = 1234.56;
float     floatType = 7890.12;
long      longResult;

// Invoke the inDoubleFloat method and write the output
// Input parameters are passed by value. Outputs and returns
// are passed by reference.
hr = pBasicTypes->indoublefloat(doubleType, floatType, &longResult);
cout << "The result of indoublefloat is: " << longResult << endl;

// Octet and Short Types
// Declare local variables for the CORBA data types
// CORBA::short -> short, CORBA::octet -> unsigned char.
short          shortType;
unsigned char  octetType;
boolean        boolResult;

// Invoke the method and display the results
// Output parameters passed by reference . . .
hr = pBasicTypes->outoctetshort(&octetType, &shortType, &boolResult);
```

(continues)

Listing 6.2 Using basic data types. (*Continued*)

```
cout << "The result of outoctetshort is: octet: " << octetType
    << " short: " << shortType << endl;

// Unsigned Types map directly in COM
// Declare local variables for the CORBA data types
// CORBA::ulong -> unsigned long, CORBA::ushort -> unsigned short
// Values are hard-coded for our simple examples.
unsigned long    ulongType = 12345;
unsigned short   uShortType = 6789;
unsigned long    ulongResult;

// Invoke the utypes operation and display the returned result
hr = pBasicTypes->uTypes(uShortType, ulongType, &ulongResult);
cout << "The result of uTypes is: " << ulongResult << endl;

// Done with the basic types, release the interface pointer.
pBasicTypes->Release();
return 1;
}
```

The next set of data types is long, double, and float. These data types are also the same in COM as in CORBA so the processing is easy. We invoke the method as `pBasicTypes->indoublefloat(doubleType, float-Type, &longResult)`; notice that the input parameters are passed in by value and that the return result is passed by reference.

Our next method uses the CORBA `octet` data type. COM does not have the concept of octet so it is mapped to an `unsigned char`, which has essentially the same meaning, an 8-bit opaque quantity. We invoke the method as `pBasicTypes-> outoctetshort(&octetType, &shortType, &boolResult)`; here we see that output parameters are passed by reference, which is also the case for **inout** parameters.

The final data types in our `BasicTypes` interface are the unsigned types. This is simple in COM since there are equivalent unsigned data types, so no overflow conditions need to be checked like in Automation. Now that we are done with the `BasicTypes` interface, we must release the interface pointer, which will decrement

Listing 6.3 IChapter4_StringTypes.h.

```
DECLARE_INTERFACE_(IChapter4_StringTypes,IUnknown)
{
   STDMETHOD(inoutstrings)(THIS_
      LPSTR VBYREF boundedString,
      LPSTR VBYREF returnValue) PURE;

};
```

the reference count on the COM view object. This is standard practice in COM programming. You don't have to worry about this in Visual Basic because it transparently takes care of managing the reference counts and releasing objects for you.

Using Strings

Next we look at how CORBA strings are mapped to COM. Listing 6.3 shows the C++ header file for the StringTypes interface from the Chapter 4 IDL. Notice that CORBA strings are mapped to an LPSTR or a long pointer to a null-terminated string.

Listing 6.4 shows the C++ code for using the strings. As always, we declare our local variables for the CORBA data types. Both the bounded and unbounded strings get mapped to LPSTRs. We set the bounded string to something that fits within the bounds and invoke the inoutstrings method. Next we set the bounded string to be longer (> 12) than the bounds defined in the CORBA IDL and invoke the method again. This time we check the HRESULT that is returned. We will get an error value of ITF_E_DATA_CONVERSION.

Complex Data Type Mappings

We've seen how easy (at least for a C++ programmer) the basic data types are to deal with from COM. In this section of the chapter we will see that the CORBA complex data types are also very straightforward from COM. This will be illustrated using the CORBA IDL and server from Chapter 5. As in the previous examples, the structure and variable names will be the same as the Visual Basic example. You may want to review the example in Chapter 5 before continuing. Listing 6.5 shows the COM C++ header file for the Chapter5_ investor interface. We will start by looking at structures.

Listing 6.4 String handling.

```
int     StringTypes()
{
    HRESULT         hr;
    LPCOLESTR       szDisplayName;
    IUnknown        *pUnk;
    IChapter3_StringTypes *pStringTypes;

    szDisplayName = L"StringType";
    pUnk = getInterfacePointer(szDisplayName);
    if (FAILED(hr = pUnk->QueryInterface(IID_IChapter3_StringTypes,
                                    (void **) &pStringTypes)))

    {
        if (pUnk) pUnk->Release();
        return 0;
    }
    pUnk->Release();

    // Strings
    // Declare local variables for the CORBA data types
    // CORBA::string -> LPSTR, CORBA::string<n> -> LPSTR
    LPSTR           resultString;
    LPSTR           boundedString;

    boundedString = "Hello world";

    // Invoke the inoutstrings method and display the new values
    // The original input string will be returned in the outString
    // parameter. The input string (inout) will be changed to all
    // upper case and returned.
    // Inout parameters are passed by reference . . .
    hr = pStringTypes->inoutstrings(&boundedString, &resultString);
    cout << "The inoutstrings method changed " << resultString
         << " to " << boundedString <<endl;

    // Now try it with the bounded string too long. This time we'll
    // check the return status.
```

Listing 6.4 String handling. (*Continued*)

```
boundedString = "Hello world from the authors of this book";
if (FAILED(hr = pStringTypes->inoutstrings(&boundedString,
                                    &resultString)))
{
    cout << "inoutstrings method failed: bounded string too long,
            Result = " << hr << endl;
}

pStringTypes->Release();
return 1;
}
```

Listing 6.5 nIChapter5_Investor.h.

```
typedef struct Chapter5_items
{
  unsigned long cbMaxSize;
  unsigned long cbLengthUsed;
  Chapter5_itemData *pValue;
} Chapter5_items;

typedef struct Chapter5_Investor_address
{
  LPSTR street;
  LPSTR city;
  LPSTR state;
  LPSTR zip;
} Chapter5_Investor_address;

typedef LPSTR Chapter5_phoneNum;

typedef LPSTR Chapter5_cellNum;
```

(continues)

Listing 6.5 nIChapter5_Investor.h. (*Continued*)

```c
typedef struct
{
  long DCE_d;
  union
  {
      Chapter5_phoneNum bizPhone; /* value = 1 */
      Chapter5_cellNum cellPhone; /* value = 2 */
      Chapter5_phoneNum faxPhone; /* value = 3 */
      Chapter5_phoneNum homePhone; /* default item */
  };
} Chapter5_phoneNumber;

interface IChapter5_order;

DECLARE_INTERFACE_(IChapter5_Investor,IUnknown)
{
  STDMETHOD(makeOrder)(THIS_
      long data[3][5],
      IChapter5_order* VBYREF returnValue) PURE;

  STDMETHOD(showOrder)(THIS_
      long data[3][5],
      Chapter5_items VBYREF theItems,
      IChapter5_order* VBYREF returnValue) PURE;

  STDMETHOD(updateAddress)(THIS_
      Chapter5_Investor_address newAddress,
      boolean VBYREF returnValue) PURE;

  STDMETHOD(_get_fullAddress)(THIS_ Chapter5_Investor_address
                                VBYREF returnValue) PURE;

  STDMETHOD(_get_name)(THIS_ LPSTR VBYREF returnValue) PURE;

  STDMETHOD(_get_primaryPhone)(THIS_ Chapter5_phoneNumber
                                VBYREF returnValue) PURE;

};
```

Using Structures

The investor interface has an attribute for the address, which is returned as a structure. CORBA structures map directly to COM structures. You can compare the structure in the Chapter 5 IDL with the Chapter5_Investor_address structure shown in Listing 6.5. We read the attribute by invoking the _get_ accessor method as shown in Listing 6.6. This is the first in a series of extracts from the C++ routine for using the complex types. Once we have the structure, we simply access each member of the structure as a standard C++ structure. The example code also illustrates passing a structure as input to the updateAddress method. Since structures are native to COM and C++, we don't have to use a factory to create a helper object as we did in Visual Basic.

Listing 6.6 Working with structures.

```
int ComplexTypes()
{
    HRESULT                    hr;
    LPCOLESTR                  szDisplayName;
    IUnknown*                  pUnk;
    IChapter5_Investor         *pInvestor;
    IChapter5_order            *pOrder;

    szDisplayName = L"Investor";
    pUnk = getInterfacePointer(szDisplayName);
    if (FAILED(hr = pUnk->QueryInterface(IID_IChapter5_Investor,
                                    (void **) &pInvestor)))
    {
     if (pUnk) pUnk->Release();
     return 0;
    }
pUnk->Release();


    ////////////////////////////////////////////////////////////////
    // Structures in CORBA map directly to structures in COM.
    // The structures are defined in the generated .h file.
    // Declare an address structure.
    Chapter5_Investor_address      theAddress;
    LPSTR                          theName;
```

(continues)

Listing 6.6 Working with structures. (*Continued*)

```
boolean                          worked;

// Get the investor's name and address by reading the
// attributes.
hr = pInvestor->_get_name(&theName);
hr = pInvestor->_get_fullAddress(&theAddress);

// Get the information from the structure and display it.
cout << "The customer is:  " << theName << endl;
cout << "                  " << theAddress.street << endl;
cout << "                  " << theAddress.city << ", "
     << theAddress.state << "  " << theAddress.zip << endl;

// Set the address in the structure for an input parameter.
theAddress.street = "436 Amherst St.";
theAddress.city   = "Nashua";
theAddress.state  = "NH";
theAddress.zip    = "03063";

// Pass the structure to the updateAddress method
hr = pInvestor->updateAddress(theAddress, &worked);

. . .
```

Using Sequences and Arrays

Let's move on to working with sequences and arrays. Listing 6.7 continues the C++ code for complex types with the processing for sequences and arrays. Arrays in CORBA map directly to arrays in COM, but there is no equivalent COM type for sequences. CORBA sequences map to a structure in COM as shown here for the sequence of items in the Chapter5 IDL:

```
// CORBA IDL
typedef sequence <itemData> items;

// COM Structure
typedef struct Chapter5_items
```

```
    {
        unsigned long cbMaxSize;
        unsigned long cbLengthUsed;
        Chapter5_itemData *pValue;
    } Chapter5_items;
```

where `cbMaxSize` represents the bound of the sequence, `cbLengthUsed` represents the number of members actually in the sequence, and `pValue` is a pointer to an array of elements of whatever type is represented by the sequence, in this case `Chapter5_itemData` structures.

In the example code in Listing 6.7, we declare our local variables for the array, sequence, and structure and then fill in the itemArray (somewhat arbitrarily), setting the "checked" member to YES and the percentage to 20 percent for each of the five available investments. We then invoke the `makeOrder` method passing in the array. The array is an **inout** parameter, so after invoking the method we print out the new array values. Next we will invoke the `showOrder` method, which will return a sequence of orderItem structures (among other things). The number of structures in the sequence is returned in the `cbLengthUsed` member of the COM `Chapter5_items` structure, so we loop that many times, printing out each item ordered.

Using Unions

CORBA unions are mapped to a structure in COM that contains a member for the union discriminator and the union itself as follows:

```
typedef struct
{
    long DCE_d;
    union
    {
        . . .
    };
} Chapter5_phoneNumber;
```

Recall from Chapter 5 that the investor's primary phone number is returned as a union. The code for this is shown in Listing 6.8. We get the `primaryPhone` attribute, switch based on the discriminator value, and print out the correct type and phone number.

Listing 6.7 Working with sequences and arrays.

```
. . .

/////////////////////////////////////////////////////////////////////
// Arrays and Sequences
// Declare local variables for the CORBA data types
// CORBA::array[x][y] -> Array[x][y], CORBA::sequence -> structure
long                    itemArray[3][5];
Chapter5_items          orderList;
Chapter5_itemData       orderItem;
unsigned long           i;

// Fill in each element of the array
for (i = 0; i < 4; i++)
{
    itemArray[1][i] = 1;
    itemArray[2][i] = 20;
    itemArray[3][i] = 0;
}

// Invoke the makeOrder method and print out the array.
hr = pInvestor->makeOrder(itemArray, &pOrder);
for (i = 0; i < 4; i++)
{
    cout << itemArray << endl;
}

// Invoke the showOrder method and print out the order
hr = pInvestor->showOrder(itemArray, &orderList, &pOrder);
for (i = 0; i < orderList.cbLengthUsed; i++)
{
    orderItem = orderList.pValue[i];
    cout << orderItem.name << " " << orderItem.price << " "
         << orderItem.quantity << endl;
}

. . .
```

Listing 6.8 Working with unions.

```
.  .  .

//////////////////////////////////////////////////////////////////
// Unions
// Declare local variables for the CORBA data types
// CORBA::union -> structure
Chapter5_phoneNumber   unionPhone;

// Get the primary phone number attribute, which is returned as
// a union.
hr = pInvestor->_get_primaryPhone(&unionPhone);

// Switch based on the value of the struture's discriminator
// member
switch (unionPhone.DCE_d)
{
    case 1:
        cout << "Business Phone: " << unionPhone.bizPhone
            << endl;
        break;

    case 2:
        cout << "Cellular Phone: " << unionPhone.cellPhone
            << endl;
        break;

    case 3:
        cout << "Fax: " << unionPhone.faxPhone << endl;
        break;

    default:
        cout << "Home Phone: " << unionPhone.homePhone << endl;
        break;
}

.  .  .
```

Using Anys

So far the CORBA complex types have mapped directly to equivalent types or structures in COM. The pesky CORBA **any** is the only exception to this. The **any** is mapped to a special interface, ICORBA_Any, as follows:

```
interface ICORBA_Any : IUnknown
{
    HRESULT _get_value ([out] VARIANT * val );
    HRESULT _put_value ([in]  VARIANT   val );
    HRESULT _get_CORBAAnyData ([out] CORBAAnyData * val );
    HRESULT _put_CORBAAnyData ([in]  CORBAAnyData   val );
    HRESULT _get_typeCode    ([out] ICORBA_TypeCode ** tc);
}
```

In most cases, a COM application can use the `_get_value` or `_put_value` methods to get and set the value of the **any**. However, the data types supported by a VARIANT cannot represent all of the possible CORBA values in an **any**, such as structs and unions. Wherever the data can be represented in a VARIANT, it will be. In other cases, the data will be returned as an IStream pointer in the variant. Some interworking bridges may not implement the IStream mechanism, in which case an HRESULT of E_DATA_CONVERSION will be returned for the _get_value method.

There are three mechanisms for determining what type of data was returned in the **any**. The simplest is to use the VARIANT type (V_VT), which works for all data types that can be represented in a VARIANT. Another method is to get the CORBA_TypeCode interface and query it for the type code kind. The last method is to get the CORBAAnyData union as follows:

```
enum CORBAAnyDataTagEnum {
    anySimpleValTag = 0,
    anyAnyValTag,
    anySeqValTag,
    anyStructValTag,
    anyUnionValTag,
    anyObjectValTag
} CORBAAnyDataTag;

typedef union CORBAAnyDataUnion
switch (CORBAAnyDataTag whichOne){
    case anyAnyValTag:
```

```
        ICORBAAny *anyVal;
    case anySeqValTag:
    case anyStructValTag:
        struct {
            [string, unique] char * repositoryID;
            unsigned long cbMaxSize;
            unsigned long cbLengthUsed;
            [size_is (cbMaxSize), length_is(cbLengthUsed), unique]
                union CORBAAnyDataUnion * pVal;
        } multiVal;
    case anyUnionValTag:
        struct {
            [string, unique] char * repositoryID;
            long disc;
            union CORBAAnyDataUnion *value;
        } unionVal;
    case anyObjectValTag:
        struct {
            [string, unique] char * repositoryID;
            VARIANT val;
        }objectVal;
    case anySimpleValTag:
        VARIANT simpleVal;
} CORBAAnyData;
```

The CORBAAnyData union contains all of the information necessary to identify and use any data type that can be returned in a union.

Let's look at some code to read an **any**. Recall from Chapter 5 that the item-Data structure contains an **any** called miscValue. Listing 6.9 shows how to get the union out of the structure and read its value. In our example, we know the value will fit into a VARIANT, so we declare a VARIANT among the local data variables. Before a VARIANT can be used from a COM program, it must be initialized. COM provides a handy helper function VariantInit for this purpose, which we use. Next, we get the **any** from the structure and then pass the initialized VARIANT into the _get_value method. We read the long value of the **any** from the VARIANT's V_I4 member. However, if we wanted to go the typecode route, we would also show how to get the typecode and kind. The values for the CORBA_TCKind are the same as those described in Chapter 5 in the section on **any**s.

Listing 6.9 Working with anys.

```
.  .  .

//////////////////////////////////////////////////////////////
// Anys
ICORBA_Any                  *pAnyMiscInfo;
ICORBA_TypeCode             *pMiscInfoType;
CORBA_TCKind                theCORBAKind;
ICORBA_TypeCodeUserException *pUserException;
VARIANT                     theVariant;
long                        theLong;

// The value of the any is returned as a variant. Use the
// handy COM VariantInit method to initialize it.
VariantInit(&theVariant);

// This time, extract the anys from the returned order list
// We also get the typecode to show how, but we don't use it here.
// We know that the value in the variant is going to be a long, so
// we don't have to bother with the VT field in our example.
for (i = 0; i < orderList.cbLengthUsed; i++)
{
    orderItem = orderList.pValue[i];
    pAnyMiscInfo = orderItem.miscInfo;
    hr = pAnyMiscInfo->_get_value(&theVariant);
    theLong = V_I4(&theVariant);
    cout << "The variant contained: " << theLong << endl;

    hr = pAnyMiscInfo->_get_typeCode(&pMiscInfoType);
    hr = pMiscInfoType->kind(&theCORBAKind, &pUserException);
}

.  .  .
```

Putting It All Together

Let's finish off the complex data types using our example, which creates the sequence of structures containing **any** as an input to the updateOrder method.

Listing 6.10 IChapter5_Order.h.

```
typedef struct Chapter5_itemData
{
    LPSTR name;
    float price;
    long quantity;
    long partNumber;
    Chapter5_misc miscInfo;
} Chapter5_itemData_itemData;

typedef struct Chapter5_items
{
    unsigned long cbMaxSize;
    unsigned long cbLengthUsed;
    Chapter5_itemData *pValue;
} Chapter5_items;

DECLARE_INTERFACE_(IChapter5_order,IUnknown)
{
    STDMETHOD(updateOrder)(THIS_ Chapter5_items VBYREF theItems) PURE;

};
```

Listing 6.10 shows the C++ header file for the `Order` interface, and Listing 6.11 shows the C++ code.

Because we are passing the CORBA **any**s as input parameters, our application is responsible for creating then. In COM we get a special factory for this, the `IAnyFactory` interface, which is similar to the way we created helper objects with a factory in Visual Basic. The `IAnyFactory` interface is available from any view object that has **any**s; in this example, we'll use the `Order` interface. We use the normal COM mechanism, `QueryInterface`, to ask the **order** interface for an `IAnyFactory`.

To keep the example somewhat simple, we will just create a sequence of two itemDatas, so we set the size of our sequence, `cbLengthUsed`, to 2. Now we start to fill in each member of the itemData structure, basically by copying the

Listing 6.11 Putting it together in an example.

```
. . .

//////////////////////////////////////////////////////////////////
// Here is our final, complicated example of how to update the order.
// To keep it fairly simple, we are just going to update the first
// two items in the sequence. We will need to create the anys for
// input so we have to declare a factory for them.
IAnyFactory            *pAnyFactory;
Chapter5_itemData      itemData1,itemData2;
Chapter5_misc          pMisc1,pMisc2;
VARIANT                variant1,variant2;
Chapter5_items         newOrderList;

// Get the Any Factory Object, available from View interfaces
// that have anys
hr = pOrder->QueryInterface(IID_IAnyFactory, (void **)&pAnyFactory);

// Set the size of the sequence.
newOrderList.cbMaxSize = 5;
newOrderList.cbLengthUsed = 2;

// Set the name, price, and partNumber from the order list
// returned from showOrder. Set the quantity to 20%. Create an
// Any and set its value to a long. The any typecode will
// automatically get set based on the value of the variant VT field.
itemData1.name =orderList.pValue[1].name;
itemData1.price = orderList.pValue[1].price;
itemData1.quantity = 20;
itemData1.partNumber = orderList.pValue[1].partNumber;
hr = pAnyFactory->CreateAny(&pMisc1);
VariantInit(&variant1);
V_VT(&variant1) = VT_I4;
V_I4(&variant1) = 5;
hr = pMisc1->_put_value(variant1);
itemData1.miscInfo = pMisc1;
newOrderList.pValue[1] = itemData1;
```

Listing 6.11 Putting it together in an example. (*Continued*)

```
// Do the same for the second itemData
itemData2.name = orderList.pValue[2].name;
itemData2.price = orderList.pValue[2].price;
itemData2.quantity = 20;
itemData2.partNumber = orderList.pValue[2].partNumber;
hr = pAnyFactory->CreateAny(&pMisc2);
VariantInit(&variant2);
V_VT(&variant2) = VT_I4;
V_I4(&variant2) = 10;
hr = pMisc2->_put_value(variant2);
itemData2.miscInfo = pMisc2;
newOrderList.pValue[2] = itemData2;

// Invoke the update order method. That didn't hurt too much . . .
hr = pOrder->updateOrder(&newOrderList);

// As always, release the reference when done.
pInvestor->Release();
pOrder->Release();
return 1;
}
```

value of the sequence returned when we invoked showOrder. When we get to the miscInfo member, rather than copying we will create the **any** using the CreateAny method of the factory. We are going to set the value of the **any** with a VARIANT, so we first have to process the VARIANT by first initializing it. A VARIANT is just a big union in which the VT member is the discriminator. Once the VARIANT has been initialized, we set its type by setting the VT field to I4 (or long) and then set the value by assigning a long value to the I4 member of the VARIANT union. Next, we set the **any** by passing the VARIANT to the _put_value method, store the **any** into the itemData structure, and place the structure into the newOrderList sequence. We do it all over again for the second itemData and then pass the sequence of item data structures in the updateOrder method.

Summary

In the previous three chapters, we have shown how to use all of the different CORBA data types from both Automation using Visual Basic and from COM using C++ as well as how interfaces are mapped between the models. However, we have glossed over many other details such as how the views get created and destroyed, how persistent CORBA references relate to transient COM interface pointers, and how exceptions are handled. In the next two chapters, we will go into detail on how these and other aspects of the two object models are mapped.

7 Integrating COM and CORBA

C hapter 3 described the significant differences between COM and CORBA regarding object identity and life cycle. This chapter illustrates how those differences arise when programming, and how you can deal with them effectively. We'll show how clients in one object system find and create objects in the other system, and how applications need to attend to certain life cycle details when using objects in another object system.

Finding Objects

One of the most common tasks performed by object-oriented applications is finding existing objects. The mechanisms provided by different object systems for doing this vary widely and are generally based on the underlying assumptions about how the object systems will be used.

Most object-oriented programming languages don't provide abstractions for locating existing objects by means of some kind of permanent identifier. Instead, they assume that the program will explicitly read stored information from a file or database, construct a new object instance, and initialize the object with the retrieved information. The object itself (the instance of the class) only exists as long as the program is running, and the program is responsible for saving the state as necessary in a well-known storage location (i.e., filename or database record) for later use. This pattern of usage reflects the assumptions of early object-oriented programs—that the program exists in isolation and all of objects used by the program are local (in the program's address space).

145

With the rise of distributed object computing, those assumptions have been shattered. Since distributed objects are not local to the programs using them, their life cycles can be independent. In many cases, clients of distributed objects can assume that the objects they need to use are "out there somewhere," existing as independent entities. Where the object is stored (or the fact that is stored at all) is hidden from the client, managed by the distributed object system and the object itself. Given this perspective, it is important that clients have a reasonable way of identifying and locating objects of interest.

Finding CORBA Objects from Automation Clients

Visual Basic (VB) programs typically use the `GetObject` function to activate Automation objects. Most COM/CORBA interworking products supply one or more ways to present a CORBA object so that it can be accessed through `GetObject`. This feature is not required by the COM/CORBA interworking Specification, but it is so useful that many bridges have implemented it.

Using Class Factories

Using `GetObject` in Visual Basic is so trivial that an example would almost be superfluous. In its typical form when used with native COM objects, the parameter to `GetObject` is a filename that indicates where the object's state is stored and what class should be created (which is inferred from the three-character filename suffix). This form will, of course, not work when a CORBA object is being mapped through a bridge. A less common alternative form allows `GetObject` to be called so the parameter string is interpreted as a custom moniker type that invokes a nonstandard moniker implementation to interpret the string and use it to bind the object in whatever way it wants. When this form is being used, the parameter string begins with the "@" character. One example of this is BEA Systems' ObjectBroker Desktop bridging product; the following is based on the example in Chapter 2:

```
Dim objAccount as DIBank_Account
Set objAccount =
GetObject("@ObjectBroker.Bridge\ADAPTER\ObjectBroker\
  Advertisements\Acct_1")
```

In this parameter string, ObjectBroker.Bridge is the ProgID of a custom moniker type provided with the ObjectBroker bridge. `GetObject` maps this ProgID to a class ID, creates an instance of the custom moniker class, and passes it to the rest of the string. In this case, the rest of the string, `ADAPTER\ObjectBroker\Advertisements\Acct_1`, is a name in a hierarchical namespace supported by the ObjectBroker bridge. CORBA object references are registered in this namespace by CORBA servers.

Some bridge products also allow a *particular instance* of a CORBA object to be associated with a COM class ID. This may seem counterintuitive (in fact, it is), but it provides a very simple way to locate well-known objects. Recall the following line from Listing 2.3 in Chapter 2:

```
Set objAcctMgr = CreateObject("CORBA.OLE.Bank_AcctMgr")
```

This `CreateObject` invocation doesn't really create the target CORBA **AcctMgr** object instance. It was created previously, and its object reference was associated with the ProgID `CORBA.OLE.Bank_AcctMgr`. To be more specific, when the CORBA object is registered (using a product-specific administrative

Product-specific Bridge Features

Distributed object technology is a rich and inherently complex field of endeavor. The range of problems that developers are addressing with CORBA technology is extraordinarily wide, from highly specialized embedded systems to ORBs running on mainframe computers. As a consequence, some of the details regarding how CORBA products work vary from implementation to implementation, often driven by differences in the requirements that specific products are designed to meet. From time to time, CORBA specifications intentionally avoid specifying certain details, leaving the matter for the product implementation to decide. This is particularly true in areas that pertain to configuring and administering the ORB and applications that use it. The COM/CORBA Interworking Specification is no exception; there are a number of details that vary from product to product. It would be extremely impractical to attempt to show how certain things are done in every available product. It would also be misleading to show product-specific features from only one bridge without describing how they might vary or generalize. We have tried to strike a reasonable balance between generic and specific, sometimes showing a particular product's solution while noting that other products may differ, and other times describing general patterns and focusing on the programming techniques that will be common among interworking products.

tool) the bridge registers a specialized class factory with a new class ID. The class factory encapsulates the CORBA object reference for the **AcctMgr** object. The bridge also registers the class ID under the ProgID, CORBA.OLE.Bank_Acct-Mgr. When CreateObject is called, it maps the ProgID to the class ID and invokes the class factory. The class factory provided by the bridge creates a view for the preexisting CORBA object. With this approach, all invocations of CreateObject with the same ProgID will return Automation views of the same CORBA object instance.

Using the CORBA Factory Object

Both of the previous techniques are not standard (though they have cognates in most bridge products). They have the advantage of being natural for COM/Automation programmers. There are other ways to find CORBA objects that are only slightly less natural but are standardized. The most useful is the CORBA factory object. The CORBA factory has two methods, GetObject and CreateObject. These are intentionally designed to be familiar and natural to Automation programmers by mimicking the form and function of Visual Basic functions of the same name.

The Automation interface for the CORBA factory is named DICORBAFactory. Here is its ODL interface definition:

```
// ODL
interface DICORBAFactory: IDispatch
{
    HRESULT CreateObject(
        [in] BSTR factoryName,
        [out,retval] IDispatch ** val);
    HRESULT GetObject(
        [in] BSTR objectName,
        [out, retval] IDispatch ** val);
}
```

The resulting Visual Basic functions take a single string parameter and return an object. Interworking products must provide an implementation of the CORBA factory and expose it in the registry with the ProgID CORBA.Factory. You can get access to the CORBA factory with the following Visual Basic statements:

```
Dim CorbaFactory as DICORBAFactory
Dim myObject as Object
```

```
Set CorbaFactory = CreateObject("CORBA.Factory")
Set myObject =
 CorbaFactory.GetObject("the.name.of.my.object")
```

The `DICORBAFactory::GetObject` method is used to obtain Automation views for existing CORBA objects. The parameter is a string that is mapped by the bridge (in some unspecified way) to a specific CORBA object instance. In general, it will be a pathname consisting of identifiers separated by periods ("."), much like COM ProgIDs. As with the previous examples, the mechanism for associating CORBA objects with names in this namespace is implementation-specific and varies from product to product. In most products, there are administrative tools that make this task easy.

The COM/CORBA Interworking Specification suggests one possible implementation of `DICORBAFactory::GetObject`, based on the CORBA Naming Service. In general, implementations of the CORBA Naming Service are distributed, federated-object directories that act as clearinghouses for objects being shared by multiple applications on a network. As such, they are significantly different in character from the local registry on Windows platforms—they are inherently distributed and highly scalable.

There is one specialized use of `DICORBAFactory::GetObject` that has a specified implementation. CORBA doesn't support global functions or static methods, so object references in CORBA programs come from operations on other objects (such as the name service `NamingContext` object). While this is a clean, consistent model, it raises a bootstrapping question—where do you get the first object reference(s) that you use to obtain subsequent references? CORBA provides an interface on the ORB pseudo-object that supplies initial object references. In essence, it acts as a very simple, flat namespace for a small number of objects under well-known names, such as the Naming Service and the Interface Repository. The method on the ORB pseudo-object is called `resolve_initial_references`:

// OMG IDL

interface ORB { // the ORB is actually a pseudo-interface

    exception InvalidName();
    Object resolve_initial_references(in string name)
        raises (InvalidName);

};

CORBA specifies names for common objects that are made available through this interface. For example, a naming context object with the interface `CosNaming::NamingContext` will be returned when you invoke `resolve_initial_references` with the string "NameService"; the Interface Repository will be returned with the string "InterfaceRepository."

Objects that are accessible through `resolve_initial_references` can be obtained from the CORBA factory by invoking `DICORBAFactory::GetObject`. The parameter to `GetObject` is formed with an initial period (".") followed by the name to be passed to `resolve_initial_references`. For example, you can obtain a view for the ORB's Naming Service in this way:

```
Dim namingService As DICosNaming_NamingContext
' assume CorbaFactory is initialized as before
Set namingService =
  CorbaFactory.GetObject(".NameService")
```

Objects obtained in this way are, for the most part, useful only to programmers familiar with CORBA and willing to cope with the CORBA-isms these mapped interfaces expose. It is not likely, for instance, that the typical Visual Basic programmer will have the need (or inclination) to use the Interface Repository. The Naming Service, however, is relatively simple and provides such a fundamental function that its use is worth discussing.

The CORBA Naming Service is probably the most commonly used CORBA object service. COM and Automation programs can use it to locate CORBA objects and to publish CORBA views of COM objects for CORBA clients. You may find that your interworking product's implementation of the CORBA factory doesn't meet your needs. The interface is rather clumsy, however, especially when mapped to an Automation interface for Visual Basic clients. The following example provides a simplified interface to the CORBA Naming Service for Visual Basic clients. It also illustrates a variety of useful programming techniques.

Using the CORBA Naming Service

A portion of the CORBA IDL for the Naming Service is shown in Listing 7.1. A complete explanation of the Naming Service is beyond the scope of this chapter, but a brief explanation should be sufficient for the needs of Automation clients trying to locate CORBA objects.

Listing 7.1 CORBA Naming Service interface.

```
// IDL
module CosNaming
{
    // Note: this is only a partial listing; see the specification
    // for the complete IDL interface

    // CosNaming uses a sequence of name components
    // instead of a single string with separators

    typedef string Istring;
    struct NameComponent {
        Istring id;
        Istring kind;
    };
    typedef sequence <NameComponent> Name;

    // exceptions used in NamingContext operations

    interface NamingContext {
        enum NotFoundReason { missing_node, not_context, not_object};
        exception NotFound {
            NotFoundReason why;
            Name rest_of_name;
        };
        exception CannotProceed {
            NamingContext cxt;
            Name rest_of_name;
        };
        exception InvalidName{};
        exception AlreadyBound {};
        exception NotEmpty{};


        // operations used in our examples:

        // bind puts an object reference into the Naming Service

        void bind(in Name n, in Object obj)
            raises(NotFound, CannotProceed, InvalidName, AlreadyBound);
```

(continues)

Listing 7.1 CORBA Naming Service interface. (*Continued*)

```
    // rebind writes over any existing binding

    void rebind(in Name n, in Object obj)
        raises(NotFound, CannotProceed, InvalidName);

    // resolve returns the object reference at the specified name

    Object resolve (in Name n)
        raises(NotFound, CannotProceed, InvalidName);

    // unbind removes the name/reference association

    void unbind(in Name n)
        raises(NotFound, CannotProceed, InvalidName);
    };
};
```

The Naming Service is organized around naming contexts. A naming context is a simple directory that associates names with object references. The references can be references to other naming contexts, which allows the contexts to be organized in a general graph. In practice, naming contexts are often organized hierarchically, like a file system, though this is not a requirement. Names are mapped to their associated object references by the `NamingContext::resolve` operation. Each individual context is a flat namespace in which a single identifier maps locally to an object, but the graph that results from connecting contexts allows compound pathnames made from a sequence of identifiers to be resolved across a chain of connected contexts.

Simplifying the Naming Service for COM/Automation Clients The way in which the Naming Service interface expresses compound names is the source of most of the service's programming inconvenience. The service and its interface were designed to be extremely generalized, capable of wrapping and integrating a wide variety of concrete directory implementations. For the sake of flexibility, the design avoids making assumptions about the forms of the names to be used (e.g., what characters may or may not be allowed in identifiers, what separators are used to express boundaries in compound names, etc.). Rather than express a compound name as a single string with separator characters, the service interface expresses them as a sequence of discrete name components. Although inconvenient, this design has proved valuable when using the Naming Service interface to federate diverse directory structures, and much of the programming awkwardness can be easily overcome with a few simple conventions (as this example will illustrate). As a further (and less justifiable) complication, each individual name component is actually a struct containing two string members, one called ID and the other kind. The ID is the name itself, used as the key to resolve object references within the context. The meaning and use of the kind field are not well defined. The intent seems to be roughly similar to filename suffixes, that is, to indicate the type or intended role of the object, but there is no required definition of its meaning or how it should be used. In practice, the kind field is almost always ignored (left as an empty string) during simple name resolution. Our example later in this section follows this practice. The kind field is useful when combined with a factory finder mechanism as shown in our example in Chapter 10.

The example in Listing 7.2 defines an Automation class in Visual Basic called `NamingServiceWrapper`. It supports a method called `GetObject` that takes a single string parameter. The parameter is a single string that contains a compound name, where the name components are separated by periods. `NamingServiceWrapper::GetObject` converts the name into the Naming Service representation of a compound name and invokes Resolve on an Automation view of the default name context provided by the bridge's ORB. The private method `BuildCompoundName` does most of the drudge work, parsing the pathname and building the array of name components. Note the use of `DICORBAFactory::CreateType` to create the compound-name pseudo-struct objects, which were explained in Chapter 5. Also note that the `Class_ Initialize` event handler obtains the view for the root-naming context as previously described by using `DICORBAFactory::GetObject` with a leading period in the name, which causes the bridge's ORB to invoke `resolve_initial_references`. In addition, the invocation of Resolve on the naming context view uses an optional parameter to receive possible exceptions. Chapter 8 will cover exceptions in detail, so we won't discuss them here.

The following example depends on these two assumptions:

- The individual names in the compound pathname don't contain periods. A slightly more clever version of this example would allow a user-defined separator character or allow separators to be escaped so they can be embedded in name components.

- The kind field of the name components is not used. Alternative pathname syntax could easily be devised to compose strings with ID and kind fields, perhaps using a different separator within each component to distinguish between the fields. Given that kind fields are rarely used, accommodating them would only serve to obscure the example unnecessarily.

Listing 7.2 VB Wrapper for CORBA Naming Service.

```
Option Explicit

Private NameContext As DICosNaming_NamingContext

Public Function GetObject(pathName As String) As Object

    ' if the pathname is not well-formed (empty or only periods, etc.)
    ' or if the resolve operation failed for any reason, GetObject
    ' returns the value Nothing

    Dim nameComponent As CosNaming_NameComponent
    Dim compoundName As Variant
    Dim namedObject As Object
    Dim anException As Variant
    Dim exceptType As ExceptionType


    ' call BuildCompoundName to parse the pathname
    Set compoundName = BuildCompoundName(pathName)
    If IsNull(compoundName) Then
        Set GetObject = Nothing
    Else
        ' get the named object from the Naming Service (name context)
        ' this invokes the view of the CORBA name context object
        Set namedObject = NameContext.resolve(nameArray, anException)
        If anException.EX_majorCode = NO_EXCEPTION Then
            Set GetObject = namedObject
        Else
            Set GetObject = Nothing
        End If
    End If
End Function
```

Listing 7.2 VB Wrapper for CORBA Naming Service. (*Continued*)

```
Private Function BuildCompoundName(pathName As String) As Variant
    Dim position As Integer
    Dim length As Integer
    Dim nameCount As Integer
    Dim compoundName As New Collection
    Dim nameSeg As String
    Dim nextDot As Integer
    Dim CorbaFactory As DICORBAFactory
    Dim nameComponent As CosNaming_NameComponent
    Dim nameArray()
    Dim index As Integer
    Dim segLength As Integer

    ' we will need the CORBA factory to create the
    ' name component pseudo-structs
    Set CorbaFactory = CreateObject("CORBA.Factory")

    ' the pathname has to be broken apart into name components
    ' (see CosNaming IDL interface)
    nameCount = 0
    position = 1
    length = Len(pathName)
    While position <= length
        ' find the next separator
        nextDot = InStr(position, pathName, ".")
        If nextDot <> 0 Then
            ' extract the next name component
            segLength = nextDot - position
            If segLength > 0 Then
                nameSeg = Mid(pathName, position, nextDot - position)
                ' create the name component pseudo-struct
                Set nameComponent = CorbaFactory.CreateType( _
                    NameContext, "CosNaming::NameComponent")
                ' set the id field to the name; ignore the kind field
                nameComponent.id = nameSeg
                ' collect the name components
                compoundName.Add nameComponent
```

(continues)

Listing 7.2 VB Wrapper for CORBA Naming Service. (*Continued*)

```
            End If
            position = nextDot + 1
        End If
    End


    ' create an array for the name components
    ' and put the components into it
    nameCount = compoundName.Count
    If nameCount > 0 Then
        ReDim nameArray(nameCount)
        index = 1
        For Each nameComponent In compoundName
            nameArray(index) = nameComponent
            index = index + 1
        Next
        BuildCompoundName = nameArray
    Else
        BuildCompoundName = Null
    End If

End Function

Private Sub Class_Initialize()
    Dim CorbaFactory As DICORBAFactory
    Set CorbaFactory = CreateObject("CORBA.Factory")
    Set NameContext = CorbaFactory.GetObject(".NamingService")
End Sub
```

Since this example closely imitates the behavior and intent of the CORBA factory object, you might be wondering why we went to the trouble. Other than being an interesting academic exercise and a good illustration of how the Naming Service works, here are some things to consider:

- Your interworking product's implementation of the CORBA factory object may not be as scalable or flexible as you would like it to be. As mentioned earlier, implementations (proper implementations, that is) of the Naming Service are inherently distributed and capable of being federated. Many

ORB vendors have made significant investments in providing high-quality naming implementations. Although it may seem like the obvious way to implement `DICORBAFactory`, there is certainly no requirement to do this.

- The mechanisms for associating object references with names in the CORBA factory's namespace are not specified, so they vary from product to product. If you are in a multi-ORB environment, or you want to design for maximum portability, you may want to consider using a technique that is (at least in theory) portable. All of the interfaces used in this example are required by the specification, and any reasonably correct implementation of the Naming Service can be used, so it should be portable between bridge products and ORBs.

Using IOR Strings

CORBA object references can be converted into strings, generally called *Interoperable Object References*, or IORs. To be precise, any object references shared among ORBs are IORs, whether they are in string form or not. The name *IOR* refers to the information contained in the reference that allows any client, regardless of the specific ORB product it was built with, to contact and use the object. IORs in string form can be exchanged and stored by any mechanism that can handle string data—you can store them in text files, send them in email messages, and so on. IOR strings are often used to initiate contact between different ORBs by having one of the ORBs publish a reference to its naming service as an IOR string. When the other ORB converts the string to a reference, it can get more objects from the Naming Service and publish its own objects there for the first ORB to access.

A COM or Automation client can use a CORBA object's IOR string as well by asking the bridge to convert it into a view. Listing 7.3 contains the Visual Basic code that will open a file containing an IOR, read the IOR, and convert it into a view. Bridges support views of the ORB pseudo-object, with the interface `DIORBObject`. The ORB view can be obtained from the CORBA factory under the name `CORBA.ORB.2`. The ORB view doesn't support all of the operations defined on the ORB pseudo-object itself because some of them have no practical use in COM and Automation clients. The operation `DIORBObject::StringToObject` converts an IOR string into a view or into the object denoted by the IOR. IOR strings are often too long (a few hundred characters) to be easily typed, and they are not human-friendly, as they consist almost entirely of hex numbers. Consequently, they are often stored in files as the following example assumes.

Listing 7.3 Using an IOR string.

```
Option Explicit

Public Function GetObjectFromIORFile(IORFileName As String) As Object

    Dim IORFile As Integer
    Dim IORString As String
    Dim TextLine As String
    Dim CorbaORB As DIORBObject
    Dim CorbaFactory As DICORBAFactory
    Dim AnException As Variant
    Dim obj As Object

    ' get the CORBA factory and the ORB object
    Set CorbaFactory = GetObject("CORBA.Factory")
    Set CorbaORB = CorbaFactory.GetObject("CORBA.ORB.2")

    ' open the file and read the IOR string
    IORFile = FreeFile
    IORString = ""
    Open IORFileName For Input As #IORFile
    Do Until EOF(IORFile)
        Line Input #IORFile, TextLine
        ' strip whitespace
        IORString = IORString & Trim(TextLine)
    Loop

    ' use the ORB view to create the view object from the string
    Set obj = CorbaORB.StringToObject(IORString, AnException)
    If AnException.EX_majorCode = NO_EXCEPTION Then
        Set GetObjectFromIORFile = obj
    Else
        Set GetObjectFromIORFile = Nothing
    End If

End Function
```

Getting the Right Naming Context

In the preceding examples using the CORBA Naming Service, the reference for the naming context was obtained (either directly or indirectly) from the `CORBA::ORB::resolve_initial_references` operation. There is no guarantee, however, that the naming context object that the bridge's ORB supplies is the same context object supplied to the remote CORBA application. The way in which initial references are assigned is specific to the ORB product. You will have to understand how your product does this in order to determine if the same name context is being used in both places.

There is a portable solution to this problem. Instead of using `resolve_initial_references` to get the naming context in both the client and server (or in different parts of the application in general), have one component of the system obtain the naming-context object from the ORB and convert the reference into string form (as shown in the preceding example). You can export that string (most likely as a file) to the other application components, where it will be converted back into an object reference (or a COM view). This approach guarantees that all of the application components will share the same naming service, even if they are constructed with different ORB products. The OMG is currently adopting a specification for making the resolution of naming context portable between different implementations. Once this is adopted, it will also become available through interworking products.

Creating and Managing Objects

All of the previous examples have assumed that the CORBA objects of interest are already in existence, have been registered with the bridge, have been put in the Naming Service, or have exported IOR strings. COM clients will often need to create new CORBA objects. There are a variety of ways to do this, and most of them involve factories of one kind or another.

Creating CORBA Objects from Automation Clients

CORBA doesn't support a uniform factory mechanism like the COM class factories. In CORBA, any object that creates other objects is a factory. The CORBA Life Cycle Service describes an interface for a generic factory, but in practice it is hardly ever used. Factories in CORBA applications tend to be specialized to the application, the object being created, and the circumstances under which the creation is expected to take place. In many cases, an object that serves an application-specific function will also act as a factory, particularly when the objects it creates are its subordinates or logical children from the application's point of view. For instance, in the banking example in Chapter 2 (see Listing 2.1), the `Bank::AcctMgr` interface acts as a factory for account objects by providing the `createAccount` operation.

One reason for this approach is CORBA's rigorous notion of encapsulating an object's state. CORBA applications generally supply the initial state as the parameters to the factory's creation method, and the state becomes an intrinsic part of the object itself, associated with its identity. The state may, of course, change over time as the object is used. CORBA clients don't (in general) maintain separate state in some storage mechanism and load it into objects after creation. It is the server's function to associate the state with a particular instance of the object. The `Bank::AcctMgr` from Chapter 2 is a good example of this kind of factory. The `createAccount` method takes *name* and *balance* parameters as the initial state of the object.

The most appropriate approach for COM programmers to take when they need to create CORBA objects will depend on the nature of the application and, in particular, whether the interfaces of the CORBA objects were designed with COM clients in mind or not. In most cases where COM clients are using preexisting CORBA objects, they will follow the object creation patterns inherent in the CORBA application's design. In many cases, however, CORBA interfaces may be explicitly designed to support COM clients by supplying factories that can be mapped into COM class factories. The COM/CORBA Interworking Specification defines an interface called `SimpleFactory` for this purpose. Here is the IDL description of the `SimpleFactory` interface:

```
//IDL
module CosLifeCycle
{
    interface SimpleFactory
    {
        Object create_object();
    };
};
```

The `SimpleFactory` interface corresponds logically to COM class factories because the `SimpleFactory::create_object` operation takes no parameters, much like `IClassFactory::CreateInstance`. The way in which a particular implementation of `SimpleFactory` is associated with a specific COM class factory is not defined in the Interworking Specification, so individual interworking products may do this in different ways.

The CORBA factory object's interface (DICORBAFactory) supports a method called CreateObject. Similar to the GetObject method on the CORBA factory, CreateObject is designed to be natural and familiar to COM and Automation programmers. The parameter is generally a series of identifiers separated by periods, similar to COM ProgIDs. The association of particular factories with names in the CORBA factory's namespace is not defined by the Interworking Specification and, thus, is determined by the bridge implementation.

For the same reasons we provided a portable implementation of GetObject on the NamingServiceWrapper class shown earlier, you may find it advantageous to use an implementation of a uniform factory mechanism based on the CORBA Naming Service. We'll extend the previous example of NamingServiceWrapper with a CreateObject method.

The CreateObject method on NamingServiceWrapper, shown in Listing 7.4, is very similar to GetObject in that it builds a compound name from the string parameter and invokes NamingContext::resolve. Instead of returning that object to the caller, however, CreateObject() assumes that the object supports the SimpleFactory interface and invokes the create_object() method to construct a new object, which it returns to the caller.

Note carefully the difference between NamingServiceWrapper::GetObject and NamingServiceWrapper::CreateObject. GetObject returns the named object already in existence; CreateObject uses the named factory object to create a new object for the caller.

Implementing Persistent, Self-activating CORBA Objects

The NamingServiceWrapper class assumes that the Naming Service is appropriately populated with CORBA object references and that the objects whose references are found there appear to be magically available at all times. In this section, we'll also show how to implement persistent CORBA objects that are activated transparently when clients use the references and how to make their references available.

Listing 7.5 shows an IDL interface that is a new variation on the banking example from Chapter 2. Some of the important differences from the simpler Chapter 2 example are as follows:

Listing 7.4 Creating CORBA objects with SimpleFactory.

```
Public Function CreateObject(pathName As String) As Object
    Dim nameComponent As CosNaming_NameComponent
    Dim compoundName As Variant
    Dim newObject As Object
    Dim anException As Variant
    Dim exceptType As ExceptionType
    Dim factory As DICosLifeCycle_SimpleFactory

    ' call BuildCompoundName to parse the pathname
    Set compoundName = BuildCompoundName(pathName)
    If IsNull(compoundName) Then
        Set CreateObject = Nothing
    Else
        ' get the named factory from the Naming Service
        ' (name context)
        Set factory = NameContext.resolve(nameArray, anException)
        If anException.EX_majorCode = NO_EXCEPTION Then
        ' invoke the factory to create the object
            Set CreateObject = factory.create_object()
        Else
            Set CreateObject = Nothing
        End If
    End If
End Function
```

- The `AcctMgr` interface was replaced with `AccountFactory`, which is derived from `SimpleFactory`.

- An `Initialize` method was added to `Account` since `SimpleFactory::create_object` doesn't have any parameters to establish initial state.

- The `AcctMgrFactory` interface was removed. The banking example from Chapter 2 used a very convenient feature that is specific to BEA Systems' ObjectBroker Desktop Connection product, which automatically maps parameterless operations called `create_object` into COM class factories. While this approach is extraordinarily convenient, it is product-specific,

Listing 7.5 Modified account interface and factory.

```
//IDL
module SimplifiedBank
{
  typedef float    Currency;

  interface Account {
    readonly  attribute  Currency      balance;
    readonly  attribute  string        name;
    readonly  attribute  long          number;

    void     Initialize      (in string   name,
                              in Currency  balance);

    Currency  Deposit    (in Currency  amount);
    Currency  Withdraw  (in Currency  amount);
  };

  interface AccountFactory : CosLifeCycle::SimpleFactory {

  };

};
```

and the resulting code is somewhat less portable. It also slightly obscures the difference between creating objects (in the CORBA sense) and finding existing objects.

In concept, the account factory object is a service that is always in existence, and there is only one account factory per bank. In the following example, we'll see how to make the account factory object available without requiring clients to create an active instance every time they want to use it.

The following section gets to the heart of one of the most significant differences between COM and CORBA life cycle and identity models. The discussion in Chapter 3 covers this topic from an architectural view; here, we'll see how this works in practice.

As described in Chapter 3, the activation state of a COM object is controlled by its clients. A client activates an object by creating a class instance and initializing it or by binding a moniker. That instance is active (i.e., existing in the address space of a running process) until the reference count goes to zero as clients release references. In contrast, CORBA object activation state is, in general, controlled by the ORB and the object servers. Clients have no idea whether the object they are about to invoke is active or, in fact, whether an appropriate server is running. By simply invoking an operation in the object reference, the client causes a chain of events that will (if necessary) start an appropriate server and activate the object. The object can decide to deactivate itself and release the resources it is using, regardless of whether clients are "holding" references to the object. The next time a client uses a reference, the object is automatically reactivated. The criteria by which an object decides to deactivate itself are the choice of the object implementer. In most cases, objects are designed to deactivate themselves when a certain time period passes with no invocations. The important point is that the decision is made locally by the object, and the programming techniques to put all of this into effect are used in the object implementation.

The Portable Object Adapter

The early versions of the CORBA specification defined an interface for object implementations called the *Basic Object Adapter* (BOA). Unfortunately, this interface was not sufficiently complete or precise to permit portable object server code. ORB vendors found it necessary to extend the BOA interface to make it useful, and their extensions were, as you might expect, divergent. As ORBs grew more popular, customer demand for portability increased. In 1996 and 1997, the OMG developed a new specification for object implementation interfaces, called the *Portable Object Adapter* (POA). This POA is a very complete, precise specification for server-side interfaces. It provides a rich programming model with many options for determining how objects behave and how they are activated. We used the POA interfaces in the following example because we wanted to use techniques that would be as broadly applicable as possible. We also wanted to use techniques that will be as long lived as possible. ORB vendors will all be providing POA support and will most likely deprecate the older BOA interfaces over time. The drawback associated with using the POA in our example is that it is a new interface, and implementations are only now becoming available. At the time of this writing, POA implementations are becoming available in the beta releases of ORB products. By the time of publication, we expect them to be generally available.

A complete discussion of the POA's features is beyond the scope of this book, and much of it would not be applicable to the main topic at hand. We will present some of the basic, most useful features here.

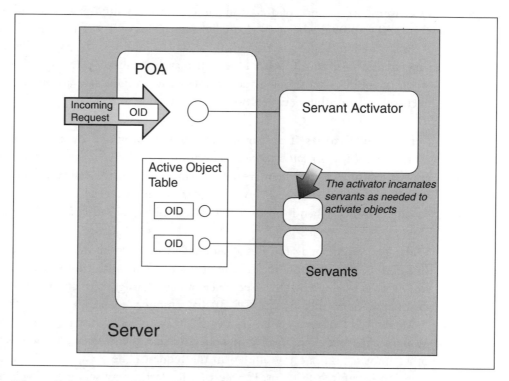

Figure 7.1 *Portable Object Adapter architecture.*

POAs are special objects that mediate between the ORB and the user-provided object implementations. Figure 7.1 illustrates the POA architecture and the important elements of the programming model. POAs act as controllers and containers of objects. When an object comes into existence, it does so in the context of a particular POA, and the name of that POA becomes part of the object's permanent identity.

The ORB supplies a root POA with a default configuration. Programmers can (and, in most cases, will) create new POAs and configure them with POA policies. Policies govern the behavior of a POA and determine the characteristics of the objects it controls.

Servants POAs manage *servants*. A servant is a programming object that supplies the implementation for a CORBA object at some point in time. This may sound confusing; we'll try to clarify. The CORBA object exists (albeit abstractly) whether it is active or not. When it is activated, some programming artifact (in most cases, an instance of a class in some object-oriented programming language) is created to provide the appropriate behavior. This object is a servant. If the object is deactivated and later reactivated, there will be a different servant. Over the lifetime of a long-lived CORBA object, it may be realized by a succession of many servants. In POA terminology, a servant is said to incarnate an object, which reflects this relationship between object and servant.

Servant Activators Transparent activation is provided by *servant managers*, or more specifically, *servant activators*. A servant activator is an object supplied by the application programmer that creates servants on demand. A servant activator is installed on a POA, and the POA will invoke a method called `incarnate` on the servant activator when it needs to activate an object to satisfy a client request.

Oids The servant activator uses a value called an *oid* to know which servant to activate and, potentially, how to find the object's state to initialize the servant. An oid is simply a byte string (in IDL, a sequence of octets) assigned to an object by the application (or, optionally, by the ORB) that uniquely identifies the ORB within its POA. An oid is assigned to an abstract CORBA object when references are created. When a client makes an invocation on a reference, the POA name and oid (as well as other information) are transmitted in the request. The server ORB uses the POA name to locate the POA or, if necessary, to start a new server that will supply the POA. When the request is forwarded to the POA itself, the POA uses the oid to look for an active servant. If there is no active servant, the POA will invoke `incarnate` on the servant activator, if one was supplied. The oid is passed as a parameter to `incarnate`. Since the application programmer supplies the implementation of the servant activator, the activator can use the oid however it wants to create and initialize the servant. In most cases, the oid identifies some stored state, like a file name or a primary key in a database. The activator will typically create an empty servant, retrieve the state, load it into the servant, and return the servant to the POA. The POA then invokes the requested method on the servant to satisfy the client and keeps the servant in its active object table until it is deactivated.

With that brief discussion as background, consider Listing 7.6. The IDL compiler supplied with your ORB will generate servant base classes for each IDL interface you compile. In Java, servant base classes have names formed by concatenating the string `POA_` and the interface name, as in `POA_Account` and `POA_AcountFactory`. The concrete implementation classes are derived from these generated abstract base classes. In the example, the classes `AccountImpl` and `AccountFactoryImpl` are the implementations of `Account` and `AccountFactory`, respectively.

Listing 7.6 Persistent CORBA object implementation using the POA.

```
import org.omg.PortableServer.*;
import SimplifiedBank.*;

package BankServerImpl;

interface SimplePersistentObject {
    public boolean Load();
    public void Store();
}

class AccountImpl extends POA_Account implements
SimplePersistentObject {

    // private state of the account

    private int _number;
    private String _name;
    private float _balance;

    // constructor and methods used by implementation

    protected AccountImpl(int number) {
        _number = number;
        _name = "";
        _balance = 0.0;
    }

    // implementation of the SimplePersistentObject interface -
    // see the accompanying text for descriptions of Load and Store

    public void Store() { }
    public boolean Load() { }

    // implementations of IDL attributes and operations

    public float balance() {
        return _balance;
```

(continues)

Listing 7.6 Persistent CORBA object implementation using the POA. (*Continued*)

```
    }

    public String name() {
        return _name;
    }

    public int number() {
        return _number;
    }

    public Initialize(String name, float balance) {
        _name = name;
        _balance = balance;
    }

    public float Deposit(float amount) {
        balance = balance + amount;
    }

    public float Withdraw(float amount) {
        balance = balance - amount;
    }
}

class AccountFactoryImpl extends POA_AccountFactory implements
SimplePersistentObject {

    private int _nextAccoutNumber;

    public AccountFactoryImpl () {
        _nextAccountNumber = 1;
    }

    public boolean Load() { }
    public void Store() { }

    public CORBA.Object create_object() {
```

Listing 7.6 Persistent CORBA object implementation using the POA. (*Continued*)

```
        byte[] accountOID = OIDUtils.IntToBytes(_nextAccountNumber++);
        String accountInterfaceID = AccountHelper.id();
        return BankServer::BankPOA().create_reference_with_id(
            accountOID, AccountInterfaceID);
    }
}

class BankActivator extends POA_ServantActivator {

    // incarnate is invoked by the POA to supply a
    // servant for the object identified by oid on demand

    public Servant incarnate(byte[] oid, POA poa) {
        int acctNum = OIDUtils.BytesToInt(oid);

        // the oid value 0 is reserved for the factory

        if (acctNum == 0) {
        AccountFactoryImpl acctFactory = new AccountFactoryImpl ();
            if (acctFactory.Load()) {
                return acctFactory;
            }
            else {
            throw new org.omg.CORBA.OBJECT_NOT_EXIST;
            }
        }
        else
        {
            AccountImpl acct = new AccountImpl(acctNum);
            if (acct.Load()) {
                return acct;
            }
            else {
                acct.Initialize("", 0.0);
                return acct;
            }
        }
```

(*continues*)

Listing 7.6 Persistent CORBA object implementation using the POA. (*Continued*)

```
    }

    public void etherealize ( byte[] oid,

        // etherealize is invoked by the POA when objects
        // are deactivated

        POA adapter,
        Servant srvnt,
        boolean cleanup_in_progress,
        boolean remaining_activations)
    {
        if(srvnt instanceOf SimplePersistentObject) {
            SimplePersistentObject pobj =
            (SimplePersistentObject)srvnt;
            pobj.store();
        }
    }
}


class BankServer {

    private POA _bankPOA;

    public static void InitializeServer(boolean firstTime) {

        // get the ORB and root POA

        CORBA.ORB orb = CORBA.ORB.init();
        POA rootPOA = POAHelper.narrow(
            orb.get_initial_references("RootPOA"));

        // create the policies to configure a POA for
        // persistent objects

        CORBA.Policy policies[] = new CORBA.Policy[4];
```

Listing 7.6 Persistent CORBA object implementation using the POA. (*Continued*)

```
policies[0] = RootPOA.create_lifespan_policy(
    LifeSpanPolicyValue.PERSISTENT);
policies[1] = RootPOA.create_id_assignment_policy(
    IdAssignmentPolicyValue.USER_ID);
policies[2] = RootPOA.create_request_processing_policy(
    RequestProcessingPolicyValue.USE_SERVANT_MANAGER);
policies[3] = RootPOA.create_servant_retention_policy(
    ServantRetentionPolicyValue.RETAIN);

// create the POA

_bankPOA = pootPOA.create_POA("BankPOA", null, policies);

// create the servant activator and install it on the POA

_bankPOA.set_servant_manager(new BankActivator);

if (firstTime) {
    AcountFactoryImpl accountFactory = newAccountFactory();
    AccountFactory.Store();
}

// create a reference for the factory and bind it
// in the Naming Service

byte factoryOID[] = OIDUtils.IntToBytes(0);
String factoryInterfaceID = AccountFactoryHelper.id();
CORBA.Object factoryRef = create_reference_with_id(
    factoryOID, factoryInterfaceID);

NamingContext namingService = NamingContextHelper.narrow(
    orb.resolve_initial_references("NameService"));

NameComponent factoryName[] = new NameComponent[1];
factoryName[0] = new NameComponent("AccountFactory", "");

namingService.rebind(factoryName, factoryRef);
```

(continues)

Listing 7.6 Persistent CORBA object implementation using the POA. (*Continued*)

```
        // convert the factory's reference into a string and
        // store it in a file

        String factoryIORString = orb.object_to_string(factoryRef);
        PrintStream ps = new PrintStream(
            new FileOutputStream("..\\factoryIOR"));
        ps.print(factoryIORString);
        ps.close();


        // turn on the POA

        _bankPOA.the_POAManager().activate();

    }

    public static void ShutdownServer() {
        _bankPOA.the_POAManager.deactivate( true, true );
    }

    public static POA BankPOA() {
        return _bankPOA;
    }
}
```

One of the major purposes of this example is to illustrate how ORBs manage persistence and activation. We've simplified the example by not coding the operations that actually perform reads and writes or queries and updates. These details tend to be voluminous, tedious, and product-specific, and they wouldn't really make the example any clearer. Instead, we hide the details behind the interface SimplePersistentObject, and let you fill in the details with your imagination. SimplePersistentObject is not a standard interface of any kind; it is an ad hoc interface contrived for this example. There are several other (no doubt, superior) approaches possible.

Here are the assumptions behind the SimplePersistentObject interface:

- The objects being loaded or stored encapsulate a unique identity that can be mapped to storage, for example, a file name or a database key.

- You load an object by creating an instance of the class that has been initialized only with the identifier and calling `Load`. All of the information needed to find the state is contained in the object before `Load` is invoked.

- `Load` returns true if the load was successful, false otherwise. If `Load` fails, the state encapsulated in the object before `Load` was invoked is unchanged.

- `Store` uses the same encapsulated identity information to store the state of the object.

The implementation of `Account` (`AccountImpl`) is relatively simple. It contains private members to hold values for the attributes defined in the IDL interface; it contains a constructor that initializes only the account number member; it contains implementations of `Load` and `Store` that use the account number as the storage key; and it contains extremely simplified implementations of the attributes and operations identified in the IDL Account interface.

The implementation of `AccountFactory` has a simple job: it allocates numbers to new accounts and creates object references for Accounts. The `AccountFactory` is a singleton object—only one instance exists (per bank server). Its implementations of `Load` and `Store` only have to worry about one instance, so there is no need to expose the storage identity. We're using the same POA for both the accounts and the account factory, so we need to reserve an oid for the factory object. It is a bit of a hack, but "account number" zero will be used to denote the factory, not an account instance.

The implementation of `create_object` allocates a new account number and creates a reference for the account object. This is the first point in the example where oids (in the POA sense) are exposed, and some explanation is warranted. An oid is a sequence of octets (a byte array in Java) that the server and the POA use together to identify a particular object. The association between an oid and the object it denotes surfaces in two places: (1) when a reference is created and (2) when a request made with the reference is received by the POA in the server. Note that a reference can be created without having a corresponding servant and without activating the object, as is the case in `create_object` on the account factory.

The `BankActivator` class is responsible for mapping oids onto servants as requests arrive. The POA invokes the `incarnate` method on the activator when a request arrives for an account object (or the account factory itself) that is not active at the time. `incarnate` constructs an instance of `AccountImpl` (the concrete servant class) and tries to load its state. If `Load` fails, we make the assumption that this is the first activation of the account, and no state has been stored yet. Presumably, the client has only recently called `AccountFactory::create_object()` to obtain the reference and is about to initialize it.

As discussed previously, the oid whose corresponding integer value is zero is reserved for the account factory. The activator checks for this and constructs an `AccountFactoryImpl` if necessary. The server initialization method ensures that there is a stored factory state, so `Load` should not fail for the factory. To illustrate an important behavior of CORBA activation, the activator throws a CORBA system exception, `OBJECT_NOT_EXIST`.

The `BankActivator` class also has an operation called `etherealize` (the complement of `incarnate`). During shutdown, the POA can be made to `etherealize` all of the currently active servants. The `etherealize` operation is also invoked when an object is explicitly deactivated. Our implementation of `etherealize` invokes `Store` on the servant. If there were explicitly releaseable resources, this is where we would release them.

The `BankServer` class represents the whole server; it has only static methods and members. The `ServerInitialize` method is important to understand. Its first two statements show how to obtain the root POA. The root POA is used to create the application's POA, which is configured to meet its requirements. `ServerInitialize` constructs a sequence of policy objects that are passed to `create_POA`. A complete discussion of POA policies and potential behaviors is far beyond the scope of this discussion. We will only briefly discuss here the policies that are used in the example:

- The `PERSISTENT` policy value instructs the POA to create references in such a way as to support the requirements of persistence. The precise details are product-specific, but this generally means that the references created by the POA will contain information that will allow the ORB to find and execute an appropriate server process if necessary.

- The `USER_ID` policy value indicates to the POA that the application will be supplying oid values when references are created. The POA can, alternatively, supply its own machine-generated oids. In most cases, implementations of persistent objects will use application-supplied oids.

- The `USE_SERVANT_MANAGER` policy value instructs the POA to use an application-supplied servant manager to locate or activate objects when necessary. POAs support other mechanisms for activation on demand that we won't discuss here. We should point out that servant activator is a subtype of servant manager. There are other variations of servant manager.

- The `RETAIN` policy value instructs the POA to maintain a table that maps active oids to servants. When this policy is in force, the POA "remembers" servants that are returned when `incarnate` is invoked on the servant activator until they are explicitly deactivated.

After creating and configuring the POA, `InitializeServer` installs an instance of `BankActivator` on the new POA. The rest of the code in `InitializeServer` (with the exception of the last statement) serves to make the account factory available to clients. The server assumes that the `firstTime` parameter will be true if this is the first time the bank server is being run and sets the next available account number to 1, assuming that there are no existing accounts. The server then creates a reference for the factory object and publishes it in the Naming Service. It also converts the reference into an IOR string and writes it to a file. Finally, the POA is activated, allowing it to begin serving requests.

Consider the chain of events that occurs when a client uses the factory to create an object and makes a request on the new object:

1. The client obtains the reference for the factory from the Naming Service. The bank server process itself may not be running at the time, or if it is, the factory may not be active.

2. The client invokes `create_object` on the factory reference. The ORB that receives the request will, if necessary, start the server. In any case, it responds to the client by telling the client ORB the address of the server, whether it had to create it or not.

3. The client ORB resends the request to the server. If the factory isn't active, the POA invokes `incarnate` in the `BankActivator`. The oid in the factory's object reference (and thus the request) will have been zero, so the oid passed to `incarnate` is zero. The activator will create an instance of `AccountFactoryImpl` and then load the last stored state. If there is no stored state, `incarnate` throws a CORBA `OBJECT_NOT_EXIST` system exception. This illustrates an important feature of CORBA object identity and life cycle models. The server application, through the agency of the servant activator, assumes responsibility for determining whether the abstract object associated with a given oid actually exists. If `incarnate` returns a servant, the associated abstract object inherently exists. If `incar-`

nate cannot or does not return a servant, then either the object doesn't exist or some other error has occurred that prevents (hopefully, only temporarily) the object from being activated.

4. Using the servant returned by incarnate, the POA invokes the create_object methods on the account factory. create_object allocates a new account number (which is turned into an oid) and creates an object reference. Note that the existence of the reference implies the existence of the abstract object. The fact that no servant exists at this time is irrelevant. The new reference is returned to the client.

5. The client invokes Initialize on the account object reference it got from the factory. When the request arrives at the server, the POA notes that the oid is not active and invokes incarnate with the oid from the reference/request. incarnate creates a new instance of AccountImpl, initializing the account number with the value converted from the oid. It then attempts to load state associated with that account number. If no state has been previously stored, the activator assumes that the account must be new and initializes it to default values.

6. Using the servant returned by incarnate, the POA invokes the Initialize method. The POA retains the servant so that subsequent invocations of the account object will not cause the activator to be invoked, unless the account is explicitly deactivated.

7. Eventually the server is shut down, at which time the POA invokes *etherealize* on the servant activator for each active object. *etherealize* stores the state of each object.

This example is hilariously unrealistic. Account information in real banking systems is (hopefully) secure and reliable, implemented with robust transactional systems, and subject to a large number of validation checks. It's only an example to illustrate object creation techniques, for crying out loud. Suspend your disbelief.

Using Persistent Objects from COM Clients

Why is this important for COM/CORBA interworking? The kind of persistent behavior exhibited by this example is typical of many CORBA applications. COM/Visual Basic programmers are accustomed to a certain view of object identity and life cycle and may design applications that use CORBA objects based on inaccurate assumptions—quite understandably. By mapping CORBA factories into COM class factories (and close imitations thereof), bridge products are potentially masking important subtleties. By seeing a concrete example of CORBA factories and life-cycle behaviors, you will hopefully be aware of the differences between creating an instance of a COM class and creating a CORBA object, even though the syntax for both operations may be identical.

Consider the earlier examples of Visual Basic clients that found CORBA objects in the Naming Service and by using IOR strings. It should now be clear why and how those examples work. The key lies in understanding the role of object references in CORBA and how they relate to their implementations.

Finding and Creating COM Objects from CORBA Clients

The COM/CORBA Interworking Specification doesn't impose any concrete requirements on bridges for making COM objects and factories available to CORBA clients in some standard way. It does suggest that COM class factories could be mapped to the `SimpleFactory` interface, but there is no standard way of associating a class factory with a CORBA view. Moreover, there is no special interface like the CORBA factory that exposes COM objects to CORBA.

So what is a poor programmer to do? You may choose to rely on the product-specific mechanisms supplied with your bridge. In many interworking products, there are easy-to-use, convenient ways to tell the bridge to automatically map certain COM class factories into CORBA factories. This mapping is often expressed through an administrative tool of some kind, often with graphical interfaces.

In the interests of portability and clarity, we'll present a simple, portable mechanism here that exposes COM objects and class factories to CORBA clients and then discuss its usage. One straightforward way to publish a particular COM object for CORBA clients is through the Naming Service. Listing 7.7 shows the code for an additional method on the `NameServiceWrapper` called `PublishObject`. `PublishObject` binds a CORBA view of the Automation object in the Naming Service.

Exposing COM Factories to CORBA Clients

COM class factories can be exported easily into CORBA. One approach is to map the `IClassFactory` interface into CORBA IDL and put views of class factories in the Naming Service. A drawback to this approach is that a large number of class factory views might need to be created and published in the Naming Service.

Listing 7.7 Exporting COM objects in the Naming Service.

```
Public Function PublishObject(pathName As String, obj As Object)
As Boolean

    Dim nameComponent As CosNaming_NameComponent
    Dim compoundName As Variant
    Dim anException As Variant
    Dim exceptType As ExceptionType

    ' call BuildCompoundName to parse the pathname
    Set compoundName = BuildCompoundName(pathName)
    If IsNull(compoundName) Then
        PublishObject = False
    Else
        ' bind the object to the name
        ' uses rebind to overwrite existing binding
        Call NameContext.rebind(nameArray, obj, anException)
        If anException.EX_majorCode = NO_EXCEPTION Then
            Set PublishObject = True
        Else
            Set PublishObject = False
        End If
    End If
End Function
```

In addition, only classes whose factories were published could be created by CORBA clients. We can avoid these problems by creating a generalized factory and mapping it into a single CORBA view. Listing 7.8 shows the Visual Basic code for this factory. The `CreateCOMObject` method takes a string parameter containing the ProgID of the class to be constructed. It simply delegates the creation to the Visual Basic function `CreateObject`. You could construct a similar class in C++ that wrapped the `CoCreateInstance` function, taking a class ID instead of a ProgID. In most cases, ProgIDs are easier to use, and the Visual Basic example is much simpler that a C++ example would be.

The following code fragment creates the `COMFactory` object and places it in the Naming Service:

Listing 7.8 Exported COM factory.

```
Public Function CreateCOMObject(ProgID As String) As Object
    Dim obj As Object
    Set CreateCOMObject = CreateObject(progID)
End Function
```

```
Dim CorbaNaming As CORBANamingWrapper
Set CorbaNaming =
 CreateObject("Chapter7Example1.NamingServiceWrapper")
Dim exportedFactory as COMFactory
Set exportedFactory =
 CreateObject("COM_CORBA.COMFactory")
Call CorbaNaming.PublishObject("COM factory",
 exportedFactory)
```

To complete the picture, we'll present a fragment of a CORBA client in Java that finds the COM factory and uses it to create a COM object. The Automation COMFactory interface is mapped by the interworking product into the following CORBA IDL:

```
//IDL
typedef unsigned long HRESULT;

exception COM_ERROR
{
     HRESULT Value;
};
module COM_CORBA
{
     interface COMFactory
     {
          Object CreateCOMObject(inout string progID)
               raises(COM_ERROR);
     };
};
```

The Java/CORBA client finds the COM factory in the Naming Service and invokes it:

```
NamingContext namingService =
    NamingContextHelper.narrow(
    orb.resolve_initial_references("NameService"));

NameComponent factoryName[] = new NameComponent[1];
factoryName[0] = new NameComponent("COM Factory", "");
try {
    COM_CORBA.COMFactory factory =
                    namingService.resolve(factoryName);
}
catch (CORBA.UserException e) {
    // handle the exception
}
Excel.WorksheetFunction func =
    factory.CreateObject("Excel.WorksheetFunction");
    Float dist = func.Poisson(numEvents, mean, false);
    LifeCycleObject lcobj =
    LifeCycleObjectHelper.narrow(func);
    lcobj.remove();
```

Life Cycle of CORBA Views

All CORBA views of COM and Automation objects support the `CosLifeCycle::LifeCycleObject` interface and implement the `Remove` operation (at a minimum). `Remove` is a parameterless operation that destroys the target object. As described in Chapter 3, the destruction of a persistent CORBA object is a deliberate act, corresponding to the destruction of the conceptual real-world object that the CORBA object represents. This is quite different than the destruction of a COM instance that occurs when all of the clients release their references and the reference count goes to zero. With persistent CORBA objects, destruction generally implies the removal of the state that the object encapsulates.

This model doesn't fit well when the CORBA object in question is a view of a COM target object. The CORBA view holds a reference for the COM object, so the reference count can never go to zero as long as the view exists. CORBA views support the `LifeCycleObject::remove` operation so CORBA clients can destroy the view and release the reference. It is important to understand the following points:

- Invoking `Remove` on a CORBA view does not destroy the target COM object in any permanent sense, as a CORBA programmer might (naturally) assume. It only releases the reference held by the view.

- CORBA clients of COM objects must be sure to invoke Remove, but only when it is appropriate, that is, when the view is no longer needed by the client that created it or any other clients that may have been passed references to it. This can be problematic. If the client that created the view passes a reference to the view to other CORBA programs, the applications must agree on some convention for determining when the view can be destroyed. At present, there is no standard way of detecting the existence of extant references in a CORBA system. When there is a need to do this, application programmers have generally developed their own conventions, tailored to the specific application.

The last two lines of the previous example illustrate how a CORBA client destroys the view in order to release to reference on the target COM object:

```
LifeCycleObject lcobj =
                LifeCycleObjectHelper.narrow(func);
lcobj.remove();
```

In this case, knowing when to invoke Remove is simple—the client created the view, used it without passing a reference to any other program or thread, and is finished with it.

Interworking products have the option of implementing views in a way that avoids this problem altogether. An interworking implementation may, at the discretion of the designers, construct views that are persistent, that are activated on demand (similar to the example in Listing 7.6), and that are capable of being deactivated or deactivating themselves. If the bridge supplies this feature, it must behave as follows:

- The view encapsulates a moniker for the target COM object. The moniker becomes part of the persistent state of the view object.

- When the view is activated, it binds the moniker, which in turn activates the target COM object.

- When the view is deactivated, it releases the reference count on the target.

This model implements a more natural correspondence between CORBA views and their COM objects. The CORBA client developer doesn't need to be as concerned with destroying the view in order to release the reference. If the view object isn't in use, it will deactivate itself, releasing the reference and allowing the resources used by the COM object to be released. The references to the view remain meaningful and useful, however, since the view will be automatically reactivated whenever a client makes a request on the view.

Know Your Bridge

When using an interworking product, it is important to know whether its CORBA views implement the moniker encapsulation feature and whether it is under your control, so you will know what the consequences of destroying (or not destroying) a view object are.

The drawback to this feature is that, like many of the other features, it is optional. Your bridge product may or may not support it. It is such a powerful feature that you should consider using if it is available, but you should understand that your application code might not be portable to other bridge products.

Summary

The transparencies provided by the bridge are powerful and useful, but they can be deceptive for naïve users. By having a clear understanding of some important aspects of the behavior of views, particularly as they pertain to the life cycle of the objects they represent, you will make your applications more robust and easier to build.

As pointed out repeatedly in this chapter, many useful bridge features are, unfortunately, optional. Whether to use them or not is a difficult decision to make. They can reduce the effort required to build your application significantly, but they introduce the risk of nonportable code and increase your dependence on a specific product. In this chapter, we have tried to focus on portable techniques that should work for any compliant bridge product and to supply you with a few useful tools to build your applications.

8 *Exceptions*

Exception handling is arguably the most complicated part of mapping between the CORBA and COM object systems. Contributing to this complexity are the fundamental differences between these exception models and the mapping of additional information from the CORBA model to COM. Another contributing factor is that COM and Automation support several different error-handling mechanisms and error objects. This requires that CORBA exceptions be mapped in many different ways, depending on the mechanism being used, but to still appear as natural as possible to the COM and Automation programmer. To understand the details of these mappings, we must first understand native exception-handling mechanisms in CORBA, Automation, and COM.

Interworking Exception Mapping

Client/server distribution introduced a whole new array of error and failure conditions into an application, ranging from communication failures and application errors in programming the communication mechanism to errors in the communication system itself. A robust error-reporting mechanism is essential to debugging and troubleshooting these applications. In addition to these errors, application servers need a way to indicate an error in the semantics of the client request and pass meaningful information back to the client application so it can inform the user or perform some meaningful recovery.

Overview of CORBA Exception Handling

CORBA was designed as a distributed communications mechanism for client/server applications, and as such it took these failure and error scenarios into account. CORBA has a rich error-reporting capability for both communication and system errors as well as for application-specific errors. All CORBA operations inherently have exception information passed as part of the request/reply protocol. Every operation has three possible outcomes, which are indicated by the `Major-Code` portion of the CORBA exception:

- No Exception
- System Exception
- User Exception

CORBA System Exceptions

A system exception indicates a communications failure, an error in programming the CORBA application, or an error in the CORBA system or operating system itself. Errors of this type can occur at the client machine, at the server machine, or somewhere in between. To distinguish between these different scenarios, CORBA system exceptions have an additional field indicating the `CompletionStatus`, which will contain one of the following values:

`COMPLETION_NO.` The request did not make it to the target system, indicating a failure at the client system or a communication failure.

`COMPLETION_YES.` The request made it to the target system before failing, indicating a failure at the server system.

`COMPLETION_MAYBE.` It could not be determined whether or not the request reached the target system before the failure occurred.

The CORBA system exception also contains a field called the `MinorCode`. This field allows CORBA to provide additional information about an error within the broader category of the standard system exceptions.

CORBA User Exceptions

A user exception indicates that the client request was successfully delivered to the server application; however, something about the client request caused the server to reject it. A simple example of this might be a bank account. If the client tried to withdraw more money than was available, the server might reject the request with a user exception of `InsufficientFunds`. Taking the example one step further, it might be useful to inform the user of the maximum amount available for withdrawal. The server would still reject the request with the `Insufficient-`

Funds exception, but as part of the exception it would also pass data indicating the maximum available.

CORBA allows for the definition of application-specific or user exceptions as part of the IDL description of interfaces. This is the biggest difference between CORBA and the COM exception model, which does not provide for extensible application-specific exception capabilities. CORBA user exceptions can be defined to include data specific to the exception. The data can be any possible CORBA data type, including complex constructed types such as sequences and structures, thus making possible complete and robust application exception handling.

Although an application could be designed to pass exceptions and data explicitly as parameters of an operation's signature, there are certain advantages to the CORBA model. First, it provides a standard mechanism for reporting errors that is consistent across all operations. Second, the CORBA system can automatically map the exceptions into standard exception-handling mechanisms, such as C++ try-catch blocks, or in the case of a COM/CORBA interworking bridge into native COM mechanisms. Finally, by declaring the exceptions as part of the interface definition in the IDL file, the client application is able to see, and thus provide code to handle, all of the possible exceptions for every operation. Since the exceptions are defined in IDL, the CORBA system will apply type checking to the exception mechanism. A server will be required to include the correct data as defined for the exception and will not be permitted to raise an exception that has not been defined in the IDL. Thus, a client application knows a priori all of the possible exceptions for each operation and is guaranteed that it will be given the data it expects, not notification of exceptions it does not expect.

Overview of Automation Exception Handling

Automation was designed to make it easy for high-level environments, like Visual Basic, to interact easily with a large variety of different objects and to support some simple, generic error-reporting mechanism. We are all too familiar with those error message boxes displayed by simple-minded Windows programs that think "OK" is an acceptable answer to an error condition. Unfortunately, this type of error handling has been the mind-set of many Windows programmers. Fortunately, this thinking is now becoming unacceptable for enterprise client/server applications.

Automation methods are invoked using `IDispatch::Invoke`, which returns a 32-bit HRESULT and can accept an optional EXCEPINFO structure. The HRESULT contains several different fields, including the following:

```
SEVERITY - bit 31
FACILITY - bits 16–30
CODE - bits 0–15
```

A value of 0 for the severity bit indicates success; a value of 1 (high bit set or negative-signed number) indicates that an error has occurred. If both the SEVERITY bit is set to failure and the FACILITY is set to FACILITY_DISPATCH, Visual Basic executes a built-in error-handling routine. The Visual Basic error handler uses the EXCEPINFO object to get additional information about the error, including the following:

SCODE. The HRESULT returned by the invocation

bstrSource. A text description of the ProgID of the object

bstrDescription. A text description of the error. This string is displayed in a message box by the default Visual Basic error handler

If an object returns an HRESULT of DISP_E_EXCEPTION, the object is indicating that an error has occurred and that it has filled in the EXCEPTINFO structure. This condition also triggers the built-in Visual Basic error handler and is utilized by interworking bridge Automation View objects.

With the advent of Dual interfaces, an additional exception mechanism has been introduced to the Automation object, the use of the OLE Error Object rather than the EXCEPINFO structure. This is the same mechanism that is used for COM objects, as described in the next section. There are two major differences between the EXCEPINFO structure and the OLE Error Object. The EXCEPINFO structure is present on both Win16 and Win32 platforms and is a per-process structure. The OLE Error Object is present on only Win32 platforms and is a per-thread object.

Overview of COM Exception Handling

Exception handling in COM is similar in many ways to Automation. All COM methods return an HRESULT that has the same format as described earlier. COM objects can return additional error information through the use of an OLE Error Object, a per-thread version of the EXCEPINFO structure containing the following information:

bstrSource. A text description of the interface of the object

bstrDescription. A text description of the error

GUID. The COM IID of the interface

In general, automation controllers do not make the HRESULT visible to programmers, so the HRESULT information is also included in the SCODE field of the EXCEPINFO structure. COM programmers can always get the HRESULT, so the information is not included in the error object. COM objects support the OLE Error Object by implementing the ISupportErrorInfo interface, which is used to get the error object from the COM object after an error has occurred.

Interworking Exception Mapping Basics

Now that you understand the basics of the different exception mechanisms, you can understand the difficulties involved in developing a simple mapping. Because COM does not support the same degree of exception handling as CORBA, the interworking architecture was forced to decide between two unsavory solutions. Either lose valuable exception data that cannot be mapped to a native COM mechanism or provide that information in a way that is not native (and perhaps natural) to the COM and Automation programmer. In typical consensus fashion, the architecture decided to provided both solutions and let the COM programmers pick their own poison. The philosophy of the interworking exception mapping can be summed up as this: Provide as much information as is possible using the native COM and Automation mechanisms and do not require a programmer to understand that CORBA is supplying more information. Also provide an optional mechanism for the knowledgeable programmer to get at the additional information that CORBA includes.

For the case of Automation, exception information is optional for the programmer. The interworking bridge's implementation of the Automation View objects provides exception information in the EXCEPINFO structure or the OLE Error Object depending on what type of invocation was made. Programmers can get all of the CORBA exception information by providing an exception object as part of the method signature. We will cover the details of this in the next section.

For COM, exception information is also optional for the programmer. The COM view objects implement the ISupportErrorInfo interface and can provide system exception information in the OLE Error Object. User exception information is returned in an optional parameter to the method. The details of this will be covered later in the chapter.

For both Automation and COM, standard CORBA system exceptions are mapped to an HRESULT that is returned directly or as part of the EXCEPINFO structure. Table 8.1 lists the mapping of CORBA system exceptions to HRE-

SULTS. CORBA exceptions are interface-specific and are thus mapped to the COM facility FACILITY_ITF, 0x40000. For each system exception, there are three possible HRESULT values, depending on the CORBA completion status: NO = 0, YES = 1, or MAYBE = 2. These control the value of bits 12 and 13 of the SCODE and, combined with the facility, result in SCODE values of 0x40xxx for NO, 0x41xxx for YES, and 0x42xxx for MAYBE. The final three hex digits (bits 0-11) are the actual exceptions.

Table 8.1 CORBA Exceptions to HRESULT Values

CORBA Standard Exception	HRESULT Constant	HRESULT Value
UNKNOWN	ITF_E_UNKNOWN_NO	0x40200
	ITF_E_UNKNOWN_YES	0x41200
	ITF_E_UNKNOWN_MAYBE	0x42200
BAD_PARAM	ITF_E_BAD_PARAM_NO	0x40201
	ITF_E_BAD_PARAM_YES	0x41201
	ITF_E_BAD_PARAM_MAYBE	0x42201
NO_MEMORY	ITF_E_NO_MEMORY_NO	0x40202
	ITF_E_NO_MEMORY_YES	0x41202
	ITF_E_NO_MEMORY_MAYBE	0x42202
IMP_LIMIT	ITF_E_IMP_LIMIT_NO	0x40203
	ITF_E_IMP_LIMIT_YES	0x41203
	ITF_E_IMP_LIMIT_MAYBE	0x42203
COMM_FAILURE	ITF_E_COMM_FAILURE_NO	0x40204
	ITF_E_COMM_FAILURE_YES	0x41204
	ITF_E_COMM_FAILURE_MAYBE	0x42204
INV_OBJREF	ITF_E_INV_OBJREF_NO	0x40205
	ITF_E_INV_OBJREF_YES	0x41205
	ITF_E_INV_OBJREF_MAYBE	0x42205
NO_PERMISSION	ITF_E_NO_PERMISSION_NO	0x40206
	ITF_E_NO_PERMISSION_YES	0x41206
	ITF_E_NO_PERMISSION_MAYBE	0x42206
INTERNAL	ITF_E_INTERNAL_NO	0x40207
	ITF_E_INTERNAL_YES	0x41207
	ITF_E_INTERNAL_MAYBE	0x42207

Table 8.1 CORBA Exceptions to HRESULT Values (*Continued*)

CORBA STANDARD EXCEPTION	HRESULT CONSTANT	HRESULT VALUE
MARSHAL	ITF_E_MARSHAL_NO	0x40208
	ITF_E_MARSHAL_YES	0x41208
	ITF_E_MARSHAL_MAYBE	0x42208
INITIALIZE	ITF_E_INITIALIZE_NO	0x40209
	ITF_E_INITIALIZE_YES	0x41209
	ITF_E_INITIALIZE_MAYBE	0x42209
NO_IMPLEMENT	ITF_E_NO_IMPLEMENT_NO	0x4020A
	ITF_E_NO_IMPLEMENT_YES	0x4120A
	ITF_E_NO_IMPLEMENT_MAYBE	0x4220A
BAD_TYPECODE	ITF_E_BAD_TYPECODE_NO	0x4020B
	ITF_E_BAD_TYPECODE_YES	0x4120B
	ITF_E_BAD_TYPECODE_MAYBE	0x4220B
BAD_OPERATION	ITF_E_BAD_OPERATION_NO	0x4020C
	ITF_E_BAD_OPERATION_YES	0x4120C
	ITF_E_BAD_OPERATION_MAYBE	0x4220C
NO_RESOURCES	ITF_E_NO_RESOURCES_NO	0x4020D
	ITF_E_NO_RESOURCES_YES	0x4120D
	ITF_E_NO_RESOURCES_MAYBE	0x4220D
NO_RESPONSE	ITF_E_NO_RESPONSE_NO	0x4020E
	ITF_E_NO_RESPONSE_YES	0x4120E
	ITF_E_NO_RESPONSE_MAYBE	0x4220E
PERSIST_STORE	ITF_E_PERSIST_STORE_NO	0x4020F
	ITF_E_PERSIST_STORE_YES	0x4120F
	ITF_E_PERSIST_STORE_MAYBE	0x4220F
BAD_INV_ORDER	ITF_E_BAD_INV_ORDER_NO	0x40210
	ITF_E_BAD_INV_ORDER_YES	0x41210
	ITF_E_BAD_INV_ORDER_MAYBE	0x42210
TRANSIENT	ITF_E_TRANSIENT_NO`	0x40211
	ITF_E_TRANSIENT_NYES	0x41211
	ITF_E_TRANSIENT_NMAYBE	0x42211
FREE_MEM	ITF_E_FREE_MEM_NO	0x40212

(*continues*)

Table 8.1 CORBA Exceptions to HRESULT Values (*Continued*)

CORBA STANDARD EXCEPTION	HRESULT CONSTANT	HRESULT VALUE
FREE_MEM	ITF_E_FREE_MEM_YES	0x41212
	ITF_E_FREE_MEM_MAYBE	0x42212
INV_IDENT	ITF_E_INV_IDENT_NO	0x40213
	ITF_E_INV_IDENT_YES	0x41213
	ITF_E_INV_IDENT_MAYBE	0x42213
INV_FLAG	ITF_E_INV_FLAG_NO	0x40214
	ITF_E_INV_FLAG_YES	0x41214
	ITF_E_INV_FLAG_MAYBE	0x42214
INTF_REPOS	ITF_E_INTF_REPOS	0x40215
	ITF_E_INTF_REPYES	0x41215
	ITF_E_INTF_REPMAYBE	0x42215
CONTEXT	ITF_E_CONTEXT_NO	0x40216
	ITF_E_CONTEXT_YES	0x41216
	ITF_E_CONTEXT_MAYBE	0x42216
OBJ_ADAPTER	ITF_E_OBJ_ADAPTER_NO	0x40217
	ITF_E_OBJ_ADAPTER_YES	0x41217
	ITF_E_OBJ_ADAPTER_MAYBE	0x42217
DATA_CONVERSION	ITF_E_DATA_CONVERSION_NO	0x40218
	ITF_E_DATA_CONVERSION_YES	0x41218
	ITF_E_DATA_CONVERSION_MAYBE	0x42218
OBJ_NOT_EXIST	ITF_E_OBJ_NOT_EXIST	0x40219
	ITF_E_OBJ_NOT_EXIYES	0x41219
	ITF_E_OBJ_NOT_EXIMAYBE	0x42219
TRANSACTION _REQUIRED	ITF_E_TRANSACTION_REQUIRED_NO	0x40220
	ITF_E_TRANSACTION_REQUIRED_YES	0x41220
	ITF_E_TRANSACTION_REQUIRED_MAYBE	0x42220
TRANSACTION _ROLLEDBACK	ITF_E_TRANSACTION_ROLLEDBACK_NO	0x40221
	ITF_E_TRANSACTION_ROLLEDBACK_YES	0x41221
	ITF_E_TRANSACTION_ROLLEDBACK_MAYBE	0x42221
INVALID _TRANSACTION	ITF_E_INVALID_TRANSACTION_NO	0x40222
	ITF_E_INVALID_TRANSACTION_YES	0x41222
	ITF_E_INVALID_TRANSACTION_MAYBE	0x42222

Handling Exceptions in Automation

Not all of the information that is returned in a CORBA exception can be mapped directly to the error-handling model of Automation, especially the data provided in a user exception. For this reason, all Automation View interfaces have a VARI-ANT **out** parameter, exceptionInfo, for the exception information. In keeping with the philosophy of not imposing CORBA on the COM programmer, however, this argument is optional. When the exceptionInfo argument is not provided, the exception will be mapped to either the EXCEPINFO or OLE Error Object. When the exceptionInfo argument is provided, several special interworking interfaces are used to provide Automation with the information from the CORBA exceptions. We will first examine error handling using the optional exceptionInfo argument and the special interworking interfaces and then using only the native Automation mechanisms.

Interworking Interfaces for Exception Handling

The interworking architecture defines several interfaces for mapping CORBA exceptions to Automation. The first interface, DIForeignException, is a base interface that is common to both system and user exceptions. It provides access to information that is relevant to both system and user exceptions, namely, the CORBA exception majorCode and exceptionId, or name of the exception:

```
//ODL
Interface DIForeignException : DIForeignComplexType
{
    [propget] HRESULT EX_majorCode ([retval, out] long *val);
    [propget] HRESULT EX_Id        ([retval, out] BSTR *val);
}

typedef enum {
    NO_EXCEPTION,
    SYSTEM_EXCEPTION,
    USER_EXCEPTION } CORBA_ExceptionType;
```

where the ExceptionType has numeric values of NO=0, SYSTEM=1, and USER=2.

System exceptions are mapped to an interface derived from this, DICOR-BASystemException, which provides access to additional system information, namely, the CORBA exception minorCode and completionStatus:

```
//ODL
Interface DICORBASystemException : DIForeignException
{
    [propget] HRESULT EX_minorCode           (
                             [retval, out] long *val);
    [propget] HRESULT EX_completionStatus (
                             [retval, out] long *val);

}


typdef enum {
    COMPLETION_YES,
    COMPLETION_NO,
    COMPLETION_MAYBE } CORBA_CompletionStatus;
```

where the CompletionStatus has numeric values of YES=0, NO=1, and
MAYBE=2.

The mapping for user exceptions is slightly more complicated. Each user exception is mapped to the interworking exception DICORBAUserException,
an interface that has no methods:

```
//ODL
Interface DICORBAUserException : DIForeignException
{
}
```

Because each user exception is different, a separate, exception-specific interface
is created for each user exception with a property accessor for that exception's data,
if any. The exception-specific interface inherits from the DICORBAUserException and follows the standing interworking naming convention DImodule_In-
terface_Exception. This is best illustrated through the following example.

Mapping IDL Exceptions to ODL

The following CORBA IDL for a bank account defines two user exceptions. InsufficientFunds is defined within the Account interface scope and indicates that the attempted withdrawal is for more than the current balance of the
account. The current balance is returned as exception-specific data as part of the
InsufficientFunds exception. The second exception, InvalidAmount,
is defined at the module scope and might be used to indicate that the attempted
withdrawal amount is greater than the maximum allowed (perhaps not too realistic,

but later on the example we will need to have more than one user exception). The `Withdraw` operation can return both of these exceptions.

```
//IDL
module Bank {
  typedef float    Money;

  exception InvalidAmount;

  interface Account {
    exception InsufficientFunds  {Money balance;};

    Money  Deposit     (in Money  amount);
    Money  Withdraw  (in Money  amount)
      raises(InsufficientFunds, InvalidAmount);
  };
};
```

In the corresponding ODL that follows, we can see how the interfaces are defined for these user exceptions. `DIBank_Account_InsufficientFunds` derives from the `DICORBAUserException` interface and has a `propget` property accessor to get the balance. `DIBank_InvalidAmount` also derives from `DICORBAUserException` but has no property accessors since the CORBA exception does not return any data.

Also notice how the exception name translation is different between the `InvalidAmount` and `InsufficientFunds` exceptions. Because `InvalidAmount` was defined at the module scope, there is no interface (e.g., Account) in the translated name. Finally, notice the optional `exceptionInfo` parameter in the method signature of withdraw. In Automation, optional parameters are always the last parameter before the `retval` parameter.

```
//ODL
library DIBank_AccountLibrary
{
    interface DIBank_Account_InsufficientFunds :
                                    DICORBAUserException
    {
        [propget] HRESULT balance(
            [retval,out] float* balance);
    };

    interface DIBank_InvalidAmount : DICORBAUserException
```

```
        {
        };

        interface DIBank_Account : IDispatch
        {
            HRESULT Deposit(
                [in] float amount,
                [in,out,optional] VARIANT* exceptionInfo,
                [out,retval] float* returnValue);

            HRESULT Withdraw(
                [in] float amount,
                [in,out,optional] VARIANT* exceptionInfo,
                [out,retval] float* returnValue);
        };
    };
```

Using the Optional Exception Parameter

When the exceptionInfo parameter is supplied in an invocation of a method on an Automation View object, the interworking bridge will fill in the parameter with a pointer to a VARIANT containing an IForeignException object. If the method succeeds, the majorCode will contain a value of NO_EXCEPTION and the HRESULT will have a value of S_OK. If the method fails, the major-Code will contain either SYSTEM_EXCEPTION or USER_EXCEPTION, and the HRESULT will have a value of S_FALSE, a value that does not have the severity bit set.

When an exception occurs, the Visual Basic or Automation program will have to examine the majorCode property of the exception parameter to determine

Using the Optional Exception Parameter

The HRESULT value of S_FALSE that is returned if an exception occurs while using the optional exceptionInfo parameter will *not* trigger the default error-handling mechanism of Visual Basic. In other words, if you use the optional exception parameter when calling a method in Visual Basic, the Visual Basic error-handling mechanism will not automatically be triggered. You can use *either* the built-in error handling or the optional exception parameter, but not both for any given method invocation.

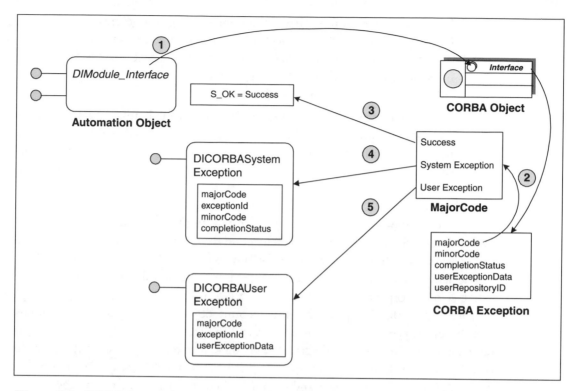

Figure 8.1 *CORBA exceptions using optional parameter.*

what type of exception it is. Figure 8.1 summarizes the usage of the optional exception parameter in Automation methods. The descriptions that follow correspond to the numbered circles in Figure 8.1:

1. An Automation program invokes a method on an Automation View object, passing in the optional `exceptionInfo` parameter to receive error information. The request is sent to the CORBA object by the interworking bridge.

2. The CORBA object processes the request. A CORBA exception object is filled in as a result. (Note that it is the ORB that fills in the CORBA exception object. If the request never reached the target object, the exception object would still get filled in accordingly). What happens next depends on the success of the operation, which is reflected in the `majorCode` of the exception.

3. If the operation was successful, the `HRESULT` is set to `S_OK`, indicating success; the operation completes successfully; and all is well and good.

4. If a system exception occurred, the interworking bridge creates a DICOR-BASystemException object, fills in the properties majorCode, exceptionId, minorCode, and completionStatus from the information in the CORBA exception; sets the HRESULT to S_FALSE, and returns the object to the caller.

5. If a user exception occurred, the interworking bridge creates a type-specific exception object that derives from DICORBAUserException, fills in the properties majorCode, exceptionId, and any exception-specific data; sets the HRESULT to S_FALSE; and returns the object to the caller.

Let's examine the code for handling errors using the optional exception parameter. Listing 8.1 shows the Visual Basic code that corresponds to the IDL shown earlier. First, we dimension variables for the routine and for exception handling. We declare a Variant called ourException, which will be our optional exceptionInfo parameter, and exceptType, which we will map to the exception majorCode. Then we get the account object and invoke the Withdraw method on it, passing in both an amount and the optional exceptionInfo parameter. Now we need to determine whether an exception occurred and what type it was. We do this by setting exceptType to the EX_majorCode of the exceptionInfo parameter and then use a Select block to switch on the exception type. If the method succeeded, then exceptType will be NO_EXCEPTION, and we will print out a message displaying the new balance. (Note that all of the Visual Basic NewLine statements have been removed from the listing to improve readability and formatting.)

Listing 8.1 Visual Basic using the optional exception parameter.

```
' Function Withdraw()

    ' Declare variables for the routine
    Dim msg As String
    Dim objAccount As DIBank_Account
    Dim Amount As Single
    Dim Balance As Single


    ' Declare variable for optional exception parameter
    Dim ourException As Variant
```

Listing 8.1 Visual Basic using the optional exception parameter. (*Continued*)

```vbnet
Dim exceptType As ExceptionType

' Get account object using subroutine
Set objAccount = GetAccountObject()

' Try to withdraw money, passing in the optional exception parameter
Balance = objAccount.Withdraw(Amount, ourException)

' Now process the exception.
' Get the exception type from the majorCode and
' switch based on the type of exception
exceptType = ourException.EX_majorCode
Select Case exceptType

  Case NO_EXCEPTION
      ' There was no error. Display the new balance.
      msg = "Withdrawal Succeeded"
      msg = msg & "    New Balance is: " _
            & Format(Balance, "Currency")

  Case SYSTEM_EXCEPTION
      ' For a system exception, the returned variant supports
      ' the minorCode and completionStatus properties.

      Dim minorCode As Long
      Dim completionStatus As CORBA_CompletionStatus
      Dim completionMsg As String

      minorCode = ourException.EX_minorCode
      completionStatus = ourException.EX_completionStatus
      ' Set text string with completion status
      Select Case completionStatus
          Case COMPLETION_NO
              completionMsg = "No"
          Case COMPLETION_YES
              completionMsg = "Yes"
          Case COMPLETION_MAYBE
              completionMsg = "Maybe"
```

(continues)

Listing 8.1 Visual Basic using the optional exception parameter. (*Continued*)

```
            End Select
            ' Format error message
            msg = "Withdrawal Failed!"
            msg = msg & "    CORBA System exception: " & ourException.EX_Id
            msg = msg & "    Minor Code: " & ourException.EX_minorCode _
                            & ", Completion Status: " & completionMsg

    Case USER_EXCEPTION
        ' If it is a user exception, the returned variant supports
        ' the properties for the defined user exceptions.
        msg = "Withdrawal Failed!"
        msg = msg & "    User exception: " & ourException.EX_Id

        ' Now we need to process the different types of user exceptions
        If TypeOf ourException Is DIBank_InvalidAmount Then
            msg = msg & "    Invalid withdrawal amount"
        ElseIf TypeOf ourException Is _
            DIBank_Account_InsufficientFunds Then
            msg = msg & "    Insufficient Funds, current balance is: " _
                        & Format(ourException.Balance, "Currency")
        Else
            msg = msg & "    Unknown exception occurred"

End Select

' Print the completion message in a Windows Message Box
MsgBox msg
```

If the method failed with a system exception, exceptType will be SYS-TEM_EXCEPTION and ourException will be a DICORBASystemException object containing a minorCode and completionStatus. We get these values from Exception and print out a message describing the system exception. Figure 8.2 shows a screen capture of our message containing the CORBA system exception information when we forced a NO_RESPONSE system exception to occur.

If the method fails with a user exception, exceptType will be USER _EXCEPTION and ourException be one of the method-specific exceptions

Figure 8.2 *Error message for CORBA system exception.*

derived from `DICORBAUserException`. The next problem is how to tell which user exception has occurred. We determine this by using the Visual Basic function `TypeOf`, which can determine the type of an interface that is contained in a `Variant`. If the exception was `InvalidAmount`, the `TypeOf` `ourException` will be `DIBank_InvalidAmount`, in which case we will print out a message identifying the error. In the case of an `Insufficient-Funds` exception, `ourException` is a `DIBank_Account_InsufficientFunds` interface. Recall that the account object will return the current balance as data in this CORBA user exception and that the data will appear as a property in our exception object. Thus, we get the returned balance from `ourException.Balance` and include it in our error message. Figure 8.3 shows a screen capture of the information that we print out for the `InsufficientFunds` exception.

Part of the information we display is the exception name, or `EX_Id`, of both the system and user exceptions. This is in the form of the CORBA fully scoped exception name, such as `CORBA::BAD_PARAM` or `Bank::InvalidAmount`. Another way to determine which type of user exception has occurred is by doing a string comparison of the exception's `EX_Id` against the CORBA name of the exceptions. However, when using this approach, you must take into consideration specific information about the interworking bridge product that you are using, namely, what version of the Interworking Specification it conforms to and, if it is version 1.0, what format is used for `repositoryId`.

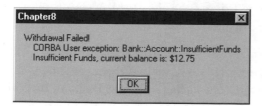

Figure 8.3 *Error message for* `InsufficientFunds` *user exception.*

Exception ID Formats and Interworking Specification Versions

The `EX_Id` field corresponds to version 1.1 of the OMG COM/CORBA Interworking Specification and supercedes the `EX_repositoryID` field that was specified in version 1.0. The information that is provided in the `repository_ID` field is not always consistent in interworking products that correspond to the 1.0 version of the OMG specification. Some products provide the fully scoped name, others provide unique repository UUIDs, and still others provide a string version of the repository identifier. Version 1.1 of the specification renamed the field and clearly specified the format of the information provided.

Using Built-in Automation Error Handling

Some programmers will not want to bother with the more complex error handling that is required when using the optional `exceptionInfo` parameter and will instead rely on the built-in error-handling mechanisms in Visual Basic or other Automation environments. In many cases, this model is sufficient to convey error information to end users, including which CORBA user exception occurred. However, the built-in mechanisms cannot handle any data returned by a user exception. If you need to utilize data returned by a user exception, you must provide the optional exception information. If your user exceptions don't return data, or you can ignore the data, then you can avoid using the optional `exceptionInfo` parameter. When you don't provide the `exceptionInfo`, the interworking bridge will automatically map the CORBA exception information to a native Automation error-handling mechanism.

There are two different error mechanisms used by Automation depending on how the method is invoked. When the method is invoked via the `IDispatch` interface, the CORBA exception information will be mapped into an `EX-CEPINFO` structure. This type of invocation, know as *late binding* in Visual Basic, occurs when a variable is declared as a generic object, for example, `Dim objAccount As Object`. Table 8.2 shows the details of mapping the CORBA exception information into this structure.

When the method is invoked via the dual interface `Vtable`, the exception information will be mapped into an OLE Error Object as shown in Table 8.3. This type of invocation, know as *early binding* in Visual Basic, occurs when a variable is declared as a specific type of object, for example, `Dim objAccount As DIBank_Account`.

Table 8.2 EXCEPINFO Usage for CORBA Exceptions

FIELD	DESCRIPTION
wCode	Must be zero
bstrSource	<interface name>.<operation name> of the CORBA interface that this Automation view represents
bstrDescription	CORBA System Exception: [<exception repository ID>] minor code [<minor code>] [<Completion Status>] of the CORBA system exception
	OR
	CORBA User Exception: [<exception repository ID>]. Spaces and square brackets are literals and are included in the string
bstHelpFile	Unspecified
dwHelpContext	Unspecified
pfnDeferredFillin	NULL
scode	Mapped COM error code from Table 8.1 to Table 8.2

Table 8.3 OLE Error Object Usage for CORBA Exceptions

PROPERTY	DESCRIPTION
bstrSource	<interface name>.<operation name> of the CORBA interface that this Automation view represents
bstrDescription	CORBA System Exception: [<exception repository ID>] minor code [<minor code>] [<Completion Status>] of the CORBA system exception
	OR
	CORBA User Exception: [<exception repository ID>]. Spaces and square brackets are literals and are included in the string
bstrDescription	CORBA System Exception: [<exception repository ID>] [<minor code>] [<Completion Status>] of the CORBA system exception. Spaces and square brackets are literals and are included in the string
bstHelpFile	Unspecified
dwHelpContext	Unspecified
GUID	The IID of the COM or Automation View Interface

The EXCEPINFO structure and OLE Error Object are very similar in the information they contain with the exception of the information about the method's result status. The status of a method invoked through IDispatch is stored in the scode member of the EXCEPINFO structure. The status of a method invoked through the Vtable is returned in the HRESULT and is not contained in the OLE Error Object. Applications that use the Vtable interface are expected to handle the HRESULT directly.

Visual Basic adds yet another object to the error-handling mix with its own Err Object. However, this turns out to be a simplification for the programmer because Visual Basic maps both the EXCEPINFO structure and the OLE Error Object to the Visual Basic Err Object transparently to the programmer. The Visual Basic Err Object contains a property called *number*, which is filled in from either the scode in the EXCEPINFO structure after an IDispatch invoke or the HRESULT from an invoke on a Vtable. In Automation, there are a fixed set of standard error codes that can be trapped by Visual Basic programs. Wherever possible, standard CORBA system exceptions are mapped to these FACILITY_DISPATCH codes. Unfortunately, the number of system exceptions that actually do map to these codes is small. Table 8.4 shows the mapping from CORBA system exceptions to FACILITY_DISPATCH status codes.

Aside from the result status, all of the other properties of the Visual Basic Err Object come directly from equivalent properties in the EXCEPINFO or Error Object. Table 8.5 shows the mapping between these three objects. Conveniently, the Visual Basic programmer does not have to be aware of these different objects and mappings, only of the information that is in the Err Object.

Let's review the Automation error processing and then take a look at some sample code. Figure 8.4 summarizes the usage of built-in Automation error handling. The following descriptions correspond to the numbered circles in the diagram:

Table 8.4 CORBA Exceptions to DISP Error Codes

CORBA EXCEPTION	AUTOMATION ERROR CODE
BAD_OPERATION	DISP_E_MEMBERNOTFOUND
INV_INDENT	DISP_E_UNKNOWNNAME
NO_IMPLEMENT	DISP_E_UNKNOWNNAME
DATA_CONVERSION	DISP_E_OVERFLOW

Table 8.5 Mapping CORBA Exceptions to the Visual Basic Err Object

ERR OBJECT PROPERTY	EXCEPINFO STRUCTURE MEMBER	OLE ERROR OBJECT PROPERTY
Number	scode	HRESULT
Source	bstrSource	BstrSource
Description	bstrDescription	BstrDescription
HelpFile	Unspecified	Unspecified
HelpContext	Unspecified	Unspecified
LastDLLError	Not Applicable	Not Applicable
Not Applicable	wCode	
Not Applicable	pfnDeferredFillIn	
Not Applicable		GUID

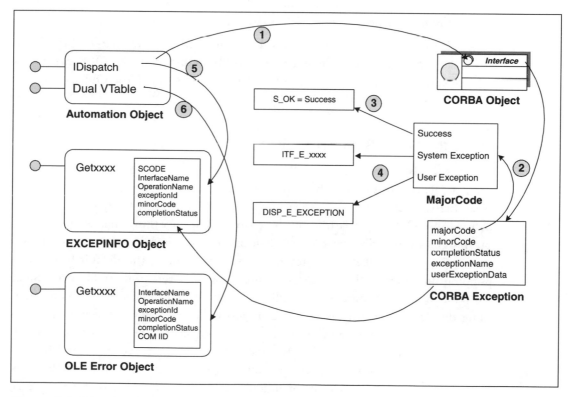

Figure 8.4 *Mapping CORBA exceptions to Automation.*

1. An Automation program invokes a method on an Automation View object and does not use the optional exception parameter. The request is sent to the CORBA object by the interworking bridge.

2. The CORBA object processes the request. A CORBA exception object is filled in as a result. What happens next depends on the success of the operation, which is reflected in the majorCode of the exception.

3. If the operation was successful, the HRESULT is set to S_OK, indicating success; the operation completes successfully; life is grand.

4. If a system error occurred, the HRESULT is set to the appropriate ITF _E_xxxx value from Table 8.1. If a user exception occurred, the HRE-SULT is set to DISP_E_EXCEPTION. In both cases, the HRESULT severity bit is set, triggering the built-in error handling.

5. If the method was invoked via the IDispatch interface, or late binding in Visual Basic, the exception will be returned in an EXCEPINFO structure. The interworking bridge will fill in the EXCEPINFO structure with the information from the CORBA exception.

6. If the method was invoked via the Dual Vtable interface, or early binding in Visual Basic, the exception will be returned in the OLE Error Object. The interworking bridge will fill in the OLE Error Object with the information from the CORBA exception.

Using the Visual Basic Err Object

The Visual Basic programmer will not see a difference between items 5 and 6 of the last section because it is hidden when the exception is mapped to the Visual Basic Err Object. Listing 8.2 shows sample Visual Basic code for the bank account defined in CORBA IDL earlier in the chapter. The first thing that we must do in our program is describe what Visual Basic should do when an error occurs. This is done using the On Error statement. If we do nothing, the default behavior—popping up a message box and terminating program execution—will occur. Since we want to perform some error handling, we must direct Visual Basic to do something different. The Resume Next option indicates that we will put our error handling in line immediately after the method invocation on the account object. Note that you must have an On Error statement before every method invocation for which you want to have your own error handling. On Error does not work at a subroutine, function, or module level. Also note that the On Error statement is not required when using the optional exceptionInfo parameter. Do you remember why?

Listing 8.2 Using the Visual Basic Err Object.

```
' Function Withdraw() continued

    ' Now try to withdraw money using the VB built-in error processing.
    ' If we want to see the error, we must use the On Error command
    On Error Resume Next
    Balance = objAccount.Withdraw(Amount)

    If Err <> 0 Then
        ' Error: get the information out of the Error Object
        ' and format a message
        msg = "Withdrawal Failed!"
        msg = msg + "    Error # " & Str(Err.Number) _
                & " was generated by " & Err.Source
        msg = msg + "    " & Err.Description
    Else
        ' Success
        msg = "Withdrawal Succeeded"
        msg = msg & "    New Balance is: " & Format(Balance, "Currency")
    End If
```

The Err Object contains information about the status of our method invocation. If it is zero, then the method succeeded. If it is not zero, then an error occurred and we will print out an error message. Because we do not have any additional information about user exceptions and we are simply displaying error messages, there is no difference in our processing between system and user exceptions. The interworking bridge does a nice job of formatting the Description string for us, which contains most of the information we would want to display.

Figure 8.5 shows a screen capture of the information message displayed when a CORBA system exception occurs. Figure 8.6 shows the display of a CORBA user exception.

It is possible to do some more intelligent error processing using the Visual Basic Err Object and a string comparison operator. The `Err Description` property contains textual information about the type of exception and the `exceptionId`. Using a comparison such as the Visual Basic `Like` operator, it is easy to parse the text for a specific pattern or string. Listing 8.3 shows how to differentiate between system and user exceptions and between different user exceptions. Of course, you

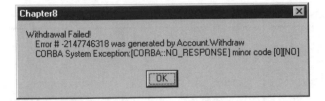

Figure 8.5 *Error message for CORBA system exception.*

wouldn't go through the trouble of determining exception type just to print out error messages; the code in Listing 8.2 does this just fine. Presumably, in addition to the comparisons that follow, there would be some different processing that takes place depending on the exception.

When it comes to distinguishing different user exceptions, I personally prefer using the optional `exceptionInfo` parameter described in the previous sections. This has the added benefit of getting data with the user exceptions. Some interesting variations are possible, such as having a standard exception handler that you pass the `exceptionInfo` object to after a method invocation and/or having your exception-handling routine `Raise` a Visual Basic error to take advantage of the message box and process termination functions that it offers.

Handling Exceptions in COM

Exception handling in COM is similar in some ways to Automation when using the dual `Vtable` interfaces and OLE Error Object. However, there are also major differences, especially in the mapping of user exceptions and in the different ways COM system and user exceptions are handled. In COM, all of the information from a CORBA system exception can be, and always is, conveyed in an OLE Error Object. The format of the information in the OLE Error Object is the same as for Automation as described in Table 8.3. The information about a CORBA user

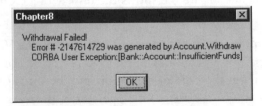

Figure 8.6 *Error message for `InsufficientFunds` exception.*

Listing 8.3 Getting exception types from the VB Err Object.

```
' Getting exception information from the VB Err Object

   If Err <> 0 Then
       ' Error: Determine what if system or user
       If Err.Description Like "CORBA System Exception" Then
           msg = "CORBA System Exception"

       ElseIf Err.Descripton Like "CORBA User Exception" Then
           ' User Exception: Print appropriate error message
           If Err.Description Like "InvalidAmount" Then
               msg = "CORBA User Exception: Invalid Amount"
           End If
           If Err.Description Like "InsufficientFunds" Then
               ' I wish I had used the optional exceptionInfo
               ' so that I'd know what the current balance was...
               msg = "CORBA User Exception: Insufficient Funds"
           End If
       End If
   Else
       ' Success
       msg = "Withdrawal Succeeded"
   End If
```

exception, and any data associated with it, cannot be conveyed in an OLE Error Object and requires that an `exceptionInfo` parameter be added to the method signature. In keeping with the interworking philosophy, this additional information is optional, and the programmer can indicate that no exception information should be returned by specifying `NULL` as the value of the `exceptionInfo` parameter. In COM, we see a different mapping for operations that do and do not have user exceptions. The mapping will only add the `exceptionInfo` parameter to the method signature when a user exception can be raised by the CORBA operation.

Listing 8.4 shows the COM MIDL that corresponds to the CORBA IDL presented earlier in the chapter. We will examine the mapping, starting with the `IBank_Account` method at the bottom of the file. Recall that the CORBA IDL for the Account interface defines no exceptions for the Deposit operation and

Listing 8.4 COM bank account MIDL.

```
// MIDL

// Structures for user exceptions
typedef struct Bank_InvalidAmount
{
} Bank_InvalidAmount;

typedef struct Bank_Account_InsufficientFunds
{
    float balance;
} Bank_Account_InsufficientFunds;

// Special User Exceptions Interface
interface IBank_AccountUserExceptions : IUnknown
{
    HRESULT _get_Bank_Account_InsufficientFunds(
        Bank_Account_InsufficientFunds *exceptionBody);
    HRESULT _get_Bank_InvalidAmount(
        Bank_InvalidAmount *exceptionBody);
}

// Exception Structure
typedef struct Bank_AccountExceptions
{
    ExceptionType type;
    LPWSTR          repositoryId;
    IBank_AccountUserExceptions *piUserException;
} Bank_AccountExceptions;

// Account interface
interface IBank_Account : IUnknown
{
    HRESULT Deposit(
        [in] float amount,
        [out] float* returnValue);

    HRESULT Withdraw(
        [in] float amount,
        [out] float* returnValue,
        [in,out] Bank_AccountExceptions *exceptionInfo);
}
```

two user exceptions for Withdraw. In the MIDL in Listing 8.4 we see that the Deposit operation has only the amount and `returnValue` as parameters. The Withdraw method has an additional parameter, `*exceptionInfo`, which is a pointer to a `Bank_AccountExceptions` structure. We will refer to this as the exception structure in the following description of the mapping.

The exception structure has three members—`type`, `repositoryId`, and `piUserExceptions`—the last of which is a pointer to a special interworking interface for user exceptions. The validity of the exception structure is related to the value of the HRESULT returned by the COM view object. The exception type is also related to the HRESULT and can have a value of either NO_EXCEPTION or USER_EXCEPTION but will never be SYSTEM_EXCEPTION. If the method succeeds, the HRESULT will have a value of S_OK, and the exception type will be NO_EXCEPTION. If a CORBA system exception occurs, the HRESULT will be one of the ITF_E_xxxx values in Table 8.1, and the exception structure will not be valid. If a CORBA user exception occurs, the HRESULT will be E_FAIL, and the exception type will be USER_EXCEPTION. These and a few other possible combinations are summarized in Table 8.6.

The second member of the exception structure, `repositoryId`, will contain the fully scoped CORBA name of the user exception, for example,

Table 8.6 Relationship between HRESULT and Exception Type

METHOD STATUS	HRESULT	EXCEPTION TYPE MEMBER	DESCRIPTION
Success	S_OK	NO_EXCEPTION	Everything is hunky-dory
CORBA system exception	ITF_E_xxxx	Invalid	Exception-type structure is not valid. HRESULT is one of the ITF status values in Table 8.1.
CORBA User Exception	E_FAIL	USER_EXCEPTION	CORBA user exception
COM Error	E_FAIL	NO_EXCEPTION	A COM error occurred that happened to have an HRESULT of E_FAIL
COM Error		Invalid	A random COM error, other than E_FAIL occurred. The exception structure is not valid.

`Bank::Account::InsufficientFunds`. This is the same format as Automation and also has the same inconsistencies with regard to the version of the Interworking Specification.

The last member of the exception structure is a pointer to an interworking-defined interface that is specific to each COM View of a CORBA object that includes user exceptions. This interface follows the naming convention `IModule_Interface`UserExceptions, for example, `IBank_Account-UserExceptions`. The interface has a `[propget]` property accessor function for every user exception that can be raised by any of the operations of the interface, for example, `_get_Bank_InvalidAmount`. The property accessor returns a structure that is specific to each user exception and contains the data associated with that exception, if any, for example, `Bank_InvalidAmount`. When a user exception occurs, the programmer gets the pointer to the `UserExceptions` interface from the exception structure and uses the property accessors to get the specific structure associated with each exception. An HRESULT value of `E_FAIL` on the `_get_xxxx` method indicates that this is not the user exception that occurred—try again. An HRESULT value of `S_OK` indicates that this is the user exception that occurred and that the returned structure will contain the data associated with the user exception.

If this sounds complicated, you're right, and most programmers will not want to deal with the complexity. You have the same choice in COM that you have in Automation. If you can do without the data from the user exception, the interworking bridge can map most of the information from CORBA exceptions to the native COM exception-handling mechanism. If a programmer supplies NULL for the `exceptionInfo` parameter, the user exception data will be mapped to the OLE Error Object. This mapping will be just like the Automation mapping described in Table 8.3 and the same as the mapping for system exceptions. Recall that system exceptions are always mapped to the OLE Error Object.

Before we get into the C++ examples in Listings 8.5 and 8.6 using this twisted maze of pointers, interfaces, and structures, let's review what we've learned so far about COM exceptions. Figure 8.7 summarizes exception handling in COM. The following descriptions correspond to the numbered circles in Figure 8.7:

1. A COM program invokes a method on a COM View of a CORBA object. The request is sent to the CORBA object by the interworking bridge.

2. The CORBA object processes the request. A CORBA exception object is filled in as a result. What happens next depends on the success of the operation, which is reflected in the `majorCode` of the exception.

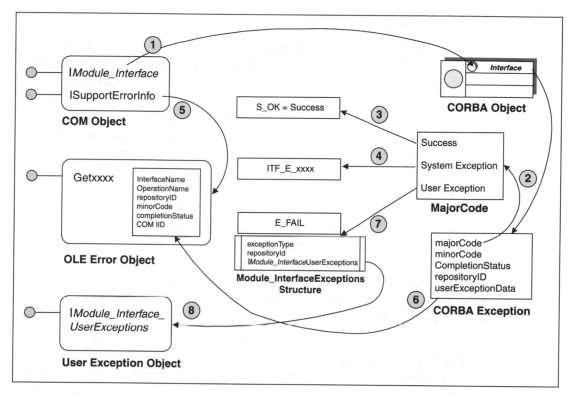

Figure 8.7 *Mapping CORBA exceptions to COM.*

3. If the operation was successful, the HRESULT is set to S_OK, indicating success, and the operation completes successfully.

4. If a system exception occurred, the HRESULT is set to the appropriate ITF_E_xxxx value from Table 8.1 and returned to the caller.

5. The caller queries to see if the COM View object supports the ISupportErrorInfo interface. It does, so the caller uses the interface to get an OLE Error Object.

6. The interworking bridge creates an OLE Error Object and fills it in using the information from the CORBA exception. The OLE Error Object is returned to the application program for error handling.

7. If a user exception occurred, the HRESULT is set to E_FAIL. The interworking bridge creates an interface-specific user exception object and fills in the interface-specific exception structure (the last parameter of the method signature) including a pointer to the user exception object.

Handling System Exceptions

CORBA system exceptions are always reported in the OLE Error Object. Listing 8.5 shows the COM C++ code for handling system exceptions that are returned from the Withdraw operation. As usual, the first thing that we do is declare variables, including some for processing the exception. The OLE Error Object implements the `IErorInfo` interface, so we declare a pointer to that as well as a pointer to the `ISupportErrorInfo` interface. We invoke the Withdraw method, not passing in an `exceptionInfo` parameter, and then check the status of the `HRESULT` returned in the variable `hr`. If a failure occurs, we will check the error object, but first we want to verify that the COM View object supports an error object. This is determined by querying for the interface `ISupportErrorInfo` and then invoking the `InterfaceSupportsErrorInfo` method on the object to determine if the interface we are using supports error objects. Finally, if it does, we use the COM helper function `GetErrorInfo` to get the error object `IErrorInfo` interface. After all that, we can get the information out of the error object. The Source and Description properties contain the same text strings as shown in Listing 8.5 in our Automation example.

Listing 8.5 Getting system exceptions.

```
// Routine for withdrawal from accounts
float Withdraw (float Amount)
{
    IBank_Account          *pIBank_Account;
    Float                  Balance;
    HRESULT                hr;

    // Declarations for Error Object exception handling
    ISupportErrorInfo      *pSErrorInfo;
    IErrorInfo             *pIErrorInfo;
    BSTR                   bstrDescriptionOfError   = NULL;
    BSTR                   bstrSourceOfError        = NULL;

    // Get the Account Object
    pIBank_Account = GetAccountObject();

    // Invoke the Withdraw method without using the exception parameter
    if (FAILED(hr = pIBank_Account->Withdraw(Amount, &Balance)))
    {
```

Listing 8.5 Getting system exceptions. (*Continued*)

```
    // Verify that the COM view interface supports error objects.
    if (FAILED(hr = pIBank_Account->QueryInterface(
                IID_ISupportErrorInfo, (void **)&pSErrorInfo)))
    {
        cerr << "ErrorInfo QueryInterface failed: " << hr << endl;
        pIBank_Account->Release();
        return 1;
    }

    if (FAILED(hr = pSErrorInfo->InterfaceSupportsErrorInfo(
                IID_IBank_Account)))
    {
        cerr << "InterfaceSupportsErrorInfo failed: " << endl;
        if (pIBank_Account) pIBank_Account->Release();
        if (pSErrorInfo) pSErrorInfo->Release();
        return 1;
    }
    if (pSErrorInfo) pSErrorInfo->Release();

    // Get the current error object.
    if (hr = (GetErrorInfo(0, &pIErrorInfo) != S_OK))
    {
        cerr << "Unable to obtain Error information:" << endl;
    }
    else{
        // fill in the error source and error description
        pIErrorInfo->GetSource(&bstrSourceOfError);
        pIErrorInfo->GetDescription(&bstrDescriptionOfError);

        cout << "Exception on interface" << bstrSourceOfError << endl;
        cout << bstrDescriptionOfError << endl;

        // Free the resources
        SysFreeString(bstrSourceOfError);
        SysFreeString(bstrDescriptionOfError);
    }

    // Release the error object.
    if (pIErrorInfo) pIErrorInfo->Release();
}
```

Handling User Exceptions

To get user exception information in COM, we need to provide an `exceptionInfo` parameter on our method invocation. Listing 8.6 shows this mechanism for error handling. We need to declare variables for the `userExceptions` object, `pIUserExceptions`, and for the different structures that we may need. `pExceptions` is a pointer to the exception structure, and then there is a structure for each user exception, `pInvalidAmount` and `pInsufficientFunds`. We invoke the Withdraw method, passing in the pointer to our exceptions structure as the last parameter. Our processing at this point is dependent on the value of the `HRESULT`. If the method succeeded, the `HRESULT` is `S_OK`. If the method failed with `E_FAIL`, then there are two possibilities to check for, which are determined by the value of the exception structure `type` member. If the type is `NO_EXCEPTION`, then some COM error returned `E_FAIL`. If the type is `USER_EXCEPTION`, then we need to determine which user exception occurred. This requires us to get the `userExceptions` object from the exception structure. We try to get each user exception structure from this interface using the `_get_xxxx` methods, so in our example we first invoke `_get_Bank_InvalidAmount`. If this request fails, then we know that it must be a different exception, so we try the `_get_Bank_Account_InsufficientFunds` method. If this succeeds, then we get the balance as a member of the returned structure. If it is a user exception, but it's not one of these two, then something is wrong. We could check for this if we wanted to because it's possible that the server may have been updated to return more user exceptions, but the client is still running an older version.

If the `HRESULT` is not `S_OK` or `E_FAIL`, then we have two other choices. It is either some other COM error, or it is a CORBA system exception. If it is a CORBA system exception, that information will be returned in the OLE Error Object, so we use the same processing as in Listing 8.5 to handle that. If we need to know that it is a CORBA system exception, we could check the `FACILITY` field of the `HRESULT` and compare it to ITF (although that is not necessarily unique), or we could do a comparison against the description field looking for the string `CORBA System Exception`.

Wrapping Up

Congratulations, you've made it through exceptions, the most complicated part of the interworking mapping, and all the other gory details of mapping CORBA ob-

Listing 8.6 Getting user exceptions.

```cpp
// Declarations for exceptionInfo and User Error processing
IBank_AccountUserExceptions   *pIUserExceptions;
Bank_AccountExceptions        *pExceptions;
Bank_InvalidAmount            *pInvalidAmount;
Bank_Account_InsufficientFunds *pInsufficientFunds;


hr = pIBank_Account->Withdraw(Amount, &Balance, pExceptions));
switch (hr)
{
    case S_OK:
        cout << "Withdrawal Succeeded" << endl;
        break;


    case E_FAIL:
        // Might be CORBA User exception of COM Error
        if (pExceptions->type = NO_EXCEPTION)
        {
            cout << "Withdrawal Failed with COM Error: "
                << hr << endl;
        }
        if (pExceptions->type = USER_EXCEPTION)
        {
            pIUserExceptions = pExceptions->piUserException;
            if (hr = pIUserExceptions->_get_Bank_InvalidAmount(
                    pInvalidAmount))
            {
                cout << "User Exception: InvalidAmount" << endl;
            }
            if (hr =
                pIUserExceptions->_get_Bank_Account_InsufficientFunds(
                            pInsufficientFunds))
            {
                cout << "User Exception: InsufficientFunds" << endl;
                cout << "Current Balance: "
                    << pInsufficientFunds->balance << endl;
            }
            pIUserExceptions->release();
```

(continues)

Listing 8.6 Getting user exceptions. (*Continued*)

```
        }
        break;

    default:
        // Might be CORBA system exception or some other COM Error
        // Do the same processing here with the Error Object
        cout << "Withdrawal Failed: " << hr << endl;
        break;

    } // end of switch

    pIBank_Account->release();
    return Balance;
}
```

jects to COM in the previous seven chapters. Next we turn our attention in the other direction, sometimes called reverse mapping. Chapter 9 will discuss the issues and techniques of mapping COM interfaces to CORBA, that is, having CORBA be the client of COM objects. We'll see how this is a useful technique in distributed object systems and later how to apply it to solve specific COM/CORBA integration problems.

9 *Bidirectional Integration*

.

This chapter describes several different approaches to bidirectional application integration. While most of this book focuses on calling from Automation or COM to CORBA, this chapter focuses on the reverse: calling from CORBA back to COM or Automation. There are a number of different ways an application can take advantage of bidirectional COM/CORBA interworking solutions. We will go through these different options, describe their advantages and disadvantages, and follow with an example of how each option works in practice. The chapter will then go into the details of mapping interfaces, methods, and data types from COM and Automation to CORBA.

Many client/server systems today have client applications that are running on sophisticated 32-bit platforms such as Windows NT or Windows95. The difference in capabilities between the client platform and server platform has almost disappeared; however, one difference is in process capacity, where there is frequently excess capacity on the client system. Thus, there is a tendency to try to move or implement some of the processing on the client, such as validating a form before sending it in, or providing some follow-up user interaction for security validation. There are also many powerful display and reporting applications that run on the client platforms that could benefit from updated data from the server. In a distributed object system, the natural way to do this is by having objects on the client system that the server can call back to report updated data or perform other tasks. When the client system is a different object model than the server, such as an Automation client and a CORBA server, this requires bidirectional integration.

Bidirectional Architectures

There are essentially three different ways to design applications that span COM and CORBA: pure client/server, client/server with callbacks, and peer-to-peer. *Pure client/server* applications are ones where the clients and servers have well-defined roles, and the application is always client-driven. That is, the client always pulls information from the server; the server never pushes information to the client. This is the type of application that we have seen in the examples thus far in this book but will not address in this chapter. Since all information is pulled from servers, this type of application does not require bidirectionality. Other types of client/server applications still have well-defined roles between the client and server, but in addition to the clients pulling information from the servers, the servers can push information to the clients. In some types of applications this can help reduce network overhead because servers can call back to clients when new information is available, instead of the clients having to continually poll the server. This type of client/server applications is called *client/server with callbacks*, or just client/server for the purposes of this chapter.

In some applications, such as three-tier applications, the roles of clients and servers are not well defined because services often act as both clients and servers at the same time. We refer to these types of applications as *peer-to-peer*. Throughout this chapter, we define peer-to-peer applications as ones where there are both CORBA and COM servers. While some applications can be neatly categorized as one of these three categories, often applications cannot be so easily pushed into one category. Different parts of applications often fall into different categories. A single application will often have aspects of each of these architectures. Let's examine the client/server and peer-to-peer architectural choices that allow a server to call back to a client more thoroughly.

Architectures for Callbacks

A client/server approach to callbacks is when the interfaces that CORBA servers will use to call back to COM or when the servers that are acting as clients are defined initially in CORBA IDL. That is, the CORBA servers are designed on the assumption that the clients will be written natively in CORBA. This means that all interfaces between application components (client and server) are defined in CORBA IDL by the server implementer. Thus, COM clients and servers must only implement interfaces whose definition comes originally from CORBA. This type of approach is often referred to as *system-centric* since all definitions must originate in one system—CORBA in this case.

A peer-to-peer approach to callbacks is when the interfaces that CORBA servers will use to call back to COM are defined initially in COM. That is, the interface to the COM clients or servers is defined in COM, and the interface to the CORBA servers is designed in CORBA IDL. This type of approach is often referred to as *system-neutral* since the definitions for interfaces originate in the system in which the server was designed.

When designing an application that spans COM and CORBA, the decision to use client/server or peer-to-peer for callbacks is often based upon a combination of the diversity of clients being implemented, the existing code base, the available developers' skill sets, and *total cost of ownership* (TCO) concerns.

A client/server, system-centric approach to application design has what, on the surface, appears to be an advantage over peer-to-peer. Since interfaces are defined independently of the implementing system, the interface can be implemented in either COM or CORBA. However, a closer examination of the problem reveals other overriding concerns. The first thing to consider is that, while the promise of being able to implement in either COM or CORBA is alluring, once an application is implemented it is rarely, if ever, reimplemented. It turns out that reducing the cost of ownership is much more important than having the ability to reimplement services in any system. The relevant components of reducing TCO are reducing initial development time, reducing ongoing maintenance costs, and allowing for easy reuse.

Applications that span both COM and CORBA are often designed by a team of developers with a variety of skill sets. Some members come to the team with a background in CORBA and C++ or Java. Others come to the team with a background in RAD tools such as Visual Basic. To reduce the initial development time of an application, the first goal is to reduce the learning curve for programmers not familiar with CORBA. Writing a client for a CORBA server in tools such as Visual Basic is relatively straightforward. However, it turns out that, with a system-centric approach, the learning curve for implementing existing CORBA interfaces as COM objects is much steeper. Thus, a system-centric approach will generally increase the time needed to develop an application that spans COM and CORBA, whereas a system-neutral approach will not. The issue of developers' skill sets also factors into ongoing maintenance costs because developers will leave and join the team over time.

Applications should be designed to take advantage of two types of reuse: the reuse of existing services built initially for other applications and the use of packaged third-party applications. A system-centric approach suffers in both cases. A client application designed for reuse would typically be constructed as a set of components that could be reused by other applications or moved into servers. To design a COM application that could be reused in a system-centric environment, both the COM component clients and component servers must be defined in CORBA but implemented and used in COM. Since COM-server development tools are very easy to use and powerful but COM-centric by their very nature, system-centric bridging tools often introduce an unnatural series of steps into COM development, which results in additional work and a steeper learning curve on the part of developers. In contrast, a system-neutral approach allows the COM component clients and COM component servers to be defined naturally in the available development environments and, later, allows components to easily migrate into being full-blown servers.

The problem of system-centric bridging solutions is magnified for packaged third-party applications because these applications already exist in COM. Using a third-party COM application such as Excel from a system-centric approach would result in a significant *wrapping* effort. Each interface in the COM application would need to have CORBA IDL defined for it and a CORBA wrapper adapted to it by hand, essentially replicating the functions performed by an interworking bridge. However, with a system-neutral approach, no wrapping is necessary, greatly reducing the overall development effort.

Given these considerations, a system-neutral (peer-to-peer) approach is typically more cost-effective over the lifetime of a project. However, every project is different, and you will need to choose which approach is more appropriate for your needs in any given situation.

Choosing an Architecture for Callbacks

When designing a new application, the first factor to examine is whether the clients will only be COM or whether there will be mix of both CORBA clients and COM clients. When there will be only COM clients, a peer-to-peer client architecture is often the best approach. If clients will be implemented in both COM and CORBA, then a client/server approach might need to be chosen. The corollary to this is that if servers are guaranteed to always be implemented only in CORBA, then a client/server, system-centric approach may be appropriate.

If the application is taking advantage of existing COM servers, for example, Excel, then a peer-to-peer, system-neutral approach is always preferred. If there are COM servers or clients being designed that might, in the future, be reused in other projects then a peer-to-peer approach would generally be preferable—especially if COM will become more common in your environment over time.

Stock Value Predictor Example

We will use an example scenario to illustrate the different approaches to bidirectionality. A real-time CORBA stock ticker server will push updated stock value information to a COM client that predicts future stock value based on past performance. The initial IDL for the CORBA server is shown here:

```
// IDL
module StockFeed
{
    interface Stock
    {
        float Current();
    }

    Interface Market
    {
        Stock Lookup(in string symbol);
    };
};
```

This CORBA server has a `Market` interface. Each instance of this interface represents a different stock market (e.g., NASDAQ, NYSE, etc.). Using the `Lookup` method on this interface, a `Stock` object can be retrieved for any given stock ticker symbol (e.g., "BEAS," "IBM," "MSFT," etc.). This `Stock` object can be used to retrieve the current value of the stock. Right now, however, this stock feed server acts only as a pure server for a client/server application; it has no way of notifying its clients of changes in the value of the stock. We will examine three different ways of having the server push information to its clients: creating a custom Automation interface, using existing COM interfaces, or mapping CORBA interfaces to COM.

Calling Custom Automation Interfaces

In this scenario, we create a custom Automation interface that will be used by the CORBA server to call back to, or push data to, the client. The scenario uses a peer-to-peer, system-neutral design. The client application is designed in two

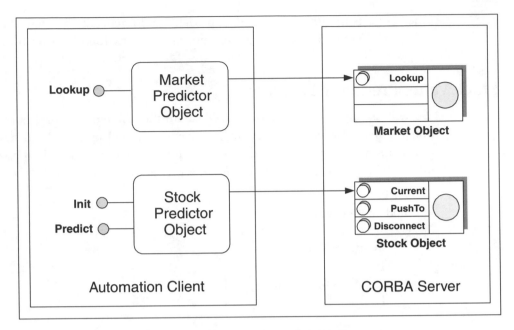

Figure 9.1 *Stock predictor example using Automation interfaces.*

different parts: a reusable stock prediction service and the GUI client interface. Figure 9.1 illustrates the components of the scenario. The steps needed to implement this application are listed in the order in which they need to be performed:

1. Design the stock prediction service—including its stock feed (push) interface.
2. Extend the CORBA server interface to be able to call back to this push interface.
3. Update the stock prediction service to connect its push interface to the CORBA server.

Designing the Stock Prediction Service

The stock prediction service will be designed, initially, as a Visual Basic in-process ActiveX DLL. The service needs to have an interface with two different functions: methods for retrieving predictions of stock value and a way for the CORBA server to push changes in stock value to the prediction object. The full code for the stock prediction service is shown in Listing 9.1. We will look at each of the classes and methods for this service individually.

Listing 9.1 Stock prediction service.

```
class module MarketPredictor (Instancing = MultiUse)

'----------------------------------------------------------------
' Retrieve a stock predictor object for a given stock market
' and stock ticker symbol.
' This method is used by COM clients.
'----------------------------------------------------------------

Public Function Lookup(      ByVal market As String, _
                             ByVal symbol As String) As Stock

    Dim factory As Object
    Dim feedSupplier As DIStockFeed_Market
    Dim feed As DIStockFeed_Stock
    Dim predictor As StockPredictor
    Dim whichMarket as String

    ' Find the CORBA stock feed supplier

    Set factory = CreateObject("CORBA.Factory")
    whichMarket = "/COSNameService/Objects/" + market
    Set feedSupplier = factory.GetObject(whichMarket)

    ' Retrieve the feed for the specified stock

    Set feed = feedSupplier.Lookup(symbol)

    ' Create the stock prediction object

    Set predictor = New StockPredictor
    predictor.Init feed

    ' Return the stock prediction object

    Set Lookup = predictor

End Function
```

(continues)

Listing 9.1 Stock prediction service. (*Continued*)

```
class module StockPredictor (Instancing = PublicNotCreatable)

Private itsFeed As DIStockFeed_Stock
Private itsValue As Single


'----------------------------------------------------------------
' Predict a future value for this stock.
' This method is used by COM clients.
'----------------------------------------------------------------


Public Function Predict(ByVal daysAhead As Long) As Single
    Dim value As Single

    ' A real prediction algorithm would go here

    If daysAhead <= 1 Then
        value = itsValue
    Else
        value = Prediction(daysAhead - 1)
    End If

    Prediction = Rnd * 10 - 5 + value
End Function


'----------------------------------------------------------------
' Initialize the stock, giving it a real-time stock market feed.
' This method is only called by the MarketPredictor class.
'----------------------------------------------------------------


Friend Sub Init(feed As DIStockFeed_Stock)
    Set itsFeed = feed
    itsValue = itsFeed.Current
End Sub


'----------------------------------------------------------------
' This method will be called when the stock value has changed.
' This method will be used by the CORBA server.
'----------------------------------------------------------------
```

Listing 9.1 Stock prediction service. (*Continued*)

```
Public Sub ValueChanged(ByVal value As Single)
    'assign value
    itsValue = value

    'do any necessary prediction calculations

End Sub
```

The service consists of two different classes: `MarketPredictor` and `StockPredictor`. These classes serve as the stock prediction parallel of the CORBA stock feed classes `StockFeed::Market` and `StockFeed::Stock`.

The `MarketPredictor` class defines one method, `Lookup`, which is used to retrieve a `StockPredictor` object for the chosen stock market and stock symbol. The `MarketPrediction` object hides the Automation Views of the CORBA objects from the other parts of the application. It creates an instance of a `DIStockFeed_Stock` view object, creates an instance of the local `Stock-Predictor` object, and ties these together using the `StockPredictor::init` method. A client of the `MarketPredictor` might use it as follows:

```
Dim market as new MarketPredictor
Dim stock as StockPredictor

set stock = market.Lookup("NASDAQ", "BEAS")
```

This retrieves a `StockPredictor` object for BEA Systems, Inc., whose NAS-DAQ symbol is "BEAS."

The `StockPredictor` object has a method, `Predict`, that can be used by Automation clients. This method would be called to retrieve a future prediction of the value of the stock. In addition to this public method, the `StockPredictor` object has two additional methods: `Init` and `ValueChanged`. The `Init` method is called by the `MarketPredictor` to provide the `StockPredictor` with an instance of `StockFeed::Stock`. The `Init` method will later be modified to connect the push interface of the `StockPredictor` with the `StockFeed::Stock` object. The other method, `ValueChanged`, is designed to be called by the CORBA server to push stock information to the stock prediction service.

Extending the Stock Feed Server

Now that the Automation stock prediction service has been defined, the CORBA stock feed server can be updated to support push functionality. To do this, the Automation StockPredictor interface must be exposed to CORBA. Most interworking products will provide a GUI tool to do this, typically the same tool that is used to expose CORBA objects to COM. The tool will read a COM-type library and then generate a CORBA IDL file from that. There are several ways to get the typelib. If the Automation object is defined in MIDL or ODL, then the Microsoft MIDL compiler can be used to create a typelib. If the Automation object is built using Visual Basic as an in-process ActiveX DLL or ActiveX executable, it will create the typelib as part of the project. This is how the type library for our example was created. The interworking product's exposure tool is used to generate CORBA IDL, which represents the StockPredictor interface. Listing 9.2 shows the generated IDL for the StockPredictor interface. We have mapped the entire module, although only the ValueChanged method of the StockPredictor object will be called by the CORBA server. The IDL file will be used with the CORBA IDL compiler to generate CORBA client stubs. These stubs will then be linked into the stock feed server.

Listing 9.2 StockPredictor CORBA IDL.

```
//IDL
typedef long HRESULT;

exception COM_ERROR
{
    HRESULT Value;
};

module Predictor
{
    interface StockPredictor
    {
        float Predict(in long minutes)
            raises(::COM_ERROR);
        void ValueChanged(in float value)
            raises(::COM_ERROR);
    };
```

Listing 9.2 StockPredictor CORBA IDL. (*Continued*)

```
interface MarketPredictor
{
    StockPredictor Lookup(
            in string market,
            in string symbol)
        raises(::COM_ERROR);
};
};
```

Once you have IDL for the `StockPredictor` object, the `Stock-Feed::Stock` object can be updated to allow information to be pushed to the `StockPredictor`. The IDL for the updated `StockFeed` CORBA server is shown in Listing 9.3.

Listing 9.3 StockFeed server.

```
//IDL
#include "predictor.idl"

module StockFeed
{
    typedef long CallbackKey;

    interface Stock
    {
        float Current();

        CallbackKey PushTo(in Predictor::StockPredictor predictor);
        void Disconnect(in CallbackKey key);
    };

    interface Market
    {
        Stock Lookup(in string symbol);
    };
};
```

Two methods were added to the CORBA server: PushTo and Disconnect. The PushTo method will be called by the StockPredictor to connect it to the stock feed. The stock feed's implementation of this method stores the predictor in a list for later use. The Disconnect method is used to disconnect the predictor from the stock feed. A recommended practice is to avoid referring directly to the StockPredictor interface in the StockFeed::Stock definition. Thus, the signature of the PushTo method would be adjusted to the following:

```
CallbackKey PushTo(in Object predictor);
```

Doing this avoids a circularity of definitions across system boundaries, that is, where a COM interface refers to a CORBA interface, which refers back to the COM interface. This circularity can lead to a catch-22 situation in which you can't create the CORBA IDL for the COM object. For example, if the StockPredictor interface referenced an object in the CORBA StockFeed module, you might not be able to create the predictor.idl for the StockPredictor. To do so, you must first create a COM view of the CORBA object that is defined in the StockFeed module; however, this requires you to load the interface repository with the IDL for the StockFeed module. Unfortunately, you can't fully load the StockFeed IDL because it includes the predictor IDL file, which you can't generate. (Note that we do not have such a circular dependency in our example.)

Once a predictor has enlisted itself with the stock feed server, if the server receives a new value for a stock it can notify each connected predictor. The CORBA server code to do this would look something like the following:

```
CORBA::Object_ptr                   pushTo = ...;
Predictor::StockPredictor_ptr       predictor;

predictor = Predictor::StockPredictor::_narrow(pushTo);
predictor->ValueChanged(Current());
```

Because the predictor object was declared as CORBA::Object in IDL, it must be narrowed to a StockPredictor object. The CORBA stub will then be used to invoke the ValueChanged operation with the current value of the stock.

Connecting the Stock Feed and the Stock Predictor

The final step in building the application is to connect the stock feed with the stock predictor. This is done with code in the Init method of the StockPredictor Visual Basic class:

```
Private key as StockFeed_CallbackKey

Friend Sub Init(feed As DIStockFeed_Stock)
    Set itsFeed = feed
    itsValue = itsFeed.Current

    key = itsFeed.PushTo(Me)
End Sub
```

To connect the stock feed and the stock predictor, one line of code was added to the `StockPredictor`'s `Init` method. The line calls the `PushTo` method of the `StockFeed::Stock` object and passes itself, `Me`, the current `StockPredictor` to be used for callback notification by the CORBA object. The `CallbackKey` is saved in a module wide variable called `key`. It will be used later to disconnect from the `StockFeed::Stock` object.

Another routine, `Class_Terminate`, is added to the `StockPredictor` class, This is a standard event routine that will get called by Visual Basic when the class is destroyed. In the `Class_Terminate` routine we call the CORBA `StockFeed::Stock` object at the `disconnect` method to inform it that we are no longer interested in receiving callback notification as shown here.

```
Private Sub Class_Terminate()
    itsFeed.Disconnect key
End Sub
```

Figure 9.2 shows an expanded view of the `StockPredictor` application with a sequence of steps that summarizes the development process just discussed. The following numbers refer to circled numbers in the figure:

1. The client application creates an instance of the `MarketPredictor` object and invokes the `Lookup` method to get a stock predictor object for a specific stock.

2. The `MarketPredictor` object creates an Automation view of the `DIStockFeed_Market` CORBA object and invokes the `Lookup` method on that object. The CORBA `Market` object creates an object reference for the `Stock` object and returns the reference for the requested stock.

3. The `MarketPredictor` creates an instance of the `StockPredictor` object and calls the `Init` method on it.

4. The `MarketPredictor` passes the interface pointer returned from the `Lookup` method on the CORBA market object into the `Init` call of the `StockPredictor`, linking it with the stock view object.

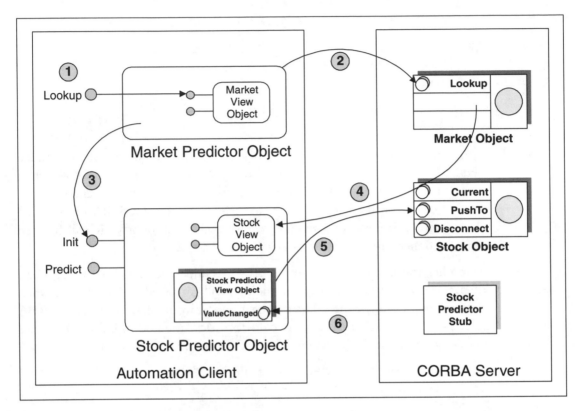

Figure 9.2 *Detailed view of stock predictor application.*

5. The `StockPredictor Init` function calls the `Pushto` method on the stock view object passing in a reference to itself. The interworking bridge creates a CORBA view of the COM `StockPredictor` object and passes a CORBA object reference to it as a parameter in the `PushTo` method on the `Stock` object.

6. When the stock data have changed, the CORBA server, acting as a client, uses the `StockPredictor` object reference and invokes the `ValueChanged` operation on the CORBA stub.

Converting the Stock Predictor into a Standalone Server

The stock prediction service was designed to be a component incorporated into a complete client application. However, at some later time you could decide to upgrade the stock prediction service to become a standalone service usable by both CORBA and COM clients. This would require a few minor adjustments.

If the new stock prediction service will be run within MTS (Microsoft Transaction Server), then the creation of the `StockPredictor` within the `MarketPredictor` would need to be modified to follow MTS standards. If the stock prediction service will be run as a standalone application server, then the Visual Basic project type would need to be modified from ActiveX DLL to ActiveX EXE. Other than these changes, nothing else is necessary.

To use the `MarketPredictor` from CORBA, however, a CORBA client needs to be able to retrieve an object reference for an instance of `MarketPredictor`. Most interworking solutions will be able to install an object reference for an instance of `MarketPredictor` in the CORBA Naming Service. When a CORBA client activates this object reference, the bridging solution will automatically create an instance of `MarketPredictor`, which can then be used by the CORBA client as a regular CORBA object.

Calling Predefined Excel Interfaces

This scenario allows the CORBA server to call directly into an Excel 97 spreadsheet to push data. As with the last scenario, this scenario uses a peer-to-peer design. The steps needed to design this application are as follows:

1. Make Excel available to be called from CORBA.
2. Extend the CORBA server interface to be able to call back to this push interface.
3. Write an Excel macro to connect its push interface to the CORBA server.

Making Excel Available to CORBA

For this scenario, we will need to use the Range interface of Excel. To make this interface available to CORBA, we first need to translate the interface from Automation to CORBA. This involves exposing the Excel interface to CORBA using the interworking exposure tool. The result will be CORBA IDL for the Range interface (and possibly other dependent interfaces). This CORBA IDL can then be used to extend the CORBA server.

Extending the Stock Feed Server

Now that the necessary Excel interface, Range, is available from CORBA, the stock feed server can be updated to support push functionality. The IDL for the updated `StockFeed` CORBA server is shown in Listing 9.4.

Listing 9.4 Stock feed server.

```
#include "excel.idl"

module StockFeed
{
    typedef long CallbackKey;

    interface Stock
    {
        float Current();

        CallbackKey PushTo(in Excel::Range range);
        void Disconnect(in CallbackKey key);
    };

    interface Market
    {
        Stock Lookup(in string symbol);
    };
};
```

As in the previous example, two methods were added to the CORBA server: `PushTo` and `Disconnect`. The `PushTo` method will be called by an Excel macro to connect the spreadsheet to the stock feed. The stock feed's implementation of this method stores the Range object in a list for later use. The `Disconnect` method is used to disconnect the range from the stock feed. To avoid referring directly to the `Excel::Range` interface in the `StockFeed::Stock` definition, the signature of the `PushTo` method would be adjusted to

```
CallbackKey PushTo(in Object range);
```

Once a spreadsheet has enlisted itself with the stock feed server, the server can notify each connected spreadsheet when it receives a new value for a stock. The CORBA server code to do this could look as follows:

```
CORBA::Object_ptr      pushTo = ....;
Excel::Range_ptr       range;
CORBA::Any             anyValue;

range = Excel::Range::_narrow(pushTo);
```

```
anyValue <<= Current();
range->Value(anyValue);
```

The `Value` attribute of an Excel Range object sets the value of the range of cells to the specified value. Thus, when a new stock value is processed by the stock feed server, the relevant cell in the Excel spreadsheet will be updated with the new stock value immediately.

Connecting Excel to the Stock Feed

The final step in building the Excel spreadsheet is to connect the stock feed to the spreadsheet. This can be done with the Excel Visual Basic for Applications (VBA) macro code shown in Listing 9.5.

Listing 9.5 Visual Basic macro script for Excel.

```
Sub FillCell()
    Dim factory As Object
    Dim market As Object
    Dim stock As Object

    ' Find the CORBA stock market object
    Set factory = CreateObject("CORBA.Factory")
    Set market =
        factory.GetObject("/COSNameService/Objects/NASDAQ")

    ' Retrieve the stock feed for the specified stock
    Set stock = market.Lookup("BEAS")

    ' Find the cell to fill with the stock feed
    Range("B1").Select

    ' Set the current value of the cell
    ActiveCell.Value = stock.Current

    ' Allow the CORBA server to update the cell as needed
    key = stock.PushTo(ActiveCell)
End Sub
```

The Excel macro retrieves the `StockFeed::Stock` object for BEA Systems, Inc. (symbol "BEAS" on the NASDAQ stock market). Once this is done, the macro selects the cell B1 using the Select method and then sets the value of the cell to the current stock value. The last line of the macro connects the cell B1 to the CORBA stock feed server so that whenever the value of the BEA stock changes, cell B1 will be updated.

Additional Flexibility

While this Excel 97 scenario is very easy to implement and use, it can have disadvantages in large deployments. If the set of Excel objects that needs to be manipulated is determined by the client macro itself, then changing the macro will require that the spreadsheet be redeployed to every client. This can be problematic and if not carefully controlled will result in higher ownership costs. Another approach is to have the CORBA server take more control over Excel itself. That is, instead of just working with the one Range object, the CORBA server could work with the entire spreadsheet and other objects. This would allow the CORBA server to update the spreadsheet automatically so that changes to the spreadsheet would not need to be redeployed by hand to every client machine. Of course, this requires much more work on the part of the CORBA server.

An additional benefit that this would enable is that prepackaged Automation applications, such as Word and Excel, could be used as servers for tasks such as reporting. A CORBA server could remotely start Excel or Word, generate a document using the objects defined by these applications, and then even e-mail that document out automatically, again using the objects defined by these applications. However, this scenario poses a similar, but opposite, skill-set issue to the problems discussed earlier: The developers skilled in writing CORBA servers are not likely to be skilled in manipulating Office tools through their Automation interfaces.

Calling CORBA-defined Interfaces

The final scenario has a Visual Basic Automation client implement an interface previously defined by the CORBA server. This scenario uses a client/server, system-centric design. Because of the differences and limitations between different Automation development environments, the COM/CORBA Interworking Specification did not define behaviors for implementing existing CORBA interfaces in Automation servers. However, we will examine a typical approach through this final scenario. The steps needed to design this application are as follows:

1. Extend the CORBA server interface to be able to call back to a CORBA-defined push interface.

2. Design the stock prediction service.

3. Update the stock prediction service to connect to the CORBA server.

Extending the Stock Feed Server

Using a client/server approach, the CORBA stock feed server can be updated to support push functionality. Listing 9.6 shows the updated IDL for the stock feed server, including the new `Listener` interface.

As in the previous examples, two methods were added to the CORBA server: `PushTo` and `Disconnect`. This time the `PushTo` interface accepts a `Lis-`

Listing 9.6 Stock feed server.

```
//IDL
module StockFeed
{
    typedef long CallbackKey;

    interface Listener
    {
        void ValueChanged(in float value);
    };

    interface Stock
    {
        float Current();

        CallbackKey PushTo(in Listener listener);
        void Disconnect(in CallbackKey key);
    };

    interface Market
    {
        Stock Lookup(in string symbol);
    };
};
```

tener object, which was previously defined in CORBA IDL. The `PushTo` method will be called by the stock predictor to connect its listener to the stock feed. The `Disconnect` method is used to disconnect the listener from the stock feed.

The stock feed server can notify the listeners whenever a stock value changes. The code to do this could look as follows:

```
Predictor::Listener_ptr Listener = ....;   //ORef passed
                                           //in PushTo

Listener->ValueChanged(Current());
```

Because the `Listener` interface was originally defined in CORBA, the server can be written without taking into account anything at all about its potential clients.

Implementing the Stock Prediction Service

The stock prediction service will be designed, initially, as a Visual Basic in-process ActiveX DLL. The service needs to have an interface with two different functions: methods to retrieve predictions of stock value and an implementation of the CORBA `Listener` interface. Because the existing `StockFeed::Listener` (`DIStockFeed_Listener` when mapped) interface must be implemented in Automation before the stock predictor can be implemented, the CORBA server's `Listener` interface needs to be translated into an Automation view and type library that can be loaded from Visual Basic using the *References* dialog. This is done using the interworking product's exposure tool, just as in any other exposures of CORBA to Automation (such as the examples in the rest of this book). The code for the stock prediction service is found in Listing 9.7. There is no change to the `MarketPredictor` class from Listing 9.1 so we will not repeat it here. We will look at each of the classes and methods for this service that are different from our previous examples.

In addition to this public method `Predict`, the `StockPredictor` object has two additional methods: `Init` and `DIStockFeed_Listener_Val`-`ueChanged`. The `Init` method is called by the `MarketPredictor` to provide the `StockPredictor` with an instance of `StockFeed::Stock`. The `Init` method will later be modified to connect the push interface of the `Stock`-`Predictor` with the `StockFeed::Stock` object.

To implement an existing interface in Visual Basic, you need to include an `Implements` statement in the class module. In this case, the statement is `Im`-

Listing 9.7 Stock prediction service.

```
'----------------------------------------------------------------
' MarketPredictor::Lookup and
' StockPredictor::Predict and Init are the same as
' Listing 9.1.
'----------------------------------------------------------------


class module StockPredictor (Instancing = PublicNotCreatable)

Implements DIStockFeed_Listener


'----------------------------------------------------------------
' This method will be called when the stock value has changed.
' This method will be used by the CORBA server.
'----------------------------------------------------------------


Public Sub DIStockFeed_Listener_ValueChanged(ByVal value As Single, _
                                 Optional ByRef excep As Variant)
    'assign value
    itsValue = value


    'do any necessary prediction calculations

End Sub
```

plements `DIStockFeed_Listener`. This tells Visual Basic that this class module will implement the `DIStockFeed_Listener` interface. In addition, the class module must define one method for each method of the `Implements` interface. These methods are named according to the name of the interface, followed by an underscore, followed by the name of the method. So, to implement the `DIStockFeed_Listener` method called `ValueChanged`, a class module method must be defined as `DIStockFeed_Listener_ValueChanged` with the appropriate signature. In this case, the implementation of the method stores the value of the stock and performs any necessary prediction calculations.

Connecting the Stock Feed and the Stock Predictor

The final step in building the application is to connect the stock feed with the stock predictor. This is done with code in the `Init` method of the `StockPredictor` Visual Basic class:

```
Friend Sub Init(feed As DIStockFeed_Stock)
    Set itsFeed = feed
    itsValue = itsFeed.Current

    key = itsFeed.PushTo(Me)
End Sub
```

To connect the stock feed and the stock predictor, one line of code was added to the `StockPredictor`'s `Init` method. The line calls the `PushTo` method of the `StockFeed::Stock` object and passes the current `StockPredictor` to be used for callback notification. Because of the method signature, the `StockPredictor` will automatically be cast to a `DIStockFeed_Listener` as it is passed in to the `PushTo` method.

We have discussed the reasons for using bidirectional interworking in an application and looked at an example scenario implemented in three different ways. These examples have implicitly presented examples of the mapping of Automation interfaces to CORBA. Now let's take a look at the mappings themselves.

Mapping Rules

The remainder of this chapter will present the details of the interworking mapping rules that cover the reverse mappings. However, unlike the previous chapters on mapping, we will not illustrate each possibility with programming examples. In general, the mappings are straightforward and what you would expect after making it this far in the book. In addition, the reverse mappings tend to be simpler because the data types in Automation and COM are mostly a subset of the CORBA data types. We will not go into much detail on the simple things, but we will cover the mappings that are not as obvious, beginning with the mapping from COM to CORBA. Much of the mapping is the same for both COM and Automation, namely, mapping interfaces, methods, properties, basic data types, and errors. These areas will be covered in the COM section.

Mapping COM Objects to CORBA

COM objects can be described in either the MIDL or ODL descriptive languages. MIDL was enhanced in Microsoft Visual Studio 97 to include and supersede

Listing 9.8 MIDL description of sample object.

```
//MIDL
library Chapter9
{
    interface Ifoo;
};

interface Ifoo : IUnknown
{
    [propput] HRESULT   property1 ([in]   proptype1  propvalue1);
    [propget] HRESULT   property1 ([out, retval] proptype1* propvalue1);
    [propget] HRESULT   properyt2 ([in]   proptype2  propvalue2);
    HRESULT   method1   ([in]   intype1 inparam1,
                         [out, retval] returntype1* returnparam1);
    HRESULT   method2   ([in]   intype2 inparam2,
                         [out] outtype2* outparam2);
};
```

ODL; therefore, we will describe an example COM object in MIDL, as shown in Listing 9.8. This object would map to a CORBA interface defined in IDL, as shown in Listing 9.9.

Let's examine the different aspects of the mapping represented by this example, starting with naming. The MIDL contains a Library construct. This gives a name to a library and identifies interfaces that are contained within it. If this is used, the library name will be mapped to a CORBA module. If no library is used, then the CORBA IDL will not have a module. The COM interface Ifoo maps to a CORBA interface with exactly the same name, Ifoo, including the leading I prefix.

Mapping COM Methods and Properties to CORBA

COM methods map to operations in CORBA. If the MIDL for the method identifies a parameter with the keyword [retval], then that argument will be used as the return type for the operation in IDL. In the example in Listing 9.8, method1 has a return value of [out, retval] returntype1 so the CORBA operation is defined to have returntype1 as its return value. If the MIDL for the method does not identify a retval, as in method2, then the

Listing 9.9 CORBA IDL mapping of COM sample object.

```
//IDL
module Chapter9
{
    typdef long HRESULT;
    exception COM_ERROR
    {
      HRESULT Value;
    };
    interface Ifoo :
    {
      attribute  proptype1  property1;
      readonly attribute  proptype2  property2;
      returntype1  method1 (in intype1 inparam1)
          raises (COM_ERROR);
      HRESULT   method2(in intype2 inparam2,
                            out outtype2 outparam2);
    }:
};
```

method is mapped directly to IDL, and the return value of the CORBA operation is HRESULT.

COM properties are indicated in MIDL using the keywords [propput] and [propget]. (This is one of the extensions to MIDL for ODL compatibility. Before these extensions, there was no concept of properties in MIDL, and these keywords were not supported.) Properties in COM map directly to attributes in CORBA. If the property has a [propput] keyword, for example, property1 in Listing 9.8, it is mapped to a standard attribute. If the property has only a [propget] keyword, for example, property2 in Listing 9.8, then it will be mapped to a readonly property in CORBA. Although it is possible to have a property in MIDL that has only a [propput] method and no [propget], CORBA does not have the concept of a write-only attribute. Such a property would get mapped to a read-write attribute in CORBA.

Mapping COM Errors to CORBA

There is one more interesting thing to examine in the mapping from Listing 9.8 to the IDL in Listing 9.9, and that is how errors are mapped. First notice that the

CORBA IDL defines HRESULT as a long. (In some interworking products, this typedef statement will be inside of a common COM/CORBA mapping include file.) In the case of method2, there is no COM return parameter so the error information is returned as the CORBA return parameter, HRESULT. However, with method1 there is a return parameter. In this case, the interworking mapping may return the HRESULT as a specially defined user exception, COM_ERROR. Notice that the COM_ERROR exception is defined to return a value containing the HRESULT and that method1 has the ability to raise this error. (Typically, COM_ERROR would also be defined in the common include file provided by the interworking product). Let's examine the circumstances under which this exception will be raised.

Developers of COM objects are expected to return error information using one of the predefined HRESULT values or to return an interface-specific error value using the FACILITY_ITF. The predefined system errors are of either the FACILITY_NULL or FACILITY_RPC type. It is possible to map these errors to standard CORBA exceptions. If the COM object returns an HRESULT that can be mapped to a CORBA system exception, it will be. If, however, the COM object returns an HRESULT with FACILITY_ITF, then the error will be mapped to the COM_ERROR user exception. Table 9.1 shows the mapping of COM FACILITY_NULL error codes to CORBA system exceptions. Table 9.2 shows the mapping of FACILITY_RPC error codes to CORBA system exceptions. If the error returned by the COM object is one of the errors in these tables, it will be mapped to the corresponding CORBA system exception. Otherwise, it will be returned in the COM_ERROR exception.

Table 9.1 COM Error Codes to CORBA System Exceptions

COM FACILITY_NULL ERROR CODE	CORBA SYSTEM EXCEPTION
E_OUTOFMEMORY	NO_MEMORY
E_INVALIDARG	BAD_PARAM
E_NOTIMPL	NO_IMPLEMENT
E_FAIL	UNKNOWN
E_ACCESSDENIED	NO_PERMISSION
E_UNEXPECTED	UNKNOWN
E_ABORT	UNKNOWN
E_POINTER	BAD_PARAM
E_HANDLE	BAD_PARAM

Table 9.2 FACILITY_RPC Error Codes to CORBA System Exceptions

COM FACILITY_RPC ERROR CODE	CORBA SYSTEM EXCEPTION
RPC_E_CALL_CANCELED	TRANSIENT
RPC_E_CANTPOST_INSENDCALL	COMM_FAILURE
RPC_E_CANTCALLOUT_INEXTERNALCALL	COMM_FAILURE
RPC_E_CONNECTION_TERMINATED	INV_OBJREF
RPC_E_SERVER_DIED	INV_OBJREF
RPC_E_SERVER_DIED_DNE	INV_OBJREF
RPC_E_CANTTRANSMIT_CALL	TRANSIENT
RPC_E_INVALID_DATAPACKET	COMM_FAILURE
RPC_E_CLIENT_CANTMARSHAL_DATA	MARSHAL
RPC_E_CLIENT_CANTUNMARSHAL_DATA	MARSHAL
RPC_E_SERVER_CANTMARSHAL_DATA	MARSHAL
RPC_E_SERVER_CANTUNMARHSAL_DATA	MARSHAL
RPC_E_INVALID_DATA	COMM_FAILURE
RPC_E_INVALID_PARAMETER	BAD_PARAM
RPC_E_CANTCALLOUT_AGAIN	COMM_FAILURE
RPC_E_SYS_CALL_FAILER	NO_RESOURCES
RPC_E_OUT_OF_RESOURCES	NO_RESOURCES
RPC_E_NOT_REGISTERED	NO_IMPLEMENT
RPC_E_DISCONNECTED	INV_OBJREF
RPC_E_RETRY	TRANSIENT
RPC_E_SERVERCALL_REJECTED	TRANSIENT

There is one exception to this rule. An attribute in CORBA cannot return a user exception. Thus, all errors thrown by the COM object during access to a COM property will get mapped to a CORBA system exception. If the exception is not one of the standard ones shown in Table 9.1, it will get mapped to UNKNOWN.

Mapping COM Data Types to CORBA

Mapping COM data types to CORBA is mostly straightforward. The basic data types all map to equivalent types in COM, as shown in Table 9.3. Structures and object references have an equivalent mapping; however, there are some minor dif-

Table 9.3 COM Basic Data Types to CORBA

Microsoft IDL	Microsoft ODL	OMG IDL	Description
short	short	short	signed 16-bit integer
long	long	long	signed 32-bit integer
	UI1	octet	unsigned 8-bit value
unsigned short	unsigned short	unsigned short	unsigned 16-bit integer
unsigned long	unsigned long	unsigned long	unsigned 32-bit integer
float	float	float	IEEE single precision float
double	double	double	IEEE double precision float
char	char	char	8-bit quantity limited to ISO Latin-1 character set
boolean	boolean	boolean	8-bit quantity, either 1 or 0
	VARIANT_BOOL	boolean	8-bit quantity, either 1 or 0
byte	unsigned char	octet	8-bit opaque data type

ferences in the constructed types arrays and unions. There are also two data types in COM that are not present in CORBA: the VARIANT and pointers. We will discuss each data type in this section.

Mapping COM Strings to CORBA

COM has several different ways to represent strings and two different types of string, ASCII and Unicode. In addition, there is also the concept of bounded and unbounded strings. CORBA has character and wide character strings that can be bounded or unbounded. Table 9.4 shows the mapping of COM and Automation strings to CORBA. Unbounded strings in COM map to unbounded strings in CORBA. Bounded strings in COM map to bounded strings in CORBA.

In CORBA, strings are null-terminated. In COM, non-Unicode strings are null-terminated, but Unicode strings are passed as a BSTR, a byte-counted string. In most cases, the mapping from a BSTR to wstring works fine. However, it is possible for a BSTR to contain embedded null characters. When a COM object returns a BSTR with embedded nulls to a CORBA client, the interworking bridge will raise the DATA_CONVERSION CORBA system exception.

Table 9.4 COM String Types to CORBA

MICROSOFT IDL	MICROSOFT ODL	OMG IDL	DESCRIPTION
LPSTR, char *	LPSTR	string	Null-terminated 8-bit character string
BSTR	BSTR	wstring	Null-terminated 16-bit character string
LPWSTR, wchar_t *	LPWSTR	wstring	Null-terminated Unicode string

Mapping Arrays to CORBA

COM allows two types of arrays to be described, fixed-length arrays and varying arrays. CORBA arrays are always fixed length. The mapping for fixed-length arrays is shown here. Notice that arrays in CORBA are one-based, not zero-based, and that the dimensions are given in the reverse order from COM:

```
//MIDL
const long n = 10;
const long m = 4;
typedef long longArray[0..10];
typedef float floatArray[n,m];
```

```
//IDL
const long n = 10;
const long m = 4;
typedef long longArray[11];
typedef float floatArray[m,n];
```

Varying length arrays, or arrays whose size must be determined at run time, are mapped to sequences in CORBA:

```
//MIDL
typedef short shortArray[];
```

```
//IDL
typedef sequence <short> shortArray;
```

Mapping Unions to CORBA

COM MIDL allows three types of unions to be described: encapsulated unions with a constant discriminator, encapsulated unions with nonconstant discriminators, and nonencapsulated unions. CORBA unions are always encapsulated with constant discriminators. The mapping for encapsulated unions with discriminators is simple and is shown here:

```
//MIDL
typedef enum (dchar,
              dlong) Union_discriminator;

typedef union switch (Union_discriminator _d)
              {case dchar: char c;
               case dlong: long l;
              }Sample_union;
```

//IDL
enum Union_discriminator
    {dchar,
     dlong};

union Sample_union
    switch (Union_discriminator)
    {case dchar: char c;
     case dlong; long l;
    };

Nonencapsulated unions and unions without constant discriminators in COM are mapped to a CORBA **any**. The type of the **any** is determined at run time by the interworking bridge during the conversion operation. An example of this mapping is shown here:

```
//MIDL
typedef [switch type( short )] union
tagSimple_union2
              {[case(0)] char c;
               [case(1)] long l;
              }Sample_union2;
```

//IDL
typedef any Sample_union2;

Mapping Variants and Pointers to CORBA

COM VARIANTS provide functionality similar to that of a CORBA **any**, except that the data types in a variant are limited to the Automation data types. A VARI-

ANT in MIDL is mapped directly to an **any** in IDL. When a CORBA client passes a CORBA **any** to a COM object expecting a VARIANT, it is possible that the **any** could contain a data type that is not legal in a VARIANT. If this happens, the interworking bridge raises a DATA_CONVERSION error to the CORBA client.

MIDL supports pointers as a data type. There is no equivalent type in CORBA for several reasons. Pointers are mainly a procedural, process-based programming mechanism that if used in a distributed system can lead to problems. More importantly, in a distributed object system, an object reference serves much the same purposes as a pointer but also provides the benefits of data encapsulation. It is recommended that pointers should not be used for distributed COM objects; however, if they are, there are some limitations to consider. It is possible to define a pointer that is cyclical, that is, it points to something that points to something that in turn points back to the beginning. Cyclical pointers must be avoided and cannot be converted to CORBA. The cycle will be determined at conversion time by the interworking bridge, and an E_DATA_CONVERSION error will be returned to the COM server. Another property of pointers is that they can be null, or point to nothing. To account for this, MIDL pointers are mapped to CORBA sequences with zero or one element. The element in the sequence will be the value of the pointer, that is, what the pointer points to, not a reference. The three different types of MIDL pointers and the corresponding CORBA types are shown in Table 9.5.

Mapping Automation Data Types to CORBA

The mapping for Automation objects to CORBA is very similar to the mappings for COM objects discussed in the last section. In particular, the mapping for inter-

Table 9.5 MIDL Pointers to CORBA

MIDL POINTER TYPE	CORBA TYPE	DESCRIPTION
Reference	sequence with one element	A non-null pointer to a single item. Cannot be cyclical.
Unique	sequence with zero or one element	A pointer to a single item. Can be null. Cannot be cyclical.
Full	sequence with zero or one element OR DATA_CONVERSION error	A pointer to a single item. Can be null. Can be used for data structures that form cyclical dependencies.

Table 9.6 Automation Data Types to CORBA

AUTOMATION TYPE	CORBA TYPE	DESCRIPTION
CURRENCY	COM::Currency	64-bit integer scaled by 10,000, fixed point number with 15 digits left of decimal point; 4 digits to the right
DATE	double	64-bit double precision float. Whole part contains number of days since 30–Dec–1899. Fractional part is time as a fraction of a day.
SCODE	long	Status portion of an HRESULT without the FACILITY or severity.

faces, methods, properties, basic types, and errors is exactly the same and will not be repeated here. There are several data types in Automation that are not represented in CORBA. These are shown in Table 9.6. Because these conversions are not exact, there are possible conversion errors associated with some of the mappings.

Mapping Automation CURRENCY to CORBA

Automation has a data type to represent money values called CURRENCY. The data type is a 64-bit double precision floating point number that represents the value with fifteen digits to the left of the decimal point and four digits to the right of it. There is no equivalent data type in CORBA with the same semantic meaning. The best mapping for CURRENCY is to a structure that holds the high and low portions of the value. The COM/CORBA Interworking Specification defines a special structure for this and creates an OMG-specified module for this and all other similar interworking structures and definitions:

```
//IDL
module COM
{
    struct Currency
    {
        unsigned long lower;
        long upper;
    }
}
```

The interworking bridge converts from Automation CURRENCY to COM::Currency at run time. It is possible for a CORBA client to create a CURRENCY structure that does not translate to a meaningful Automation CURRENCY value. If this occurs, the interworking bridge raises the CORBA DATA_CONVERSION system exception.

A similar situation can occur when a CORBA client passes a double to a COM object as a date. If the double does not represent a meaningful date, the interworking bridge raises the CORBA DATA_CONVERSION system exception. Thus, for every parameter passed as a currency or date, the bridge must do both a conversion between the formats and a validity check. We have also seen this situation when mapping from CORBA to Automation, for example, when mapping unsigned CORBA types to Automation signed types.

Mapping Automation SAFEARRAYs to CORBA

Automation has the concept of a SAFEARRAY, which is a structure that describes a multidimensional array. The SAFEARRAY contains size and boundary information for the array, reference to the array data, and other *"safety"* features describing each element (that are not applicable to the mapping). The type of the element is determined before run time, but the number of dimensions and the bounds for each dimension are determined at run time.   The interworking bridge uses the SAFEARRAY APIs to unpackage and repackage the SAFEARRAY into a CORBA sequence. When the SAFEARRAY is multidimensional, the corresponding position of an element in the sequence can be calculated. Consider a SAFEARRAY with three dimensions: $d0$, $d1$, and $d2$. The position of element $[x0][x1][x2]$ in the CORBA sequence will be as follows:

$$position[x0][x1][x2] = x0{\times}d1{\times}d2 + x1{\times}d2 + x2.$$

For example, a SAFEARRAY with dimension 4, 5, 6 maps to a linear sequence with a run-time bound of $4{\times}5{\times}6 = 120$ elements, yielding valid offsets from 0 to 119 into the sequence. The offset of an element at location [2][3][4] would be $2{\times}5{\times}6 + 3{\times}6 + 4 = 82$.

Creating View Objects from CORBA

Chapter 7 deals with the creation of objects in detail. However, it is worthwhile to review here the different ways that a CORBA client can get a reference to a COM object. The method used in our examples is to pass an object as a parameter in a method. For example, the PushTo method on the Automation View of the CORBA Stock object took an interface pointer to an Automation object. When the method was translated to an invocation on the remote CORBA object, the

Automation interface pointer was turned into a CORBA object reference to a CORBA view object. The CORBA server did not have to do anything special to get the object reference. This is the simplest and most common method for callback situations.

Another method is to register an instance of a view object with the CORBA Naming Service. This could be done explicitly by the server for the COM object or by the interworking bridge when the instance of the view object was created (as part of some server process). A variation on this method is to have a special server for all of the CORBA View objects (that are not passed as parameters in the callback case) on a COM system. This server would be constructed by the interworking product as part of the normal exposure mechanism. One of the functions of the server would be to register instances or factories with a CORBA name service. The COM/CORBA Interworking Specification does not cover the implementation of publishing COM objects to CORBA clients. Some interworking products have chosen this *Bridge Server* approach.

One method that is attractive is to map a COM class factory to a CORBA `Lifecycle SimpleFactory` interface. Both interfaces return an object and take no parameters for input, so the mapping is easy to do. The special bridge server would register the CORBA factory in the name server and provide the implementation of the `SimpleFactory` interface. The simple factory would then call the COM class factory to get an instance of the object and return the interface pointer to the caller. The interworking bridge would automatically convert the interface pointer into a reference to the CORBA view object as it was returned.

As shown here, there are many ways for the CORBA client to get an object reference to a COM object. The simplest and most portable is to pass the object reference to the CORBA object as part of another method call. This is supported by virtually all interworking products. Beyond that, several options for implementing your own solutions are described in Chapter 7, and different interworking products have provided their own value-added solutions to the problem. Once the CORBA client does get the reference, powerful applications can be implemented using a combination of COM and CORBA objects.

Summary

Distributed object systems allow processing to be distributed between the client and server. This includes having the server call back to the client for some functions or notify the client of a change. We have discussed the differences and benefits of the client/server-with-callback approach and the peer-to-peer approach to distribution. We have also addressed the differences between a system-centric and a system-neutral approach to defining interfaces. These were illustrated with an example that was implemented in three different scenarios. Finally, we explored the details of the mapping so you would be able to implement your own callback mechanisms. In the next chapter, "Building an ActiveX Control," we will use this information to build a callback mechanism into an ActiveX control.

10 *Building an ActiveX Control*

A big advantage of client/server programming is the separation of interface and implementation, specifically the separation of a graphical user interface from the implementation of a business process (i.e., business object). This separation makes it easier to reuse both the user interface and the business object. ActiveX controls are a COM technology designed to facilitate the reuse of user interfaces as standard building blocks, or *components*, of a client user interface application. This chapter will show you how to build ActiveX controls that interact with remote CORBA business objects.

The emphasis of the chapter will be on the various aspects of using CORBA objects inside of ActiveX controls rather than on building ActiveX controls generally. There are many excellent sources for learning how to build ActiveX controls, such as *ActiveX Controls Inside Out* by Microsoft Press, that provide general information. This chapter will first present an overview of ActiveX controls and discuss their use as client components in a COM/CORBA environment. We will then illustrate the use of CORBA objects with three example ActiveX controls, two built using Visual Basic and the other using Visual C++. The Visual Basic control will display summary information about a combined investment portfolio. In the next example, we will extend the Visual Basic control to use events. The Visual C++ control will use COM objects to implement a useful COM/CORBA interworking design pattern for movable objects.

Overview of ActiveX Controls

ActiveX controls provided a standard for implementing reusable components in the COM and Automation object system. ActiveX controls are one model for implementing client components. (Another popular model for client components is JavaBeans.) Let's look at how ActiveX controls implement the features of client components.

ActiveX Controls Are Client Components

Components provide a specific service to a client application, typically involving a graphical user interface for a business process. The component can be reused by many different client applications, which can be constructed by combining several components together. Components by themselves are not executable programs. They must be included in some sort of application, or *container*, to execute. For them to be reusable in different applications, the interaction between the component and the container application must conform to some standard set of interfaces. In COM, these interfaces are defined by ActiveX and provide all of the functions necessary for the component and container to interact. Figure 10.1 shows a high-level view of these functions as four main categories of interaction:

User Interface. The display of data to the user and interaction with the user to gather input.

Methods. Typically, the business functions that this component is an interface to. The methods are described and implemented by the component and invoked by the container. Methods are the container's entry point into the component.

Events. Occurrences that can take place in the component and need to be conveyed to the container, such as notification of data change. The events are described and issued by the component and received by the container. Events are the component's entry point into the container.

Properties. Environmental characteristics of the control. There are both common characteristics, such as background color or font size, and application-specific characteristics, such as file paths. Common properties would exist in a standard property page while the application-specific properties would typically be implemented in a custom property page.

There are many components, perhaps thousands of different ones, but relatively few containers. The most common containers for ActiveX controls are Web browsers, Visual Basic (or other Automation controllers), and desktop applications such as Microsoft Word. It is not possible, nor desirable, to have these containers know about all of the different controls beforehand. Instead, there needs to be a standard mechanism by which the container can discover what methods, events,

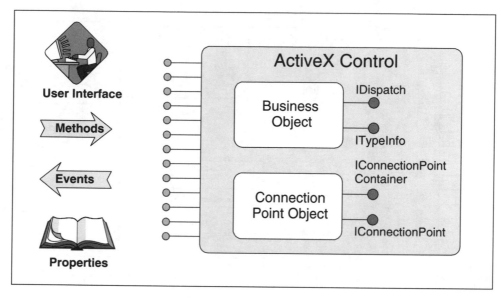

Figure 10.1 *The structure of an ActiveX control.*

and properties a control has. This mechanism is also part of the interfaces specified for ActiveX controls. The description of a control's methods and properties are relatively straightforward, but coordinating events bring a new degree of complexity to the equation. The container has to determine what events a control can issue, determine what interfaces the events want to invoke in the container, and then dynamically construct those *callout* interfaces. (This is certainly one reason there are only a few containers.) ActiveX controls use the COM `IConnectionPoint` and `IConnectionPointContainer` interfaces to facilitate this coordination of a control's events and the container's implementation of those event callout routines.

Figure 10.1 shows an ActiveX control as being composed of two principal objects, a business object and a ConnectionPoint object. The ActiveX control itself implements the external interfaces for control/container interaction but delegates responsibility for the control's methods to the business object and responsibility for events to the ConnectionPoint object. This chapter will show how to use a COM or Automation View of a CORBA object to implement the business object part of the ActiveX control and how to use callbacks to implement the events portion. The standard part of the ActiveX control will get created for us by our development environment, such as Visual Basic. We will use the development environ-

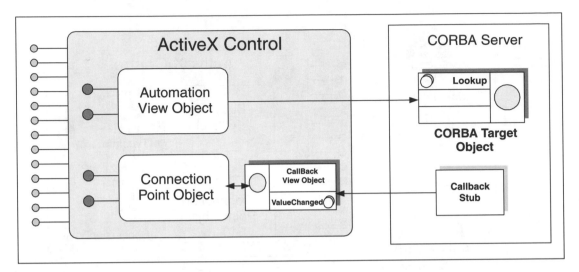

Figure 10.2 *ActiveX control interaction with CORBA objects.*

ment to tie these three pieces of the control together. Figure 10.2 shows the interaction of CORBA objects with the internal objects of the ActiveX control. The
business object portion of the control is an Automation View of the remote
CORBA object. The ConnectionPoint object uses a callback object to receive notification from the remote CORBA server.

Our first example will use Visual Basic, the easiest way to build an ActiveX
control, and will not have events. The second example will use Visual C++ and
MFC (Microsoft Foundation Classes) to build a nonvisual control using COM objects rather than Automation. This example will use a movable object to present
complex CORBA structures as fine-grain properties on the control. The third example will again use Visual Basic and will extend the first example by adding
events using a callback with the CORBA server.

Considerations for Using CORBA Objects

There are several aspects to consider when incorporating CORBA objects into an
ActiveX control, namely, reusability, obtaining the CORBA object, and performance. Obviously, a primary goal of implementing client applications as ActiveX
controls is to be able to reuse those components in other applications. The design
of both the client control and the business object will determine their reusability.
There are two factors that influence the reusability of a control: the specificity of

its functions and the environments in which it can operate. In simple terms, the more closely tied to a specific task a control is, the less flexible and reusable it will be. Consider the example of a control for a bank account. If the control is tied specifically to a checking account, if might not be usable for a savings account. On the other hand, if it is more generic, the same control can probably be used for both types of accounts. Of course, it requires more foresight, design, and code to build generic versions of controls, so there is a trade-off to be made. The potential reuse of a control must justify the additional work and complexity of a more generic design.

One of the characteristics of successfully reusable designs is flexibility. Specifically, a good reusable design will anticipate factors that are likely to be different in different environments and design in flexibility around them. A good design will also try to anticipate changes in requirements and environments over time and provide for extensibility in these areas that will not break backward compatibility. Now let's consider the environments that a control can operate in, specifically, an ActiveX control for a remote CORBA object. One of the areas that is different in a lot of CORBA systems is the way in which object references are obtained. Some of the more popular methods for getting object references are a naming service, a factory and factory finder, a trader service, and a shared file. Even within the same system, there can be different methods for obtaining references. It is easy to design flexibility for this into a control. One method is to design a control that is passed to the object as a parameter on initialization. This control can be combined with code that obtains an object reference or with another control that is specifically designed to obtain object references for a specific environment.

The last technique points out an important characteristic of controls. They can be combined together to form more powerful, composite controls. Figure 10.3 shows such a composite control. In this figure, we have constructed the application-level ActiveX control from several other controls. One control (or more) is used to provide the visualization to the user, and another set of controls is used to gather input from the user. These controls are then tied together through some local processing with a nonvisual control that represents the business object.

The nonvisual control illustrates a useful construction technique for COM objects that helps to minimize network traffic under certain conditions. Programs that use Automation objects and ActiveX controls expect to deal with fine-grained properties to get specific bits of information. CORBA objects are typically designed to minimize network traffic and thus pass large amounts of data in a single message. These two different approaches present inherent mismatches when bridging from one model to the other, and these mismatches are the root of much of the complexity of the Automation mappings. This should be old news to you by now. The worst–case situation occurs when a CORBA object has an attribute that is made up of a complex data type, a structure, for example. The structure is passed to an Automation program as a helper object that contains properties for each member of the structure. When the application program reads each member of the structure, the interworking bridge has all of the information cached locally, and no additional network messages are incurred. However, when the application program sets a property on the helper object, the interworking bridge cannot know when that application is done setting properties. Thus, the bridge must invoke `set_attribute` on the CORBA object each time the Automation program changes a single member of the CORBA structure, resulting potentially in many extra network messages. COM objects, however, do not have this problem because the CORBA complex types map much more naturally to them. (Many CORBA designers would argue that the use of structures as attributes is a bad idea, but I have seen them used more than a few times. Obviously, it is a bad idea in an environment that will include Automation clients.)

Figure 10.3 shows how a simple, nonvisual control can be constructed to avoid this problem. In this figure, the nonvisual control is built using C++ and a COM View object. The COM object deals directly with structures and then presents the members of the structures as fine-grain properties of the control. This technique

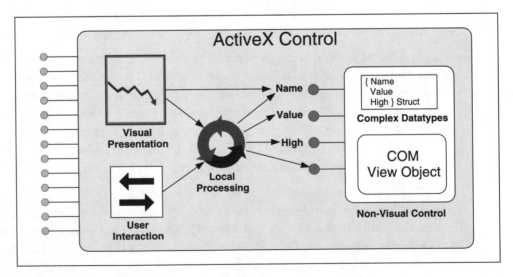

Figure 10.3 *Compound ActiveX control construction.*

provides the opportunity for additional filtering and processing. For example, the CORBA structure might contain some information that is necessary to the application but also some information that you do not want to make available to Visual Basic applications. The nonvisual control could simply not present the restricted information. Consider another example in which a structure contains several different values. Your application may typically need all of the individual values as well as some calculated value, such as a weighted average. The nonvisual control could provide this additional level of processing and present the result as a property of the control. There are obviously many opportunities to provide your own "custom" mappings from the CORBA object to something that is easier or more useful in your application using this technique.

We have discussed several techniques involving design, getting object references, and using nonvisual controls that we will demonstrate throughout the examples in the chapter. Let's start by building a simple control in Visual Basic.

Building a Control in Visual Basic

Visual Basic is the easiest development environment in which to build an ActiveX control. In version 5.0 of Visual Basic, Microsoft added several new project types: ActiveX executable, ActiveX DLL, and ActiveX control. Using the ActiveX control project in Visual Basic 5 makes it extremely easy to build an ActiveX control for a CORBA target object. (Although it may be possible to build an ActiveX control using Visual Basic version 4.0, it is not recommended and we will not do it here.) When building an ActiveX control, the project must have a component called a *User control*. The user control is much like *the form* in a standard Visual Basic project. It has a visual presentation that can contain other controls, such as a text box, and code associated with the presentation, such as `_click` routines and a `form_load` routine. You can treat the user control just like a form, although there is one major difference. An ActiveX control is intended to be embedded inside of another application, such as a Web page or a Visual Basic project. When you embed an ActiveX control into another application, it is the visual presentation of the user control that you add to your form.

Getting Summary Information for an Investment Portfolio

In the post–deregulation age of merger mania, a huge conglomerate has acquired and merged several financial service corporations, namely, a bank, a brokerage house, and an insurance company. The new parent company, Financial Mega Corporation

(FMC), wants to develop several new customer applications that deal with the combined assets of any given customer across the three financial institutions. One obvious function is to display the total assets of a customer on a single form. The same function will be used in several different applications, such as a customer-accessible Web page for home banking and a Visual Basic application intended for a customer service representative. This makes it a perfect application for an ActiveX control.

A customer who has accounts with all three institutions would have three different account numbers—not a very friendly interface. A new way to access all accounts from a single identifier is needed, so FMC introduced a new entity called the customer portfolio, which contains identifiers to all of the customer accounts. A CORBA object called the `PortfolioManager` manages the customer portfolio and provides access to all of the other accounts distributed among the other financial corporations. Our example is to build an ActiveX control called the `PortfolioSummary` that collects all of the information about the different customer accounts and then displays it in a single form.

We want the `PortfolioSummary` control to be reusable in several different scenarios that may involve different ways of getting the CORBA `PortfolioManager` object. However, we don't want the control to dictate how the object must be obtained, so we have designed our control to have an `initialize` method that accepts the `PortfolioManager` object as an input. This lets the application obtain the object reference in the most appropriate manner. FMC uses the CORBA Life Cycle Service to obtain object references. Factories are used to create object references, in much the same way that COM class factories are used. One difference is that access to these factories is distributed on the network through the use of a Life Cycle Service factory finder server. CORBA servers register their factories with the factory finder, and clients use the factory finder to find factories. Our client application uses the Automation view of the factory finder to get an Automation view of the CORBA `PortfolioManager` object. Figure 10.4 illustrates our example application.

There are two CORBA objects involved in the scenario illustrated in Figure 10.4: the factory object `FMCFactory` and the portfoliomanager object `PortfolioManager`. The CORBA IDL for these objects in shown in Listing 10.1. This illustrates another difference between CORBA and COM factories. The `FMCFactory` object accepts the customer's `portfolioID` as an input and returns a `PortfolioManager` specifically for that customer. Recall that in COM, class factories do not accept input parameters. (Although it is possible to have a "custom factory" in COM that does accept input, these are cumbersome to

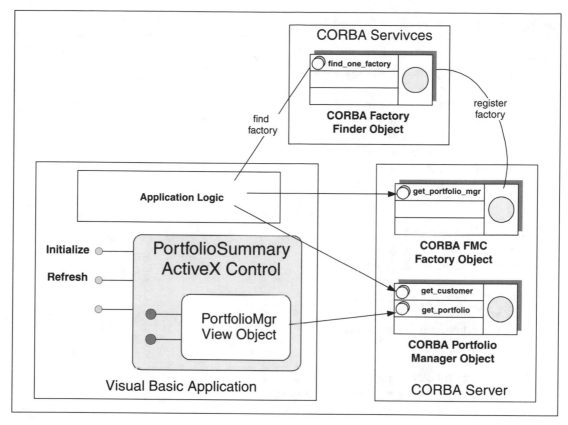

Figure 10.4 *PortfolioManager ActiveX control example.*

implement and thus, in practice, are very rarely used.) In COM, you use the factory to first create the object and then initialize it as a separate operation, which requires an extra network message. We can see how the different design centers of the two object models have influenced this behavior. CORBA is optimized for networking and thus has a model that requires fewer messages. COM is structured around generic tools and thus has a standard factory interface for all objects, which makes it possible for any tool to be able to create any object.

From the example IDL, we see that the `PortfolioManager` can return a structure that contains customer information such as name, address, and so on with the `get_customer_info` operation. The `get_portfolio_balance` operation also returns a structure, this one containing cash and equity balance amounts for each of the different financial services of FMC. Our ActiveX control

Listing 10.1 PortfolioManager CORBA IDL.

```
// IDL
module FMC    //Financial Mega Corporation

  struct CustomerInfo {
    FirstName    first_name;
    LastName     last_name;
    char         middle_initial;
    Address      customer_address;
    Phone        phone_number;
  };

struct PortfolioBalance {
    float      bank_cash_value;
    floa       bank_equity_value;
    float      brokerage_cash_value;
    float      brokerage_equity_value;
    float      insurance_cash_value;
    float      insurance_equity_value;
  };

  interface PortfolioManager {
    PortfolioBalance    get_portfolio_balance();
    CustomerInfo        get_customer_info();
  };

  interface FMCFactory {
    PortfolioManager get_portfolio_manager(in long Id);
  };
};
```

will provide a visual presentation for the information returned by the get
_portfolio_balance operation.

Creating a Visual Basic Project for an ActiveX Control

Throughout this chapter we will take advantage of the many features in Visual Basic to build our controls. The samples from this chapter are available at our Web site: http://www.wiley.com/compbooks/rosen. This project is in the directory "\Chapter10\VisualBasic\Example1." The first thing we need to do is create a

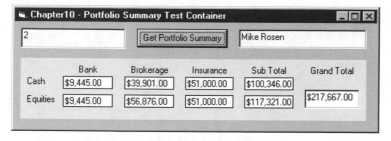

Figure 10.5 *PortfolioSummary ActiveX control screen.*

new project in Visual Basic. Select the "New Project" item from the Visual Basic File menu and choose "ActiveX Control" as the project's type. This creates a "User control" item in the project. The user control consists of both code and a visual form, much like a standard EXE project. Figure 10.5 shows a screen capture of our control and test project. The lighter-shaded portion at the bottom of the screen is the embedded user control form of our ActiveX control. In this form, we use a specialized version of the TextBox control, called the Masked Edit box, which will automatically display the text in a variety of formats, such as money values, as we have chosen. To include this, or any other control, in your project choose "Components ..." from the Visual Basic Project Menu.

The code portion of the user control is shown in Listing 10.2. Our control has two public methods, `Initialize` and `Refresh`, and two private subroutines, `UpdateForm` and `CheckException`. The public methods will be available to users of the control, whereas the private methods will not. Visual Basic has a wizard that helps you create headers for routines. From the Tools menu, choose "Add Procedure ..." and then select between "Public or Private Subroutine," "Function," "Property," or "Event." For subroutines, the wizard doesn't do much besides create the `Public Sub ...` and `End Sub` lines in your code, and I usually just do this manually. However, the wizard is more useful for creating properties and events, and I usually use it for these. Let's examine each of the routines in our control. The first thing we do in the user control code is declare a module-wide variable `objPortfolioManager` for the `PortfolioManager` object. We set this object's value in the `initialize` routine, which we have made public. The user of our portfolio summary control will have already created the `Portfo-lioManager` object and will pass it in to the control in the `initialize` routine. After setting our copy of the `PortfolioManager` object, we call our internal routine to update the values in the form. The second public method, `Re-fresh`, does nothing more than call the same internal routine.

Listing 10.2 Portfolio summary ActiveX control.

```vb
' Declare an object for the Portfolio Manager
'
Private objPortfolioManager As DIFMC_PortfolioManager


'----------------------------------------------------------------
' Initialize method. Here, the containing program passes
' in the portfolio manager object for this control to use
'----------------------------------------------------------------
Public Sub Initialize(portfolioManager As DIFMC_PortfolioManager)
    Set objPortfolioManager = portfolioManager
    Call GetSummary
End Sub


'----------------------------------------------------------------
' Refresh method. The containing program invokes this
' method to refresh the display.
'----------------------------------------------------------------
Public Sub Refresh()
    Call GetSummary
End Sub


'----------------------------------------------------------------
' UpdateForm subroutine. The above public methods both call
' this subroutine to actually do the work.
'----------------------------------------------------------------
Private Sub GetSummary()

    Dim Exception As Variant
    Dim objPortfolioBalance As DIFMC_PortfolioBalance
    Dim cashSubTotal, equitySubTotal As Single

    ' Get the portfolio balance structure

    Set objPortfolioBalance =
            objPortfolioManager.get_portfolio_balance(Exception)
    If checkException(Exception, "Getting cash balances") Then
        Exit Sub
```

Listing 10.2 Portfolio summary ActiveX control. (*Continued*)

```
End If

' Get and display the cash values

meBankCash.Text = objPortfolioBalance.bank_cash_value
meBrokerageCash.Text =
              objPortfolioBalance.brokerage_cash_value
meInsuranceCash.Text =
              objPortfolioBalance.insurance_cash_value
cashSubTotal = objPortfolioBalance.bank_cash_value + _
              objPortfolioBalance.brokerage_cash_value + _
              objPortfolioBalance.insurance__cash_value
meSubTotalCash.Text = cashSubTotal

' Get and display the equity values

meBankEquity.Text = objPortfolioBalance.bank_equity_value
meBrokerageEquity.Text =
              objPortfolioBalance.brokerage_equity_value
meInsuranceEquity.Text =
              objPortfolioBalance.insurance_equity_value
EquitySubTotal = objPortfolioBalance.bank_equity_value + _
              objPortfolioBalance.brokerage_equity_value + _
              objPortfolioBalance.insurance_equity_value
meSubTotalEquity.Text = equitySubTotal

meGrandTotal.Text = cashSubTotal + equitySubTotal

End Sub
```

UpdateForm is where we do most of the work of the control. First, we declare the necessary variables for the routine. The portfolio balance information is returned as a CORBA structure, so we need to declare our helper object for the structure. Then we call the get_portfolio_balance method, using the optional exception parameter. We pass the exception to another internal routine for exception handling. CheckException is a generalized version of the exception checking code from Listing 8.1 that formats an error message in a message box. It is not repeated in Listing 10.2, but it is in the project on the Web site. Finally, the routine takes the portfolio values from the `objPortfolioBalance` helper object, calculates totals, and displays them in the Masked Edit boxes. The next step is to test the control.

Testing the ActiveX Control in Visual Basic

An ActiveX control needs to run within a control container. Visual Basic is not only an easy way to construct controls but is also a container for running them. This makes it a handy container to use for testing, especially since Visual Basic allows you to integrate the control and the test projects together into a single project group. From the Visual Basic File menu, choose "Add Project ..." and then choose "Standard EXE" as the new project type. This will create a project group and add the new project to it. It will even automatically add the user control as a component in the test project. From within the project group, we can run the test project, which will invoke the user control. We can then set debugging breakpoints in the code for both the test and user control. There is only one trick to using project groups. Before the user control can be added to the test form, the form and properties for the user control must be stored. This is accomplished by closing the user control form window. Once that is done, the user control becomes available as a component in the test form's control tool palette. Select the user control and drop it onto the test form and then resize it to include the full visual form of the user control. In our project, we have also added two text boxes and a command button to our test form, as shown in Figure 10.5. The code for our test project is shown in Listing 10.3.

Our FMC project uses CORBA factories and factory finders to get object references. This is illustrated in the `Form_Load` routine of our test project. We use the standard interworking CORBA Factory to get an Automation View of the CORBA factory finder. We will use a specialized class of the factory finder, `Tobj.FactoryFinder`, which is provided by the interworking product we've used in this example. The specialized `Tobj.FactoryFinder` has some additional convenience methods such as the `find_one_factory_by_id` method that we are using. This method provides two additional functions to our client. First, it allows us to pass in a simple string identifier of the object we want rather than construct the CORBA name component structure required by the standard CORBA `find_factories` method. The standard CORBA method will return a sequence of factories that match our search criteria. The client would then choose one of the available factories from the sequence. The specialized method that we are using here returns only one factory and instead lets the factory finder perform the load balancing among the available factories. All we do on form load is to get the CORBAFactory and the FMCFactory.

Listing 10.3 Portfolio control test module.

```
' Module scope declarations

Private objCORBAFactory As DICORBAFactoryEx
Private objFactoryFinder As DITobj_FactoryFinder
Private objFMCFactory As DIFMC_FMCFactory
Private objPortfolioManager As DIFMC_PortfolioManager


'----------------------------------------------------------------
' Form_Load subroutine. Get the CORBA and FMC Factories
'----------------------------------------------------------------
Private Sub Form_Load()

    ' Use the CORBA factory to find the factory finder.
    ' Use the factory finder to get the Portfolio Manager factory
    ' Use that to find the portfolio manager

    Set objCORBAFactory = CreateObject("CORBA.Factory")
    Set objFactoryFinder =
        CORBAFactory.GetObject("Tobj.FactoryFinder")
    Set objFMCFactory =
        objFactoryFinder.find_one_factory_by_id("FMCFactory:1.0")
End Sub


'----------------------------------------------------------------
' cmdGetSummary_Click subroutine. This routine is called when
' the "Get Summary" button is clicked. It just calls the
' PortfolioSummary control.
'----------------------------------------------------------------
Private Sub cmdGetSummary_Click()

    Dim PortfolioID As Long
    Dim custInfo As DIFMC_CustomerInfo
    Dim strCustomerName As String
```

(continues)

Listing 10.3 Portfolio control test module. (*Continued*)

```
' Use the PortfolioID from the text box and get a portfolio
' manager. Get the customer info from the manager and
' display the user's name.

PortfolioID = CLng(txtPortfolioID.Text)
Set objPortfolioManager =
            objFMCFactory.get_portfolio_manager(PortfolioId)
Set custInfo = objPortfolioManager.get_customer_info
strCustomerName = custInfo.first_name + " " + custInfo.last_name
txtCustomerName.Text = strCustomerName


' Call the PortfolioSummary control's initialize method
' passing in the manager object. That will update the
' portfolio summary display.

ucPortfolioSummary.Initialize objPortfolioManager

End Sub
```

When using the test form, we enter a `portfolioID`, and click the "Get Portfolio Summary" button to initiate our test. This brings us to the `cmdGet-Summary_Click` routine in our test code. The first thing we do in this routine is to get a `PortfolioManager` object from the `FMCFactory`, passing in the `portfolioID` as input to the `get_portfolio_manager` method of the factory. We do two things with the `PortfolioManager` object that is returned to us. The customer's name is obtained from the `custInfo` structure that the portfolio manager returns from the `get_customer_info` method, and we display it in a text box on the test form. The second thing we do is pass the `PortfolioManager` object to the `initialize` method of our user control. This will invoke our user control and cause its form to be updated. It's that simple.

Building and Distributing an ActiveX Control

After testing out the control, there are two more steps to perform. We need to build the user control as an .ocx file and register it so it can be used by other projects. From the Visual Basic File menu, choose "Make FMCSummary.ocx" (or whatever you called your user control). This will build the .ocx file and register it in the system registry on your system. However, if you went to the trouble of building an ActiveX control, you probably want to be able to use it on other systems also, which means it needs to be registered there as well. Again, Visual Basic comes to the rescue with its Application Setup Wizard, which is an option in the Visual Basic program group.

The Application Setup Wizard will build a setup program to install and register your control. As part of this process, it will determine what dependencies (constituent controls) your control has and optionally add them to the setup program. By default, it will include all files, but you can select which files you want to be part of your distribution kit, so, for example, you can choose whether or not to include the Visual Basic 5.0 run time in your kit. If you include it, then your control can run on any desktop system whether or not Visual Basic has been previously installed. Unfortunately, it is also 844 KB in size, which will probably dramatically increase the size of your kit.

The wizard is not smart enough to know that your control is made of Automation views of CORBA objects and that these objects also have to be registered on the client system. However, the wizard will let you add files to the installation kit that it builds. This feature can be used in combination with a feature of some interworking bridge products to easily build a complete distribution kit. Many interworking products will let you build what is called a *deployment package*. The deployment package will perform the exposure operations for the CORBA objects and register them in the system registry. Direct the Application Setup Wizard to add the deployment package files to the distribution kit it builds.

Adding Events to a Visual Basic Control

We now know how to build and test a simple ActiveX control that uses a CORBA object. The next example will expand on our previous one to use callbacks and show how to tie them into events on the ActiveX control. We will add an event called `DataChange` that will notify the control's container that the data values have changed. To accomplish this, we will add a callback object, `SummaryEvent`, to the control, as shown in Figure 10.6. The `Refresh` method of the control is no longer necessary since any changes in data are automatically pushed to it, so we have removed it from our new control. The CORBA `PortfolioManager` object has been modified to support the `PushTo` and callback operations. Both the `portfolioManager` view object and the `SummaryEvent`

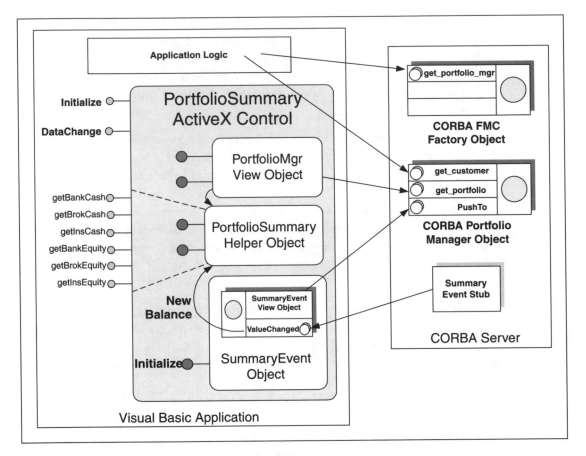

Figure 10.6 *Portfolio summary ActiveX control with events.*

object can return a new `PortfolioBalance` helper object. We have also enhanced the control to provide each of the portfolio balance values as properties so
they can be accessed programmatically in addition to being displayed in the controls form.

Listing 10.4 shows the new code for the portfolio summary control. Let's start
by looking at the implementation of the `SummaryEvent` callback object. The
first thing we do is declare our event. It is easy to use the "Add Procedure ..." wizard from the Visual Basic Tools menu for this. It will provide both the event declaration and the subroutine template for you. The `SummaryEvent` object will
raise an event to tell the portfolio summary control that the data have changed.
The `Initialize` routine is very similar to the initialization of our stock predic-

tor object in Chapter 9. A `PortfolioManager` object is passed in and saved in a class member variable. The CORBA `PortfolioManager` object has been modified to support the `PushTo` operation, as shown in the following IDL.

```
//IDL
interface PortfolioManager {
    PortfolioBalance       get_portfolio_balance();
    CustomerInfo           get_customer_info();
    CallbackKey            PushTo(in Object callback);
    void                   Disconnect(in CallbackKey key);
};
```

In our `Initialize` routine, the portfolio manager `PushTo` operation is called, passing it the `SummaryEvent` object. The callback key is saved for later use. When the data have changed at the CORBA object, it will call back to the `ValueChanged` routine of the `SummaryEvent` object, passing in a new portfolio balance object. Because the `SummaryEvent` object is a different class than the portfolio summary control, they cannot share global data. Instead, the data must be passed between them. We will use the `newBalance` event to do this. When the `ValueChanged` routine is called, it will raise the `newBalance` event, passing on the new portfolio balance object to the portfolio summary control, where an event-handling routine will process it. The last routine of the `Sum maryEvent` class, `Class_Terminate`, will get called when the class is destroyed. In this routine, we call the CORBA `PortfolioManager` object at the `Disconnect` method to inform it that we are no longer interested in receiving callback notification.

In the `PortfolioSummary` user control module we declare the `Data-Change` event. The event can be handled by the control's container to update its own use of the data obtained from the portfolio summary. Next, we have the module-wide variable declarations. We have added several new variables to the list from our last example. `SummaryEvent` is the callback object that we will pass to the CORBA portfolio manager. We also added member data to hold the values from the portfolio balance object.

Like the previous example, an application creates a `PortfolioManager` object and passes that in to the `portfolioSummary` control's `Initialize` routine. After setting the local variable for the portfolio manager, we need to create and initialize the `SummaryEvent` callback object, also passing in the `Portfolio Manager` object. Finally, we get a `PortfolioBalance` object from the portfolio manager and call the `getSummary` routine. We have changed the getSummary routine in several ways. When the CORBA portfolio manager calls the callback object, it will pass in a new PortfolioBalance helper object to the SummaryEvent object, which will then be passed to our portfolio summary control. We now have two different ways to get the portfolio balance object, so we have removed obtaining the PortfolioBalance helper object from the getSummary routine. The other change is that we store each of the values from the portfolio balance in member variables of the control. We still display the values in our Masked Edit boxes, but we have also made them available as properties.

The SummaryEvent object has an event called newBalance. Our routine to receive that event is simply called SummaryEvent_newBalance. The event handler routine sets the local portfolio balance object and then calls getSummary to update the display and the local member variables with the new balance information. Finally, we raise the DataChange event to signal the control container of the data change. The last part of the listing shows the property get routines to return the individual balance information.

Listing 10.4 Portfolio summary ActiveX control with events.

```
class module SummaryEvent (Instancing = PublicNotCreatable)

Public Event newBalance(newValue As DIFMC_PortfolioBalance)


Private objManager As DIFMC_PortfolioManager
Private key as FMC_CallbackKey
'-----------------------------------------------------------------
' Initialize the stock, giving it a real-time stock market feed.
' This method is only called by the MarketPredictor class.
'-----------------------------------------------------------------
Friend Sub Initialize(manager As DIFMC_PortfolioManager)
    Set objManager = manager
    key = objManager.PushTo(Me)
End Sub


'-----------------------------------------------------------------
' This method will be called by the CORBA server
' when the stock value has changed.
'-----------------------------------------------------------------
Public Sub ValueChanged(newValue As DIFMC_PortfolioBalance)
```

Listing 10.4 Portfolio summary ActiveX control with events. (*Continued*)

```
        RaiseEvent newBalance(newValue)
End Sub


'------------------------------------------------------------------
' This method will be called when the SummaryEvent object is
' destroyed. It will call the PortfolioManager Disconnect method
'------------------------------------------------------------------
Private Sub Class_Terminate()
    objManager.Disconnect key
End Sub

UserControl PortfolioSummary

' Event Declarations:
'
Public Event DataChange()
'
' Module-wide declarations
'
Private objSummaryEvent As SummaryEvent
Private objPortfolioManager As DIFMC_PortfolioManager
Private objPortfolioBalance As DIFMC_PortfolioBalance
Private bankC, brokerageC, insuranceC As Single
Private bankEq, brokerageEq, insuranceEq As Single


'------------------------------------------------------------------
' Initialize method. Here the containing program passes
' in the PortfolioManager object for this control to use
'------------------------------------------------------------------
Public Sub Initialize(manager As DIFMC_PortfolioManager)
    Set objPortfolioManager = manager
    '
    ' Create and initialize the SummaryEvent Object for callbacks
    '
    Set objSummaryEvent = New SummaryEvent
    objSummaryEvent.Initialize (objPortfolioManager)
    '
    ' Get a PortfolioBalance and call routine to update properties
```

(continues)

Listing 10.4 Portfolio summary ActiveX control with events. (*Continued*)

```
    '
    Set objPortfolioBalance =
            objPortfolioManager.get_portfolio_balance
    GetSummary

End Sub

'----------------------------------------------------------------
' getSummary - Read the new values from the PortfolioBalance
' object. Set the control's property values and update the display
'----------------------------------------------------------------
Private Sub getSummary()
    Dim cashSubTotal, equitySubTotal As Single
    '
    ' Set the controls public property values
    '
    bankC = objPortfolioBalance.bank_cash_value
    brokerageC = objPortfolioBalance.brokerage_cash_value
    insuranceC = objPortfolioBalance.insurance_cash_value
    bankEq = objPortfolioBalance.bank_equity_value
    brokerageEq = objPortfolioBalance.brokerage_equity_value
    insuranceEq = objPortfolioBalance.insurance_equity_value
    '
    ' Display the cash values
    '
    meBankCash.Text = bankC
    meBrokerageCash.Text = brokerageC
    meInsuranceCash.Text = insuranceC
    cashSubTotal = bankC + brokerageC + insuranceC
    meSubTotalCash.Text = cashSubTotal
    '
    ' Display the equity values
    '
    meBankEquity.Text = bankEq
    meBrokerageEquity.Text = brokerageEq
    meInsuranceEquity.Text = insuranceEq
    equitySubTotal = bankEq + brokerageEq + insuranceEq
```

Listing 10.4 Portfolio summary ActiveX control with events. (*Continued*)

```
        meSubTotalEquity.Text = equitySubTotal

        meGrandTotal.Text = cashSubTotal + equitySubTotal

    End Sub

    '----------------------------------------------------------------
    ' This routine is called by the SummaryEvent object calls when
    ' it is notified of ValueChanged by the CORBA object.
    '----------------------------------------------------------------
    Private Sub SummaryEvent_newBalance(
                                newValue As DIFMC_PortfolioBalance)
        Set objPortfolioBalance = newValue
        getSummary
        RaiseEvent DataChange
    End Sub


    '----------------------------------------------------------------
    ' Return the appropriate value for each propget method
    '----------------------------------------------------------------
    Public Static Property Get BankCash() As Variant
        BankCash = bankC
    End Property
    Public Static Property Get BankEquity() As Variant
        BankEquity = bankEq
    End Property
    Public Static Property Get BrokerageCash() As Variant
        BrokerageCash = brokerageC
    End Property
    Public Static Property Get BrokerageEquity() As Variant
        BrokerageEquity = brokerageEq
    End Property
    Public Static Property Get InsuranceCash() As Variant
        InsuranceCash = insuranceC
    End Property
    Public Static Property Get InsuranceEquity() As Variant
        InsuranceEquity = insuranceEq
    End Property
```

The original test project from the last example will still work with our new control, but it will not take advantage of any of the new features we have added. To test these, we have enhanced the test project to receive the `DataChange` event and to read the individual balance properties of the control. We have not repeated the code for the test project here since these are simple modifications.

Building a Control in C++ Using MFC

Visual Basic is only one of many good tools for building ActiveX controls. Visual C++ also has a lot of features that make building controls easy, especially with the use of MFC and the Class Wizard. Any ActiveX control can have some form of visual presentation, or it can have only local processing functions and be known as a nonvisual control. Visual Basic is a much easier tool for building visual controls, but Visual C++ offers some real advantages for building nonvisual controls. Of course, it is possible to build visual controls in C++, but it is more difficult than in Visual Basic. It is also possible to build nonvisual controls in Visual Basic, but you do not get the same advantages that are possible with C++. Visual C++ also supports building controls using the Active Template Library (ATL). ATL allows you to build a smaller, more efficient control but at the cost of more complexity for the developer. In the following example we will build a nonvisual control using Visual C++ and MFC.

C++ programmers would most naturally want to program to COM objects that lend themselves to programming languages rather than to Automation objects that easily support scripting capabilities. In other words, they would want to use COM Views of CORBA objects instead of Automation Views. This provides an opportunity to deal directly with complex CORBA data types rather than with helper objects. The use of C++ to build nonvisual reusable components using COM objects is a powerful technique for integrating COM and CORBA systems. A nonvisual control can be used to hide areas from the Visual Basic programmer where CORBA is visible, such as the use of the CORBA Factory for creating objects. Our example control will use COM objects and hide two areas of complexity from the end user of the control. First, we will hide the complexities of creating the CORBA object, and, second, we will present all of the values of a CORBA structure as fine-grain properties of the control. We will incorporate these construction techniques with a useful distributed object design pattern to illustrate a powerful and flexible technique for creating reusable ActiveX components that provide a higher level of functionality than the simple Automation or COM Views.

The Movable Object Design Pattern

The Movable Object Design Pattern is a generic technique for moving data from a server system to a client system, where it can be processed locally. When the local processing is done, the entirety of the data can then be sent back to the server to update the data store. This pattern is particularly useful for moving large amounts of data, such as an entire form, to a client system. At the client system, the user interacts with the local version of the data where it can be preprocessed and validity checked before being sent back to the server for processing within the actual business systems. One advantage of using this pattern is that it allows processing to be moved from the server to the client systems. Another advantage is that network messages are greatly reduced down to two calls, one to get the data and a second to update it. The pattern does, however, impose an additional semantic on the client. The client must indicate that it is done with the data by explicitly signaling some sort of *submit* operation. This is a common semantic when using a form but is not a common technique for programmers dealing with the properties of an object or control. Figure 10.7 shows the construction of an ActiveX control that implements the Movable Object Design Pattern.

The CORBA server has an object that is responsible for managing some state, possibly backed by data in a database or other data store. The data manager object has two operations that explicitly deal with the state. The first operation, `get-State`, requests that the manager object send the state (data) to the client. The

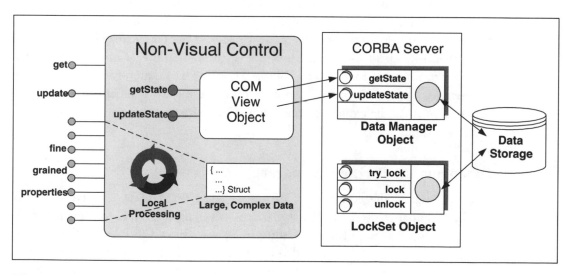

Figure 10.7 *Movable object ActiveX control.*

state will typically be sent as a structure or another constructed data type. The second operation, updateState, requests that the manager object update the permanent store of data with the new values provided by the client. The ActiveX control has two corresponding functions that simply call the data manager object to get and set the data. In addition to these housekeeping functions, the ActiveX control has local fine-grain properties that present subsets of the total data to the user in small, manageable amounts. Some local processing may also be done in the control, such as moving the data from the coarse-grained networking structures to the fine-grained properties. More sophisticated processing can be also be done, such as providing calculated or composite data. The use of properties to get and set data is a much more natural programming technique, but it does not scale well to a distributed environment. The Movable Object Pattern gives your application the best of both worlds.

One aspect of the Movable Object Pattern is that the data are moved to the client machine for processing. Moving the data to the client has two implications. First, the object receiving the data must be knowledgeable about how to process it. In essence, the encapsulation of data that is key to object systems has been delegated by the server to the local processing object. Second, when the data are moved to the client system, there are two copies of the data: the actual data in the permanent data store and the copy that is being used by the client. Whenever there are multiple copies of data, there is an opportunity for things to get out of synch. These possible errors must be accounted for in the manager object. Another complication is that more than one client can ask for the same data at a time, so there could be three or more copies of the data. The concurrency control of the data is another responsibility of the data manager. If the data manager object allows more than one client to get the same data at the same time, it must implement it own versioning and merging capabilities. Locking is frequently used to prevent concurrent access to data. This can be achieved using the standard functions of a database, or it can be explicitly implemented by the server using a LockSet Object, as shown in Figure 10.7.

Enhancing the Portfolio Manager

The first step in the construction of a new PortfolioInfo ActiveX control will be to enhance the CORBA PortfolioManager object to implement the Movable Object Design Pattern. Listing 10.5 shows the CORBA IDL for the new PortfolioManager. The individual operations to get balance and customer information have been replaced by the new movable object operations of get-

State and updateState. You will also notice the PushTo and Disconnect operations that we added to support callbacks. A new structure has been added, PortfolioInfo, that contains all of the data of both the CustomerInfo and PortfolioBalance structures. The PortfolioInfo structure is what gets passed in the getState and updateState operations. The CORBA server needs to be updated to support these new operations. Our implementation will not allow more than one client to have the same portfolio information so we don't need to worry about the concurrency problems.

Listing 10.5 Enhanced FMC IDL file.

```
// IDL
module FMC    //Financial Mega Corporation

typedef long CallbackKey;

  struct CustomerInfo {
     FirstName     first_name;
     LastName      last_name;
     char          middle_initial;
     Address       customer_address;
     Phone         phone_number;
  };

  struct PortfolioBalance {
     float      bank_cash_value;
     float      bank_equity_value;
     float      brokerage_cash_value;
     float      brokerage_equity_value;
     float      insurance_cash_value;
     float      insurance_equity_value;
  };

  struct PortfolioInfo {
     customerInfo        customer;
     PortfolioBalance    portfolio;
  }

interface PortfolioManager {
  PortfolioInfo    getState();
  void             updateState(in PortfolioInfo  newState);
```

(continues)

Listing 10.5 Enhanced FMC IDL file. (*Continued*)

```
    CallbackKey    PushTo(in Object callback);
    void           Disconnect(in CallbackKey key);
  };

  interface FMCFactory {
    PortfolioManager get_portfolio_manager(in long Id);
  };
};
```

Implementing the ActiveX Control in C++

We have used Visual C++, MFC, and the Class Wizard to build the ActiveX control. The easiest way to do this is to create a new project in Visual C++ and select "MFC ActiveX Control Wizard" as the project type. Answer the few questions and, voilà, the wizard creates everything that your project needs to build an ActiveX control. The next step is to use the Class Wizard, which is available from the View menu, to add the methods and properties that your control will have. We have added methods to the control to `Initialize`, `getPortfolioInfo`, and `setPortfolioInfo`. We have added properties to get and set each item in the `CustomerInfo` structure and to get each item of the `PortfolioBalance` structure. Listing 10.6 shows the pertinent code segments, that is, code that we have added, from the PortfolioInfoCtl.cpp file that the wizard created. For simplicity, we are only showing the code that deals with the customer information in the listing, not the portfolio balance. The `Initialize` routine is called by the user of the control who passes in the `portfolioID` that they are interested in. It is in `Initialize` that we hide all of the CORBA object creation details from the user. The same methods that we used in the earlier examples are used here to get the `PortfolioManager` object. First we create the CORBAFactory using the standard `CoCreateInstance` call. Notice that we use the `CORBA.Factory.COM` progID to get the COM version of this, rather than the Automation version. Then we use the CORBAFactory to get the `FactoryFinder` object, which we use to get the `FMCFactory` object, which we in turn use to get the actual `PortfolioManager` object. We save the interface pointer in our member data and then release all of the other objects on our way out of the routine.

The `getPortfolioInfo` routine is straightforward. We call the `getState` method on the portfolio manager, which returns the `portfolioInfo` structure. We then get the customer information from the `customerInfo` reference structure inside of `portfolioInfo` and populate our control's member data with the values from the structure's members. This is also where we would get the portfolio balance information and populate our member data with that information. We have the opportunity to provide some additional value based on local calculations, such as providing properties for the cash and equity subtotals and portfolio grand total.

The `setPortfolioInfo` routine does almost the opposite of the get routine. We create a structure for the `portfolioInfo` and fill it with the values from our internal member data. The data in the `PortfolioBalance` information is read-only and will not be affected by the `updateState` operation, so we just leave this data uninitialized. Finally, we call the `updateState` operation, passing in the `portfolioInfo` that we just created.

The control can now be initialized and state gotten and updated, so the final thing to add is the ability to deal with each piece of state as a separate property. We finish off Listing 10.6 with routines that do this for the customer address. In the `GetCustomerAddress` routine, we simply return the value from our internal member data. Automation properties want to deal with strings as BSTRs, but COM objects use LPSTRs, so we have chosen to store the strings internally as a `CString` data type. All we need to do to convert it to a BSTR is use the convenient `AllocSysString` member function. In the `SetCustomerAddress` routine, we just set the member data to the new value. This would be a good place to add more value to the control by providing code to do some validity checking of the new data before setting the properties. You could also add some checking in the `setPortfolioInfo` routine to verify relationships between data.

Listing 10.6 Movable object control in C++.

```
// Private member data (from PortfolioInfoCtl.h)
//
Long     m_portfolioId;
CString  m_firstName;
CString  m_lastName;
CString  m_address;
CString  m_phone;
IFMC_PortfolioManager   *m_pManager;


// Routine called by the user of the control to associate
// it with a portfolioID
//
```

(continues)

Listing 10.6 Movable object control in C++. (*Continued*)

```cpp
void CChapter10Ctrl::Initialize(long PortfolioId)
{
    m_pManager = NULL;
    m_firstName = "";
    m_lastName = "";
    m_address = "";
    m_phone = "";

    GUID guid;
    ICORBAFactory        *pCorbaFactory;
    ITobj_FactoryFinder  *pFactoryFactory;
    IFMC_FMCFactory       *pFMCFactory

    // Create a CORBA factory to get the FactoryFinder from.
    //
    CLSIDFromProgID(L"CORBA.Factory.COM",&guid);
    CoCreateInstance(guid,NULL,CLSCTX_INPROC_SERVER,
                    IID_ICORBAFactory,(void**)&pCorbaFactory);

    pFactoryFinder = pCorbaFactory->GetObject(
                                "Tobj.FactoryFinder");
    pFMCFactory = pFactoryFinder->find_one_factory_by_id(
                                "FMCFactory:1.0");

    // Get the Portfolio Manager and set our classes member data.
    //
    m_pManager = pFMCFactory->get_portfolio_manager(m_portfolioId);

    pCORBAFactory->release();
    pFactoryFinder->release();
    pFMCFactory->release();

    return;
}

// Routine called by the user of the control to get the object
// state moved here from the server
```

Listing 10.6 Movable object control in C++. (*Continued*)

```
void CChapter10Ctrl::getPortfolioInfo()
{
    FMC_PortfolioInfo        pPortfolioInfo;

    // Get the portfolio info from the portfolio manager and
    // get the customer info from that. Set member data from
    // the returned information.
    //
    pPortfolioInfo = m_pManager->getState();
    m_firstName = pPortfolioInfo->customerInfo.first_name;
    m_lastName = pPortfolioInfo->customerInfo.last_name;
    m_address = pPortfolioInfo->customerInfo.customer_address;
    m_phone = pPortfolioInfo->customerInfo.phone_number;

    return;
}


// Routine called by the user to set the Portfolio data
//
BOOL CChapter10Ctrl::setPortfolioInfo()
{
    FMC_PortfolioInfo        pPortfolioInfo;

    // Create a structure and set the values from
    // our local member data
    //
    pPortfolioInfo->customerInfo.first_name = m_firstName;
    pPortfolioInfo->customerInfo.last_name = m_lastName;
    pPortfolioInfo->customerInfo.customer_address = m_address;
    pPortfolioInfo->customerInfo.phone_number = m_phone;

    // Call the portfolio manager to update the state
    //
    m_pManager->updateState(&pPortfolioInfo);

    return TRUE;
}
```

(continues)

Listing 10.6 Movable object control in C++. (*Continued*)

```
// Routines to get and set the Customer address properties
// of the local control. Does not change the CORBA object
// until setPortfolioInfo is called
BSTR CChapter10Ctrl::GetCustomerAddress()
{
    return m_address.AllocSysString();
}


void CChapter10Ctrl::SetCustomerAddress(LPCTSTR lpszNewValue)
{
    // This would be a good place for some validity checking
    m_address = lpszNewValue;
    SetModifiedFlag();
}
```

Using an ActiveX Control in a Web Application

ActiveX controls are an important technology for building reusable client components. They evolved from OLE Controls, specifically to support Web-based applications. Let's examine some application scenarios for ActiveX controls built using CORBA objects. We will concentrate on the aspects of using our CORBA-based ActiveX controls, not generally on how to build Web pages using ActiveX controls. There are two different Web-based application scenarios for using ActiveX controls: inside an enterprise on the corporate intranet or outside the enterprise on the Internet.

Using ActiveX Controls in an Intranet

The intranet can be characterized as a relatively controlled and managed environment. All of the machines on the network are owned and managed by the company. The machines will typically be connected directly to a high-speed LAN providing ample bandwidth for applications. The intranet may be isolated from external access through a firewall and may allow trusted security within the company. In this environment, system administrators can install required software on client systems. Such software may include internal business applications, standard tools such as Microsoft Office, and infrastructure components such as an interworking bridge product. When the interworking bridge is installed on the client system, the ActiveX control that accesses the CORBA object can run inside the Web page on the client system.

Having the ActiveX control inside the Web page is the fastest and easiest way to implement a solution. Using any HTML editing tool such as Microsoft Front Page or ActiveX Control Pad, simply insert the ActiveX control into the page, and then add some VBScript to perform functions on it. Imagine that we changed the ucPortfolioSummary control from our first example to take a portfolio id as input to the initialize routine, rather than a PortfolioManager object. This would probably be a better design if the ActiveX control is planned for use inside a Web page, instead of as a building block for other Visual Basic applications. The following HTML code, generated by ActiveX Control Pad, shows a very simple use of the control. We inserted the control into the HTML page using the "Edit" "Insert ActiveX Control" menu option. ActiveX Control Pad created the object tag shown. The object tag places the control in the Web page, but something else must be done to cause the control to perform any operations. We have used the Script Wizard capability of ActiveX Control Pad to create a very simple VBScript. In general, a script performs some function in response to an event. The script below will be executed when the window_onLoad event occurs, when the window is loaded into the browser. In this case, we will call the Initialize method on the control passing in the PortfolioID of 2034. When the Initialize method is called, a request will be made through the interworking bridge to the CORBA PortfolioManager object. The portfolio summary results will be displayed in the ActiveX control inside the Web page.

```
<HTML>
<HEAD>
<TITLE>Sample ActiveX Page</TITLE>
</HEAD>
<SCRIPT LANGUAGE="VBScript">
<!--
Sub window_onLoad()
ucPortfolioSummary1.Initialize (2034)
end sub
-->
</SCRIPT>
<BODY>
    <OBJECT ID="ucPortfolioSummary1" WIDTH=7 HEIGHT=8
    CLASSID="CLSID:69445757-F761-11D1-8627-
```

```
00400525778B">
        <PARAM NAME="_ExtentX" VALUE="159">
        <PARAM NAME="_ExtentY" VALUE="212">
    </OBJECT>
</BODY>
</HTML>
```

A more realistic page would probably have a form to enter the portfolio Id, and a button to request information. The `Initialize` method would then be called as a result of a button_click event, passing in the data from the form.

Using ActiveX Controls from the Internet

The Internet provides a very different environment for applications. It can be characterized as uncontrolled where the client machines are not owned or managed by the company. Typically, machines will be connected to the network through low speed connections, such as a modem, and will probably be required to enter the corporation through a firewall. Once inside the firewall, clients will gain access to corporate resources only through an intermediary *Web server*. In this scenario, the client machines do not have an interworking bridge on them. Instead, they use the HTTP protocol to communicate to the Web server, and the Web server communicates to the corporate CORBA objects. The ActiveX controls that are built to access the CORBA objects operate inside of Active Server Pages (ASP) in an Internet Information Server (IIS) environment. The machine with the IIS server and Active Server Pages has the interworking bridge installed on it. Figure 10.8 illustrates this configuration.

An Active Server Page is an application that processes files made up of both HTML and scripting code. The ASP executes the script, translates it into HTML, and returns the entire page to the client browser. An ASP is invoked from an HTML page, typically one that contains a form in which users enter input data. When the user is done entering data, the request is sent to the ASP. The *Action* attribute of the form specifies the target ASP as shown in the following HTTP tag.

```
<FORM METHOD="POST" ACTION="summary.asp">
```

The following code shows the VBScript portion of the `summary.asp` needed to execute the above form action. In the code, we create a `ucPortfolioSummary` ActiveX control and initialize it using the `PortfolioId` passed in from the form. ASP's require the use of a `Server` object. Object creation is done using the `CreateObject` method of the `Server` object as shown here.

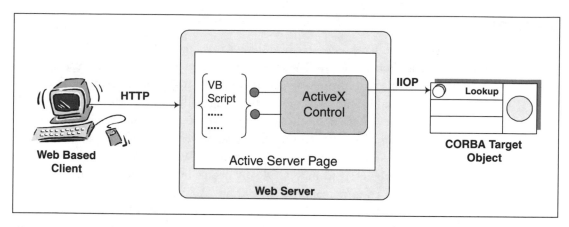

Figure 10.8 *Using ActiveX controls in an Active Server Page.*

```
portfolioID = CLng(Request.Form("PortfolioID"))
Set Summary = Server.CreateObject("Chapter10.ucPortfolio-
   Summary")
Summary.Initialize portfolioID
```

When the `Initialize` method is called, a request will be made through the interworking bridge to the CORBA `PortfolioManger` object. The portfolio summary results are returned to the ActiveX control inside of the ASP, translated to HTML, and displayed on the form in the client's Web browser.

Note that there are some differences in operating in the ASP server environment instead of a pure client environment. For example, error and status reporting become more complex. It is not acceptable to pop up a message box to report an error because the user of the ActiveX control is the ASP server. It cannot display or respond to a message box but can handle an error returned in an OLE Error Object.

A sophisticated user of ASPs can implement a session concentrator function and object pool between the HTTP clients and the CORBA objects. Instead of creating a new ActiveX control for every client, the ASP application can maintain a *pool* of objects and reuse them for each different client request. This cuts down on the total number of objects that are needed and also amortizes the cost of object creation among many clients. This of course, requires that the ActiveX control and CORBA object be designed to be reuseable. The pool of objects can be created on demand, or at the `Application_OnStart` event described in the global.asa file.

Summary

In this chapter, we have seen several different ways to build and use ActiveX controls that act as clients to CORBA objects. The simplest case was built using Visual Basic and presented data from a CORBA object visually on a form. Data change notification was added to the control by tying callbacks to the native ActiveX event mechanisms. We used another technique to build a reusable, nonvisual component for moving data between the client and server in a way that is both natural for the programmer and efficient on the network. We have also seen how an ActiveX control can be used to hide CORBA details from client programmers or to provide your own custom-mapping algorithms. ActiveX controls provide a useful framework for building reusable client components for CORBA as well as for COM objects. There are many possible variations, from the simple to the complex. Finally, we presented design considerations and showed how to use the ActiveX controls within Web-based applications. In the next chapter, we will discuss many other application design considerations for using CORBA objects from COM and ActiveX clients.

11 *Using COM/CORBA Bridges in Distributed Systems*

B uilding manageable, scalable distributed systems can be a complicated and difficult task. Distributed systems of any size inevitably involve integrating several diverse technologies—networking between different hardware and OS platforms, bridging between communication protocols, various programming languages, and so on. COM/CORBA bridging is an example of the technologies that emerge to enable this kind of integration.

In addition to the programming issues that are involved when you use COM and CORBA together, you will face many issues caused by the fact that the application or system you are building is distributed. Although both COM (in particular, DCOM) and CORBA do a great deal to hide the low-level mechanics of distributed computing, it is impossible to build effective distributed systems by starting with single-process or single-host designs and then distribute them by sprinkling the magic dust of distributed object technology on them. Distributed computing is an inherently difficult task that (at least with today's technology) can't be automated away. Even though you can avoid the gritty details of marshaling data into buffers and managing sockets, you still need to design distributed interfaces differently than you would local interfaces, and you need to understand how the performance and operational requirements of distributed systems affect your architecture and design decisions.

A generalized discussion of distributed computing is far beyond the scope of this book. Instead, this chapter will focus on two areas:

- Some general considerations for designing and using distributed object inter-faces
- Issues that are specific to using COM and CORBA together in distributed systems

The discussion of the first point (general considerations) focuses on some fairly practical, rule-of-thumb techniques and principles that are driven by our experiences working with people and organizations making their first forays into distributed object technology. There are a handful of fundamental issues that almost everyone (even an intelligent, experienced person like yourself) collides with, often painfully, when first learning and applying distributed object technology. In this chapter, we will try to show you where at least some of the rocks are under the water's surface.

The second discussion (issues specific to distributed COM/CORBA bridging) is somewhat problematic. As pointed out in other chapters, there is considerable room for variation between specific bridging products. The impact of this varia-tion on programming details is limited—compliant products must support the same programming model (i.e., the same data type mappings, interface mappings, names and GUIDs of standard interfaces, etc.), with the possible differences mainly being optional features that may or may not be present. The COM/CORBA In-terworking Standard intentionally puts absolutely no restrictions or limitations on how a bridge is implemented or on the operational characteristics of a bridging product. It is in these areas (bridge implementation and operational management) that most distribution issues arise, and the detailed solutions are product-specific in most cases. Rather than make an attempt to cover the entire space of available products with detailed solutions, we will describe the general issues and the design decisions faced by bridge implementers. COM/CORBA bridging technology is evolving quickly; new products (and new versions of established products) with more sophisticated architectures and features are appearing on the market rapidly. We believe you will be better served by an understanding of principles than by a cookbook of ephemeral solutions.

Distributed Interface Design

The fact that you are using COM and CORBA technologies together means that you are almost certainly building a distributed system, that you are invoking meth-ods from some client machine on objects running on a remote machine. The design of the distributed interfaces has a profound effect on the efficiency and usability of your application or system. You may or may not have control over the design of the interfaces that you are invoking remotely. They may be part of a preexisting legacy application, or they may be the responsibility of a separate development group within a large organization. If so, it can only be hoped that the interfaces supplied to you are reasonably well designed for distributed use (which is, in terms of unwarranted optimism, roughly the equivalent of panning for gold in your shower). If the interface design is lacking, all is not necessarily lost. We will describe some strategies you may be able to employ to ameliorate the problem. But first, we'll start the discussion by assuming you have control of the remote interface design.

Request Latency

The first important thing to understand when designing distributed interfaces is that the time it takes to execute the method (from the client's perspective) is roughly three orders of magnitude larger than a local method invocation. The latency of a small remote request is typically measured in milliseconds rather than microseconds (on a LAN between conventional workstations or servers). In most cases, request latency isn't affected significantly by the size of the request (i.e., the size of the request parameters) until the messages become relatively large—several hundred bytes of parameter data. There are three major sources of request overhead:

Parameter marshaling. The client's ORB (actually the stub in CORBA terminology, or the proxy in COM terminology) takes the request parameters in their in-memory form and packs them into a flat, contiguous buffer to send over the network and unpacks the results to return to the caller. The server ORB does the inverse of this. When passing large parameters or parameters with complex structures, this overhead can become significant.

OS overhead. After marshaling a request, the ORB calls the operating system to send the request buffer to the destination. Many programmers underestimate the amount of overhead this entails. In many cases, requests between two processes on the same machine incur almost as much request latency as requests between two machines on a fast, relatively quiet LAN. Much of this latency is due to the context switching between the user process and the system, or between two user processes.

Communication. Ultimately, the marshaled requests must flow between machines through some transmission medium. The overhead of communication seems intuitively obvious, but in fact reality is often counterintuitive on this point. Communication overhead is difficult to predict without careful modeling and baseline measurement. Many people underestimate it by following naïve assumptions.

The balance struck between these three effects depends on the relative speed of processing and communication, which is constantly shifting. With conventional technologies available today, parameter marshaling times for the relatively small requests in typical business applications tend to be lost in the noise of the OS and communication overhead. As network bandwidths improve over time, this balance will change.

These observations provide a strong incentive for you to reduce the number of remote requests by making each one do as much useful work as possible—getting the most functional bang per request buck. The amount of data exchanged and work performed by a request is called *request granularity*. The challenge of designing distributed interfaces is to increase the granularity of requests without destroying the usefulness of the interface by making it abstruse or specialized to a very narrow usage pattern. Good distributed interfaces are almost always a compromise between formal object-oriented design principles and the harsh realities of real-world constraints.

Increasing Request Granularity

To show how to reduce the frequency of requests and increase their functional granularity, we'll consider a simple example that is often used to illustrate object-oriented interfaces—a spelling checker interface:

```
interface SpellChecker {
    typedef sequence<string> wordList;
    boolean check(in string word);
};
```

This interface checks one word at a time, a reasonable granularity for local invocations. The overhead of a local method invocation (i.e., a function call) is a small fraction of the work required to look up a word in a dictionary. When you consider this as a distributed interface, however, the amount of work required to make the remote request (marshaling, system calls, transmission) hardly seems worth the meager results—a single word checked. Also consider that it is most often the case that an entire document (or a large part thereof) is checked at once.

Operate on Blocks

We can increase the amount of useful work done per request by redesigning the interface to check many words with a single request:

```
interface RemoteSpellChecker {
    typedef sequence<unsigned long> indexList;
```

```
    typdef sequence<string> wordList;
    indexList checkMultiple(in wordList words);
};
```

This approach makes the interface slightly less obvious to the reader, and it narrows (very slightly) the general applicability of the interface by building in the assumption that words will be checked in blocks. This interface is more cumbersome to use if you only want to check a single word. The validity of this interface is based on understanding the patterns of usage, by observing that words are typically checked in blocks.

Although this example is not particularly realistic, it illustrates some extremely important principles:

- Useful increases in request granularity can only be achieved by understanding and exploiting common patterns of use. Commonly recurring patterns are aggregated into fewer requests that do more work.

- Interfaces that are designed to be coarse grained are only cost-effective to the extent that applications that use them follow the patterns assumed in their design. By definition, there is some loss of generalization.

Aggregate Attributes

Another example will illustrate a common pattern in distributed interface design. Many interfaces are designed with a set of discrete properties or attributes—public data values that can be examined and modified. In some cases, exposed attributes constitute a major portion of the interface. Object-oriented design principles generally encourage designers to keep attributes small and separately accessible, especially when they are logically orthogonal. This design principle is based on the assumption that the object is local. If a client needs to examine several attributes, it calls their accessor functions sequentially. It is often the case that clients using these interfaces access several attributes to complete a single logically cohesive action. When the object is remote, this requires that several high-cost network requests be made to access a relatively small amount of data. Consider this example interface:

```
interface Book {
    attribute string name;
    attribute string author;
    attribute string ISBN;
    attribute float retailPrice;
};
```

Interfaces designed for distributed access often aggregate attributes into a single composite data structure that can be accessed in a single request:

```
interface RemoteBook {
    struct bookDescription {
        String name;
        String author;
        String ISBN;
        Float retailPrice;
    };
    bookDescription describe();
};
```

This is a useful compromise if it fits typical client access patterns—that is, if attributes are accessed in clusters. Even when the client typically accesses two or three attributes together, the cost savings achieved by reducing the number of requests usually far outweighs the cost of sending some attributes that aren't needed by the client.

Iterate in Blocks

Another useful pattern that illustrates the compromises required for distributed interfaces involves what we call *block iterators* or *enumerators*. Iterators are a common object-oriented pattern for traversing collections. Most iterator classes designed for local use return a single object or datum from the collection that corresponds to programming patterns that iterate (hence the name) over the collection processing one element at a time. When the application is processing a large number of small objects, accessing them remotely one at a time is extremely inefficient. To solve this problem, you can design iterator interfaces that return collection elements in blocks:

```
typedef string elementType;
typedef sequence<elementType> elementList;
interface BlockIterator {
    elementList nextBlock(in unsigned long maxElements, out boolean more);
    void destroy();
};
interface remoteCollection {
    unsigned long size();
    BlockIterator make_iterator();
};
```

A particular advantage of this approach is that the client has some control over the granularity of the requests because it can specify the maximum number of elements it will accept in a request.

Summarizing Granularity Issues

It would be helpful if there were a mechanized process for designing successful distributed interfaces, but none is available. The approach to designing successful distributed interfaces is simple in concept but difficult in practice:

- Analyze the functional behavior of the application, noting in particular the common request patterns that can be aggregated and encapsulated in a small number of requests.

- Analyze the performance characteristics of the deployment environment and gain a thorough understanding of the quantitative effects of different design choices. Intuition and simple models can be very misleading. If at all possible, base your analysis on careful measurements of cases that approximate the deployed applications as closely as possible.

- Designs for efficient distributed interfaces often conflict with basic object-oriented design principles. Don't be hidebound by purist views to the extent that you can't make useful compromises.

- There is a trade-off between the network efficiency of using complex datatypes and the programming complexity of using them, especially within Automation clients. A rule of thumb is to limit CORBA constructed data types to three or four levels and to avoid using CORBA **anys** whenever possible. If very complex data types are required, then COM objects should be used rather than Automation objects.

Distributed Interface Stability

Successful distributed interface design involves considerations other than performance. Perhaps the single most important difference between local interfaces and distributed interfaces is this: distributed interfaces embody a much greater commitment to stability. The economic impact of changing a distributed interface is (generally) orders of magnitude greater than that of changing local interfaces. In emerging models of enterprise systems, distributed interfaces are the integration medium for all of the information systems in the business and, quite likely, between the business and the external world. As such, this technology is often used at the boundaries between organizations and consequently between different software development organizations. In the past, different organizations within a large business developed their own applications independently, usually with very little thought (if any) given to the possible uses of their application outside of their immediate organizations or to the potential need to integrate them with other applications built by other organizations. The results are often called "stovepipe" systems, meaning an unconnected (or poorly connected) collection of applications that work in isolation. Such systems are usually redundant and inconsistent, and data exchange is usually crude and often requires human intervention (i.e., reading data from one system and manually entering it into another).

Distributed object technology is proving to be an extremely effective solution to this problem. Stovepipe applications can be encapsulated by object-oriented interfaces that provide abstractions of their function as well as access to their information and services to other applications and organizations within the enterprise. For this approach to succeed, these interfaces must be extremely stable. Organizations and development teams throughout the enterprise must be able to assume safely that these trans-enterprise interfaces will not change. Major software modifications within the applications of a single organization can be very problematic and expensive, even when the change is contained within the efforts of a single development group. Changes in interfaces that cross organizational boundaries can be (in fact, may inevitably be) disastrous.

Software systems must nonetheless evolve as the business itself grows and changes. Change in the system must be accommodated without invalidating the interfaces that extant applications depend on. Applications that are modified to extend their function can be given new alternative interfaces to express the extensions, possibly derived from the previous interfaces. The updated services must be able to support both interfaces simultaneously for as long as there are other applications in the enterprise that use the previous interfaces. This approach works, but has its obvious drawbacks. If interfaces are designed with built-in flexibility, it may be possible to accommodate some degree of functional evolution without changing the interface structure.

Flexibility in Distributed Interfaces

Flexibility in object-oriented interfaces is almost a self-contradiction. Much of the benefit of object-oriented interfaces resides in their ability to represent a particular well-defined functional abstraction, to capture as much as possible of the essential nature of the function or service that the interface embodies. To the extent that an interface does this successfully, it is inflexible—it cannot be used to represent a different abstraction. The operation signatures and parameter data types constitute the constraints that specialize the interface. The specialization that limits flexibility is also what makes the interface meaningful as a representation of some function. Relaxing some of the constraints for the sake of flexibility diminishes the crispness of the interface and its value as a representation of a particular function.

Designing distributed interfaces is an exercise in compromise—finding a useful balance between functional precision and flexibility—just as it is requires compromises for the sake of efficiency. It is easy to go overboard, defining an interface that is so flexible that it expresses no functional abstraction whatsoever:

```
interface TooFlexible {
    any perform_some_action(in any parameters);
    // the action to be performed is implied by the parameter value
};
```

(You can imagine the equivalent COM interface with a `VARIANT` parameter and return value.) As a functional abstraction, this interface is roughly the equivalent of sockets. We present it as an extreme case, partly for the sake of humor, but it pains me to note that we have seen it more than once in proposed system designs.

Simply saying that interfaces should be flexible is much easier than telling you how to do it. Building an interface that is a good balance of flexibility and functional usefulness must be based on a thorough understanding of the system's requirements, in particular, what is likely to change and what is not. The following are some general rules of thumb, provided as examples of the kinds of design decisions you will be faced with:

Avoid enumeration types. Enumeration types in OMG IDL and in many programming languages are not extensible. Simply adding a new value makes the interface syntactically invalid, most likely forcing you to support a new alternative interface to the service in question. This can be avoided by defining the value to be some standard integer type and defining constants that correspond to enumeration values. New values may be added without changing the typing structure of the interface, but you must be careful that clients of the interface always check for values that are meaningless to them and exhibit some reasonable behavior.

Avoid low-precision numeric types. Some of the largest, most costly debacles in the history of computing can be traced back to statements like "we'll never have more that a thousand of these things," or "this program will be replaced long before the year 2000."

Avoid fixed-size arrays and bounded sequences. See the previous comment.

Use wide character types, even if you don't think you'll ever need them. If you have ever had to internationalize a large application, you'll understand.

On the other hand, don't go overboard and reinvent sockets in a frenzy of overgeneralization:

Avoid the temptation to use CORBA anys (or COM VARIANTs) for everything. anys may be flexible, but they make programming very awkward (and programs obscure), causing it to lose almost all power of expression.

Avoid multifunction operations. Overgeneralization sometimes leads to multifunction operations, where one of the parameters is a discriminant that tells the target object what action to take. In extreme cases, the target object becomes an interpreter, and the parameters are essentially a mini-program. Building one of these Frankenstein's monsters can make you feel very clever, but the townspeople will eventually be at your door with torches and pitchforks.

It is difficult to understand the implications of distribution on interface stability and the most useful balances of flexibility and expressive precision. Such understanding is only gained through experience.

Distribution Issues Specific to COM/CORBA Interworking

When the OMG first undertook work to define a standard for bridging COM and CORBA, DCOM did not exist. Customers needed a solution to their integration problems that would work with their existing environments—nondistributed COM/OLE and CORBA 2.0. At the same time, it was obvious that DCOM would emerge as an important technology sometime in the near future and that it would most likely have a significant effect on interworking architecture. Consequently, the OMG decided to divide the work into two parts, unimaginatively named Part A and Part B. The requirement for Part A was to define a bidirectional mapping between nondistributed COM as it existed at the time and CORBA 2.0. Part B was intended to address changes and additional issues raised by DCOM, and its schedule was accordingly longer—dependent on the availability of DCOM.

The programming model is almost entirely unaffected by the addition of DCOM. The mapping of data types, operations, and so on is orthogonal to the distribution medium. The Part B specification focuses mostly on the interoperability issues that arise between bridging products that emerge from the addition of DCOM and some problems of parameter locality and reference chains, which are described in more detail in the following sections.

Bridge Location

The differences between Part A and Part B obviously affect distribution, primarily because Part B offers more choices regarding how applications can be distributed and, more specifically, where the bridges themselves can live and execute. With Part A, the bridge—the software that makes the transformation between COM and CORBA invocations and owns the view objects—necessarily lives on the Windows platform (see Figure 11.1). The CORBA side of the bridge handles all of the distribution, so the communication protocols are managed by the ORB (e.g., IIOP). With the introduction of DCOM into the picture in Part B, the bridge can live anywhere—on the COM platform, on the CORBA platform, or on some intermediate machine. The choice of where the bridge is implemented has important implications for the performance and manageability of the system and involves many trade-offs.

Note that the distinction between the COM platform and the CORBA platform is imprecise. Wherever the bridge lives, the hardware/OS platform must necessarily support elements of both COM and CORBA. This discussion assumes that some of the platforms in the client system are primarily COM platforms used to run programs built with COM technology, and other platforms are primarily used to run CORBA applications or services. A Windows machine in a distributed system may be primarily used to run Visual Basic client programs, and at the same time be a fully functional CORBA platform (if you are running a Netscape browser, this is in fact the case). Though technically imprecise, the labels "COM platform" and "CORBA platform" indicate the roles the machines are playing and make the discussion of distributed COM/CORBA easier.

Bridging on the COM Platform

Most of the system architectures we have seen built with COM/CORBA bridges use Windows platforms as desktop clients in a classic multi-tier client/server system, using COM/ActiveX to manage graphical user interfaces (GUIs), and using CORBA to implement shared services and business applications on a variety of different platforms (e.g., Windows NT, various flavors of UNIX, and MVS). This architecture reflects the origins and design centers of both technologies. All of the bridging products that have been available (until recently) implement Part A, so the bridge lives on the Windows client. This architecture embodies certain trade-offs.

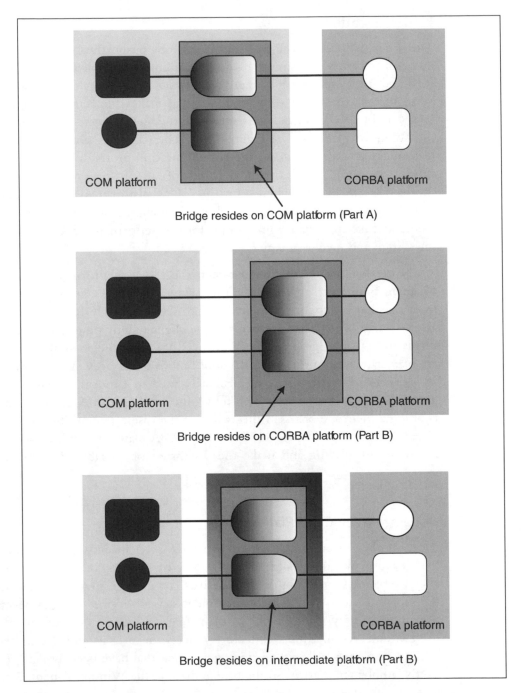

Figure 11.1 *Possible bridge locations.*

- The computational burden of bridging is on the client machine. I have been involved in many heated debates over whether this is a good thing or a bad thing. My own opinion is that it is an advantage. In most client/server systems, computational cycles are much more available on client machines than on server machines. Desktop machines, especially in thin-client architectures, usually spend 99 percent or more of their cycles waiting for human input. The untapped computing resources represented by tens of millions of computationally idle desktop Pentium machines is staggering. Computational cycles on server machines, on the other hand, are centralized, shared resources—always scarce commodities in large systems. Executing the bridge on client machines distributes that load, offering an inherently scalable solution. It should be noted that this observation is true regardless of which technology is used to implement clients and servers. It is quite possible, though uncommon at present, to build a system with CORBA clients and DCOM servers.

- CORBA is the primary distribution infrastructure. Whether or not you view this as an advantage may be regarded as a religious issue. It is not our intent to use this book as a platform on the battlefield of the DCOM/CORBA struggle, but we (the authors) make no pretense of being nonpartisan. Where distributed infrastructure is the issue, we are staunchly in the CORBA camp. So you probably should expect a few potshots.

- CORBA implementations have been around much longer than DCOM and are much more mature as software products. Most Microsoft supporters usually don't disagree with this point.

- There is mounting empirical evidence that CORBA ORBs are significantly better-performing and more scalable distribution platforms than the current implementation of DCOM. This may, of course, change in the future as DCOM matures. There are, however, some aspects inherent in DCOM's architecture that adversely affect its scalability (see the section on Effects of Object Identity and Life Cycle later in this chapter for a discussion of this issue).

- CORBA's design center is a distributed infrastructure; COM's design center is not.

- CORBA is inherently, fundamentally platform-neutral—available on an extremely wide variety of hardware/OS combinations (ironically, CORBA is available on more Microsoft OS platforms than DCOM, including Windows 3.1 and even Windows CE). DCOM is being ported to non-Microsoft platforms, but the industry in general seems reluctant to accept DCOM as a serious cross-platform solution. It is almost certain that the DCOM implementation on Microsoft platforms will always be more complete, more mature, and better supported than implementations on other platforms.

• Perhaps most importantly, CORBA is the product of an open process: the shared, jointly controlled property of the OMG member community (over 800 members to date, including Microsoft). It cannot be manipulated by any single commercial entity for mercenary or malicious reasons (or any other reasons, for that matter). It has dozens of diverse, robust implementations available from different suppliers, including some fairly high-quality free implementations.

• Bridging software must be installed and managed on all of the client machines. This is definitely a minus. Most of the bridge implementations available today have relatively small disk and memory footprints, but this has not proved to be a significant problem for enterprises using bridge technology. The main source of problems is system management overhead. Bridge software must be configured and managed in deployed systems, a burden that increases with the number of client machines. This burden is relatively small with current products and is decreasing further as bridge products mature and acquire integrated system management capabilities. The techniques that are evolving to reduce system management costs in client software, in the quest for the mythical "zero-maintenance" client, apply to bridges as well as any other software.

Bridging on the CORBA Platform

In practice, to date, CORBA platforms have usually played the server role in client/server applications built with COM and CORBA together. In the context of this discussion, *CORBA platform* and *server* will be used synonymously. Many of the observations here about bridging on the CORBA platform are the converse of those in the previous section on bridging on COM.

The computational burden of bridging is on the server. The server's computational load in a client/server application usually increases more or less linearly with the number of clients, up to the point where the saturation of some resource begins to occur. Consequently, server throughput is a major limiting factor in system scalability. As systems grow, the pressure to stretch server performance as far as possible can become overwhelming. Any overhead that grows proportionally with the number of clients or the rate of requests becomes a prime target for reduction.

Bridging overhead on a server is per-request—it contributes immediately and directly to scaling limitations. This factor is less important in systems that aren't approaching their performance limits. As in the discussion of COM bridging, this observation is equally valid when the roles are reversed, and CORBA clients are calling DCOM servers.

DCOM is the primary distribution infrastructure. From our comments in the previous section, you can probably guess that we think this is a bad thing, though not religiously. DCOM is an integral part of the Microsoft Back Office infrastructure and is supported intimately by Microsoft development environments. For shops that are primarily committed to Microsoft server solutions and are using CORBA as a way to integrate legacy applications, this is an attractive approach.

Bridging software is installed on a small number of centralized machines, making system management easier.

Bridging on an Intermediate Platform

It is possible to configure a bridge so that it acts as a protocol gateway running on an independent platform. In the resulting system, both DCOM and CORBA distribution mechanisms are used. Neither the client nor the server platform is required to be aware of the bridge's existence. This architecture offers more interesting and potentially useful trade-offs.

Request latency is greatly increased. Each request is subjected to at least twice as many network transfers as it would be if the bridge resided directly on either the client or the server. Since network communication is a major source of request overhead, this usually constitutes significant performance degradation. Note that the primary effect is on latency but not necessarily total bandwidth. In particular, if the bridging machine is also acting as a gateway between two physical networks, with DCOM on one side of the gateway and CORBA on the other, the total bandwidth may be relatively unaffected. The viability of this bridging architecture for your system depends on the nature of the system's performance requirements, specifically, whether latency or bandwidth is more critical.

Deployment and management overhead is limited to the machine(s) running the bridge. Isolating the bridging function in this way can greatly reduce the operational management costs of bridging. It also allows more flexibility for system configuration. For example, your system requirements may prohibit you from running bridges on client machines, but there may not be a bridge product available for your legacy server platform. In this case, you may have no other choice than to use an intermediate bridge.

Object Technology Domains This architecture can also be used to isolate networks and keep DCOM and CORBA protocols separated. Many IT organizations find it necessary to partition their networks to keep protocol families and all of the infrastructure that supports them separated. This is usually done to simplify network operational management, but there are other reasons that may justify the decision to use this architecture, in spite of the increases in latency. Consider DCOM and CORBA as domains—spaces within which some characteristic is uniform, with recognizable boundaries beyond which those characteristics differ. Different system characteristics define different domains, all of which coexist on the same physical network, overlaying each other. Looking at distributed systems as a set of overlapping domains at different levels can be very useful (see Figure 11.2). Here are some examples of domains that are important in distributed systems:

> **Addressing domains.** There are abstract spaces (sets of machines or processes) in which certain network addresses are meaningful. For example, IP host addresses are valid throughout the Internet, so the Internet constitutes a single, very large addressing domain. Machines with Internet addresses may simultaneously have addresses in other protocol families, such as Novell protocols (IPX/SPX), in which case these two addressing domains are superimposed on each other. A network gateway between IP and Novell protocols is a bridge that joins those two domains. At lower levels of a protocol stack, addressing domains correspond to physical domains, that is, sets of machines that are all connected via the same physical networking technology, such as an Ethernet or token-ring network.

> **Policy domains.** Enterprise networks are usually partitioned into spaces where different management policies are enforced, from assigning user IDs and permissions to allocating resources and limits, and so on. It is important to clearly define the policy domains for system management and administration purposes, and they are as much sociological entities as they are technological.

> **Object technology domains.** These domains are the primary topic of this book. Sets of machines, processes, and users that interact via DCOM and CORBA constitute object technology domains. Within DCOM domains, the defining uniform characteristics are data representations, protocols, object identity and addressing mechanisms, and so on—these are the essential elements of DCOM. Likewise with CORBA. A COM/CORBA bridge sits at the boundaries of these two domains, joining them, making interaction possible.

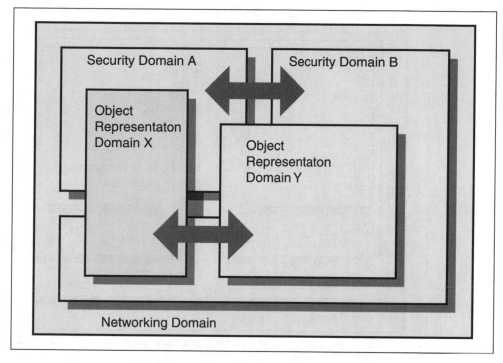

Figure 11.2 *A distributed system as superimposed domains.*

Most of this book deals with the basic elements that define these object technology domains and that are important to programmers building applications that have elements in both domains. Object technology domains are very abstract in the sense that they are dependent on (and defined in terms of) a fairly deep stack of layered network and software technologies that support their existence, and they are relatively complex domains to define and describe.

Note that the concept of bridging—the joining of two functionally equivalent but distinct domains—is generally applicable. Most kinds of domains can be bridged: file system domains, network protocol domains, and so on. Bridges usually take the form of hardware and/or software. As networks and the applications they support grow more complex, the problems associated with managing and bridging various domains are compounded. Many system architects control this complexity by making a particular set of machines share a consistent set of domains at many levels of abstraction (see Figure 11.3.) A particular set of machines on the same physical network (a low-level domain) also uses the same transport protocols, management policies, security mechanisms, administrative policies, and so on.

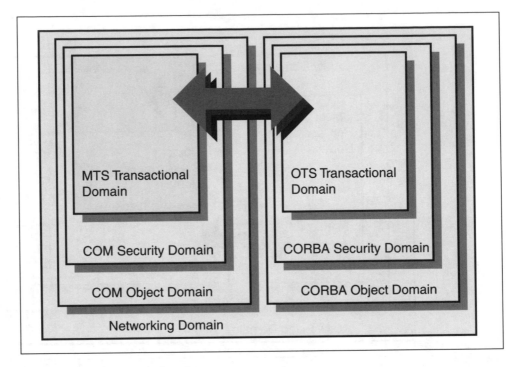

Figure 11.3 Congruent domains.

When a system is organized in this fashion, bridges that connect the domains at different levels are colocated (at least logically, if not physically). The point at which you connect two different physical networks becomes the point at which you also mediate between administrative policies, higher-level protocols, and possibly object technologies. Intermediate COM/CORBA bridges are attractive solutions in systems with this architecture since they have distinct physical locations and logical locations at various levels of abstraction. If you distribute the COM/CORBA bridges among clients or servers, it becomes impossible to make the boundaries of the object technology domain congruent with other physical and logical domains.

The advantages to this approach are not merely matters of administrative convenience. Sometimes using a gateway machine between object technologies is a practical necessity. Object technology domains are inextricably related to other domains, interacting with them in intimate ways. One increasingly important instance of this is security. Security domains are complex, involving both technological characteristics (e.g., authentication protocols and encryption schemes) and policy characteristics (e.g., principal identities, key management, the management of permissions and capabilities). Bridging between security domains is extremely complicated and is generally considered a research topic. COM /DCOM and CORBA have very different security models. At present, there are no commercial solutions that bridge between these security domains. The existing deployed systems that use COM/CORBA bridges tend to live within isolated *trust domains*—spaces within which everyone is assumed to have general permission to access resources, such as the departmental networks protected by firewalls.

It is becoming increasingly obvious that trust domains are not viable in the long run. As DCOM and CORBA continue to mature and be deployed in enterprises, their security models will not only have to coexist, they will also have to be bridged, so that principal identities, authentication certificates, and permissions in one system will be automatically (but securely) mapped to the other system at run time. When this technology emerges, it is likely that isolated gateways between object technology domains and their corresponding security domains will be a necessity. The same observation is applicable to other complex domains that are closely associated with object models, such as transactional domains.

It should also be noted that in large systems the addition of routers and gateways allows communication and computational loads to be isolated, distributed, and balanced. In a carefully designed and managed network, the latency introduced is negligible compared to the performance increases that are gained.

Summary of Bridge Location Issues

At the time of the writing of this book, bridge implementations that support COM/CORBA Part B are not yet widely available, so there isn't a large body of experience to draw from. Moreover, until such products are more available and mature, these discussions are mostly of academic value. The important points to consider are as follows:

- At present almost all applications of COM/CORBA bridges fall into the first category, with the bridge executing on a Windows client machine. This is a proven, viable architecture for a wide range of current applications. It plays to the strong points of both technologies—COM as a local component-based integration medium and CORBA as a robust, scalable distribution platform.

- The second alternative, bridging on a CORBA server, is attractive to organizations that are committed to a predominantly Microsoft solution for the client and middle tiers of multitier systems but that also need to integrate legacy or external systems that are easily accessible through CORBA.

- The third alternative, bridging on an isolated gateway machine, is likely to be an increasingly attractive approach for very large systems, where operational management issues are extremely important. This architecture will also become advantageous in the future as COM/CORBA bridges begin to address higher-order services—security, transactions, and so on.

Mechanical Issues

There are a few technological details of bridging technologies that are worth noting because of their implications for distribution strategies.

Effects of Object Identity and Life Cycle

Chapter 3 described the important differences between COM and CORBA identity and life cycle models. These differences create an important difference in the way communication is managed. COM's reference-counting mechanism requires object implementations (class instances) to know whether or not there are active clients that hold references to the object. In general, the object will remain in existence until all references are released. This is problematic in distributed systems. A client in a distributed system may crash or become disconnected in such a way that the server object cannot determine what has happened. If a client holding a reference crashes without releasing it, naïve assumptions could cause the server object to remain active indefinitely, consuming resources unnecessarily. DCOM solves this problem by having clients send periodic messages at a fairly low rate to the server, indicating that the client is still alive and holding a reference. If a server fails to receive these "pings" for some specified period, it assumes that the client has died and releases the reference(s) itself.

A naïve view of this scheme might lead you to believe that a network could become saturated with ping messages. This is generally not the case. DCOM includes a sophisticated mechanism for concentrating or coalescing ping messages, so that one message exchange between two host machines can convey all of the status information regarding the active references being shared between the applications running on those machines. The rate of pinging increases with the number of interacting machines, not with the number of objects or active references, and the rate is relatively low. There is little or no available experience with this protocol on very large systems, however, so the effects of pinging in very large networks is not well understood and could be problematic.

Excessive ping traffic is not the major drawback of this scheme. The server's only clue that a client has crashed is a lapsing of the ping messages. There are a variety of possible causes for this, however, such as transient network traffic that saturates communication channels for a sufficiently long time. The rate of pinging is slow enough that this is very unlikely to happen on high-speed LANs, but it poses a serious problem across low-bandwidth WANs. The Internet is probably the worst case since there is so much variability in message latency. It is extremely difficult to predict delays in such a large system, and accordingly it is difficult to determine with any certainty whether a machine has failed or not by observing network traffic (in fact, it is theoretically impossible). As a result, there is the real potential that a server may conclude that a client has died and released its references, when, in fact, the client is still quite alive. If the server destroys the object because the references were released and the client subsequently sends a request that reaches the server, the server raises an exception to indicate that the object no longer exists. If the client making the request happens to know the identity of the object's storage or to have a moniker for the object, it can re-create an equivalent object with the appropriate state. If, however, the client obtained the interface pointer to the object from some other context and doesn't have a moniker, it may lose the capability to access the object altogether.

CORBA avoids this problem altogether by disassociating the object activation state from the client state. Servers manage resources according to their own policies. Servers can deactivate objects, close connections, or even terminate execution without disrupting a client's ability to access its objects. When the client program makes a request, the ORB does whatever is necessary to satisfy the request—activate the object, open a new connection, or execute a new server process—without disturbing the client application.

Locality of Automation Parameters

Since Automation doesn't support direct equivalents to CORBA structs and unions, they are mapped as Automation objects that encapsulate the same information model. When a CORBA struct is passed through a bridge to a COM recipient, the bridge builds a Automation helper object that is local to the receiving context and encapsulates a copy of the data in the struct when the parameter was passed. The helper object is a new, independent artifact. If the Automation program modifies its property values, the original struct in the CORBA program is unaffected. This model is consistent with the semantics of CORBA structs—they are copied, creating independent, local values. When the receiving side isn't a single COM program, but a component in a distributed DCOM system, this picture becomes more complex. If the COM program that received the helper object initially passes its interface pointer to a remote COM program, it is passed by reference. If the remote program sets any properties, they become remote invocations of property set functions. This situation causes two problems. First, the local copy semantics intended for the original CORBA data type are no longer being observed; the helper object becomes (in the DCOM world) a shared, remotely accessed object. Second, potentially serious scaling problems are introduced. Each invocation of a property accessor becomes a remote invocation, with all of the incurred overhead costs.

The Part B specification corrects this by defining mechanisms that allow objects representing CORBA value data types (e.g., structs) to be copied when passed to remote DCOM applications. The new extensions don't change any APIs that are typically seen by the user, but they do change the semantics of Automation helper objects. When you are using a bridge product that supports Part B extensions, you should be careful to note the different behavior.

Reference Chains

Consider this scenario: a CORBA object reference passes through a bridge; a DCOM view is created. For all intents and purposes, the DCOM view is a fully functional DCOM object, with its own identity. The DCOM application that initially received the view passes it to another DCOM application. This second DCOM application passes the reference through the bridge to a CORBA application. The bridge might not be able to recognize that the DCOM reference is really a reference to a view of a CORBA object, so it might create another CORBA view of the DCOM view (see Figure 11.4). It would obviously be more efficient if the bridge could determine which CORBA object it is actually invoking through this chain of views of views and substitute the direct CORBA object reference. Part B defines extensions that allow bridges to detect and eliminate (or at least shorten) reference chains in most cases, even when the chain passes through different bridges. The details are only interesting to bridge implementers, but it is useful to understand that chains can occur and may not be entirely eliminated by the bridges. It is also interesting to note that reference chains are not specific to COM/CORBA interworking; they can occur whenever two object systems are bridged by building proxy objects (views, in our case), and bidirectional interworking is supported.

Summary

This has only been a brief introduction to distribution issues. Even with technologies such as DCOM and CORBA to automate many difficult mechanical details of

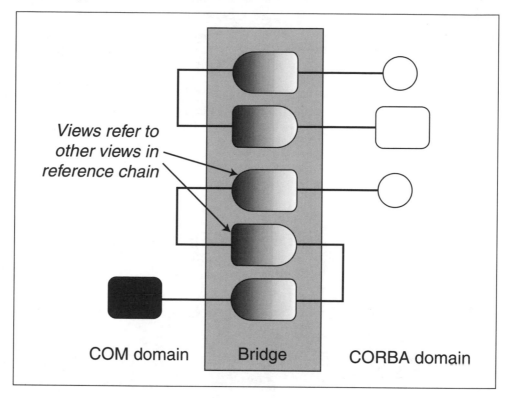

Views refer to
other views in
reference chain

COM domain   Bridge   CORBA domain

Figure 11.4 *Reference chains.*

distribution, building successful large-scale distributed systems is still very much an art, a practice of wizards. The ability of COM/CORBA bridging technology to make heterogeneous distributed systems easier will continue to evolve and improve over time, as you can already see in the advances made from Part A to Part B. Almost all of the changes in Part B introduced mechanisms for bridge implementers to use and do not affect the programming model at all. This is an indication that the basic mapping between object models is sound—Part B was produced when several Part A products had already been in use for some time, but no major changes to the mapping were found necessary.

We hope this chapter has offered some useful guidance and will help you avoid some of the more obvious obstacles. You will learn much more than we could ever write in a chapter when you start building your first serious distributed COM /CORBA application (if you haven't already done that).

12 *Conclusions and Futures*

This chapter completes our examination of COM/CORBA interworking architecture and programming. We will summarize the key points we have learned throughout the book and try to draw conclusions based on that information. Finally, we will take the bold step of trying to predict where the technology will go over the next few years.

Where We Have Come From

In the introduction, we stated the primary thesis of this book as this: COM's strengths best cast it in the role of a component-oriented programming model for managing presentation and user interaction. CORBA's strengths best suit it to the roles of distributed infrastructure and as an integration medium. As such, these technologies are complementary, and together they constitute a powerful tool kit for building complex enterprise applications.

We have shown how the COM/CORBA interworking architecture and bridging products support this premise. You can certainly write COM-based clients for CORBA applications today! In addition, we have provided informed opinions on the relative merits of each technology as applied to different aspects of an overall enterprise solution. We sincerely hope that you have found this interesting, insightful, and not too biased. Our approach throughout the book has been to provide you with a mix of architectural discussions, general considerations for application design, and concrete programming examples of COM and Automation-based clients for CORBA objects. All of this has been in keeping with our main goals in this book: (1) *When you are presented with interworking pro-*

gramming problems, you will understand the issues involved in writing the code to solve the problem and will be able to relate it to some similar programming tasks presented in our examples, and (2) *when you are presented with problems unlike any of the examples presented in this book, you will be well equipped to tackle them with confidence in your design judgment.* We hope we have achieved these goals. Please let us know how we did and what we could improve.

The Mappings

One of the primary design goals of COM/CORBA interworking is to allow programmers in one object system, such as COM, to use objects in a different system, like CORBA, as though they were native objects. Although a programmer in one model does not have to be proficient in the other, it has been impossible to completely hide the fact that object systems are being bridged. This is most obvious when creating objects in the other object system, thus spanning different creation models and naming services.

Most of this book, and indeed the COM/CORBA interworking architecture, deal with mapping from CORBA to COM or Automation and vice versa. In many cases, this mapping is simple and straightforward. However, in other cases, mismatches in the two object models present complexity for the programmer. The worst examples of this are when using complex CORBA types from within Automation and when handling CORBA exceptions in either COM or in Automation clients. Despite these few minor annoyances, however, the mapping is quite complete, workable, and effective. We have explored the details of these issues and shown how to build robust, full-function clients for CORBA objects using popular and powerful COM-based development environments.

The interworking architecture is fully bidirectional, allowing CORBA applications to be clients of COM objects. This is most commonly utilized when you are having CORBA objects call back to COM objects or use standard desktop tools such as Excel. Again, we have included working examples that help you understand how and why you should implement these capabilities in your application.

ActiveX Controls

In some sense, the first nine chapters of the book were a lead-up to building ActiveX controls as clients of CORBA objects. This is in no way meant to imply that the earlier applications were somehow less valid or unimportant. There will certainly be lots of Visual Basic, Visual Basic for Applications, PowerBuilder, Delphi, and C++ applications written for CORBA objects (at least, as builders of inter-working products, we certainly hope so). Rather, the ActiveX controls we built were a culmination of all of the previous techniques that we have learned. ActiveX controls, however, provide more than just the opportunity to combine techniques. They provide the perfect mechanism to add client-side value to CORBA business objects and distribute them as reusable application components. The issues of object creation, data type mappings, and exceptions can all be encapsulated within the control and made invisible to its users. The pool of CORBA-aware COM programmers can be kept small and can concentrate on providing reusable controls for use throughout the enterprise. We expect to see this as a popular scenario in large development organizations.

This has been a quick summary of the things that we hope you have learned from the book. First, you have learned that COM/CORBA interworking provides a complete integration architecture for enterprise applications that allows you to take advantage of the complementary strengths of each technology. Second, you have discovered that it is easy to build COM-based clients that integrate the complete capabilities of CORBA business objects into standard desktop environments and tools. And, finally, you have found out how to go about building those clients. Now let's take a look at where this technology might be headed.

Where We Have Yet to Go

COM/CORBA interworking Part A, where CORBA is the distribution mechanism from the desktop to the enterprise, has been the focus of this book and of the currently available interworking products. As of this writing, interworking products that support Part B of the specification are not widely available. But this is quickly changing and may have changed by the time you read this chapter. To see where this bridging technology is heading, it is useful to examine the trends in both the COM and CORBA markets. The markets are evolving in two general directions that are important to COM/CORBA interworking: the Internet and the enterprise.

The Internet

The Internet is having a profound impact on the way we do business, both inside and outside of enterprises. Inside the enterprise, the intranet is being used for internal communications, project coordination, human resources, and dozens of other applications that require a distributed but restricted environment. Outside the enterprise, Internet use is exploding in the new area of electronic commerce. Web server and electronic commerce server products are fighting for market share in this new business area. Let's examine how COM/CORBA fits into these different scenarios.

In the case of an enterprise intranet, it is probably a valid assumption that the client is coming from a known and managed computer system. It is not unreasonable to expect certain software to be installed on the client, such as an interworking bridge, or for the client to have authorization to access certain resources within the corporation. In this scenario, the client will usually access CORBA objects directly from an ActiveX control or view object on its system, which goes through an interworking bridge somewhere.

For an Internet, these are not valid assumptions. You definitely do not want Internet users to have direct access to your corporation's resources. This is where Web servers come in. The Web server acts as a secure entry point into the corporation for external clients and provides a variety of functions. First, the server acts as a concentrator, funneling requests from many clients over just a few connections to the actual resources. The server also provides security checking and may be integrated with some sort of firewall product for increased security. In this scenario, the Web server is actually the client of the CORBA system. The external client uses the HTTP protocol to communicate with the Web server, and the Web server communicates with the enterprise CORBA servers using an interworking bridge. A common implementation of this scenario is to have an ActiveX control that accesses the CORBA object. The ActiveX control is embedded in an Active Server Page implemented on an Internet Information Server system.

Both the Internet and intranet applications are more concerned with developments in client/server-style interworking.

The Enterprise

Another hot area of technological innovation and competition is the computing infrastructure for the enterprise. Enterprise systems have additional requirements than simple client/server applications. In addition to the functions of distribution, enterprises have some or all of the following requirements:

Openness. An open, standards-based solution available from multiple vendors and on a wide variety of hardware/software platforms.

Security. Ranging from authentication to authorization to encryption.

Transactions. The ability to coordinate multiple, distributed resources together into an all-or-nothing unit of work.

Scalability. The ability to support tens of thousands of clients, thousands of servers, and millions of concurrent objects.

Configuration. The ability to dynamically add, remove, or shift resources within an application without shutting the application down.

Manageability. The ability to manage and monitor the operation of the entire application from a single system.

Availability. The characteristic that services are always available when needed. The ability to failover to other existing systems in the event of failure.

Reliability. The ability of a system to operate 24 hours a day, 7 days a week, 365 days a year without interruption or failures.

Interoperability. The ability to interoperate with other vendors, other object models, and existing legacy applications.

A new breed of product, called the Object Transaction Manager (OTM), is emerging to satisfy these additional requirements. All of the major CORBA vendors are introducing products in this space (such as BEA Systems' M3 product and IONA's OrbixOTM). Interestingly, these are also the vendors that are most active in the interworking product area. Many other companies are introducing products into this space, such as IBM and several major database and web application server vendors. Microsoft is also going after this market segment with its MTS product. It will eventually become important to provide interworking solutions that span the entire range of enterprise requirements, from security and transactions to availability and reliability.

A common problem in enterprise computing, and one to which CORBA is particularly well suited, is the integration of disparate existing, or legacy, systems into a common connected infrastructure. This type of integration is typically done between server systems and represents a peer-to-peer relationship rather than a client/server relationship. As DCOM and MTS become more prevalent, services that are deployed on DCOM systems will increasingly need to be integrated into CORBA networks on a peer-to-peer basis.

Client/Server Interworking

By client/server interworking, we mean scenarios where the interworking primarily involves clients in one object system accessing services in another. This also includes the use of callbacks. Advances in client/server interworking are likely to come in two areas: locality of the interworking bridge and integration of additional distributed services.

Products that support COM/CORBA Part B will allow client systems to use DCOM to communicate off of their system rather than needing to have an interworking bridge installed on each client. In the last chapter, we discussed at length the trade-offs between, on the one hand, installation and management requirements and, on the other, the utilization of available computing resources. The most likely solution to relaxing bridge locality lies in the introduction of a standalone *bridge server* that relieves the client of the need to install interworking software but does not move the computing to the business server systems. A bridge server also provides the opportunity to bridge many of the services and other requirements of peer-to-peer communications. It may come as no surprise that the major CORBA vendors are also working on implementations of bridge server products.

Another possible solution to bridge locality is to have the bridge implemented in the CORBA ORB, as a separate protocol stack. In other words, the ORB could communicate simultaneously with either IIOP or DCOM. Although this is theoretically possible, it does move the processing to the server system and does not provide the advantages of the standalone server, so we are less likely to see this solution offered in many products.

Services Integration

Another area of improvement will probably come in the integration of services from one domain to another. For example, we saw how to manually connect a callback object to an event in an ActiveX control. It is also possible for an interworking product to automatically map from the CORBA event model to the COM IConnectionPoint model. The COM/CORBA Interworking Specification does not address service mapping, so solutions in the area will be proprietary, at least initially. This type of integration may focus on presenting CORBA services as native COM interfaces rather than trying to provide full bidirectional mappings between services. The likely areas of integration will be the following:

Naming. We already have some integration in naming today; for example, the CORBAFactory can create an interface pointer for an object in a CORBA namespace. Some solutions also offer namespace monikers that provide this functionality without the need to use the CORBAFactory. As Windows NT 5.0 becomes more common, we will see integration with the Active Directory Services, which allow native COM interfaces to be used to get views for CORBA objects.

Life cycle. It is possible to map a CORBA Simple factory to COM Class factory interfaces so that standard functions such as Visual Basic `CreateObject` or COM `CoCreateInstance` can be used to create views of CORBA objects. There are some interworking solutions that offer this mapping today.

Events. The CORBA event model is fairly complex. There are several possibilities for mapping CORBA events to COM interfaces. The most likely solution maps CORBA Typed Event Channels to IConnectionPoint interfaces. Recently, CORBA introduced the notification service, which is a higher level service built on top of the event service. We may see mappings to the notification service instead of widely available mappings to the event service.

Security. COM clients are used to a single logon for their domain. Some interworking products may map these existing credentials to equivalent CORBA protocol objects. This mapping will probably not occur until NT 5.0 appears with Kerberos-based authentication.

Peer-to-Peer Computing

As DCOM and MTS services become more widely deployed, Object Transaction Manager vendors will be increasingly motivated to provide full peer-to-peer interoperability between COM and CORBA domains. This will require a full, bidirectional mapping of at least the following services:

- Naming
- Security
- Transactions

Some services will not be offered as one-way (client/server) mappings but will only be available as bidirectional solutions. This will probably be the case for transactions where interoperability may be based on the emerging Transaction Internet Protocol (TIP). Other services like events or notification may only see one-way mappings. Yet other services, perhaps asynchronous messaging, may never see standard mapping solutions.

Whatever happens with bridge servers and service mapping, it is a safe bet that both CORBA and COM systems will be used together in enterprise computing and that interworking will become more important over time. To that end, CORBA OTM vendors will continue to compete to provide the best interoperability solution for the enterprise.

Well, how's that for speculation? We'll check back in a year or two to see how our predictions did. In the meantime, we hope that you have enjoyed our book and have found it to be a valuable resource. Thanks for reading it!

Recommended Readings

Books on CORBA:

Orfali, R., D. Harkey, J. Edwards. *Instant CORBA*. (New York: John Wiley & Sons, Inc., 1997).

Orfali, R., D. Harkey, *Client/Server Programming with JAVA and CORBA,* 2nd ed. (New York: John Wiley & Sons, Inc., 1998).

Siegel, J. *CORBA Fundamentals and Programming*. (New York: John Wiley & Sons, Inc., 1996).

Books on COM:

Chappell, David. *Understanding ActiveX and OLE*. (Redmond, WA: Microsoft Press, 1997).

Denning, A. *ActiveX Controls Inside Out*, 2nd ed. (Redmond, WA: Microsoft Press, 1997).

Books on Objects:

Fowler, M. *UML Distilled*. (Reading, MA: Addison-Wesley, 1998).

Gamma, E., R. Helm, R. Johnson, J. Vlissides. *Design Patterns, Elements of Reusable Object-Oriented Software*. (Reading, MA: Addison-Wesley, 1995).

Taylor, D. *Object-Oriented Technology: A Manager's Guide,* 2nd ed. (Reading, MA: Addison-Wesley, 1998).

Index

What's on the Companion Web Site

This book provides a lot of different programming examples. To make these examples more useful to you, we have made all of the code available on our Web page. For each chapter, there is a directory containing the Visual Basic or COM client code. In many cases, we have also included the CORBA server code.

Another section of the Web page points you to a variety of related resources that will complement the information in this book:

- Links to CORBA Interworking products (BEA, Iona, Inprise)
- Links to articles
- Links to related sites
- Patterns, Doug Schmidt
- Recommended reading list

CD-ROM Contents and Organization

Information on the Web site is divided up into several directories as follows:

Chapter2\Server\
Chapter2\VBClient

Chapter4\Server\
Chapter4\VBClient

Chapter5\Server
Chapter5\VBClient

Chapter6\COMClient

Chapter7\VBExamples\NameService
             \GetObjectfromIOR
             \CreateObject
             \ExportingCOM
Chapter7\CORBA\POA

Chapter8\Server
Chapter8\VBClient
Chapter8\COMClient

Chapter9\VBClient
Chapter9\COMClient

Chapter10\Server
Chapter10\VBClient\Example1
                   \Example2
      \COMClient\Example3